Kneeling Theology

Kneeling Theology

ANTON ŠTRUKELJ

FOREWORD TO THE GERMAN EDITION
by Christoph Cardinal Schönborn

FOREWORD TO THE RUSSIAN EDITION
by Archbishop-Metropolitan Thaddäus Kondrusiewicz

FOREWORD TO THE AMERICAN EDITION
by Archbishop Elden Francis Curtiss

THE CATHOLIC UNIVERSITY OF AMERICA PRESS
WASHINGTON, D.C.

Most of this volume was originally published in two German books:
Kniende Theologie, EOS Verlag, Sankt Ottilien © 2003.
Vertrauen. Mut zum Christsein, EOS Verlag, Sankt Ottilien © 2012.

The paper used in this publication meets the minimum requirements of
American National Standards for Information Science—Permanence of
Paper for Printed Library Materials, ANSI Z39.48-1984.

∞

Cataloging-in-Publication Data is available from the Library of Congress
ISBN: 978-0-8132-3577-6
eISBN: 978-0-8132-3578-3

"Hans Urs von Balthasar coined the expression: theology on its knees. He knew that theology is suspended between the abysses of adoring obedience and of humble love. He knew that theology can come into action only at the touch of the living God, which happens in prayer."

Joseph Cardinal Ratzinger, "Homily at the Funeral Liturgy of Hans Urs von Balthasar, Luzern, July 1, 1988," in *Hans Urs von Balthasar, His Life and Work*, edited by David L. Schindler (San Francisco, Ignatius Press, 1991), 292.

"Every time I read the works of Joseph Ratzinger, Benedict XVI, it becomes clear to me that he pursued 'theology on his knees' and still does: on his knees, because we see that he is not only a preeminent theologian and master of the faith, but a man who really believes, really prays. We see that he is a man who embodies holiness, a man of peace, a man of God. And so he embodies in an exemplary way the essence of all priestly work."

Pope Francis, Foreword to Joseph Ratzinger/Benedict XVI, *Teaching and Learning the Love of God: Being a Priest Today* (San Francisco, Ignatius Press, 2017), 11.

CONTENTS

ACKNOWLEDGMENTS

God granted me the grace to meet and know many saintly persons: Pope St. John Paul II, St. Mother Teresa of Calcutta, and my great teachers: Archbishop Anton Vovk and Professor Anton Strle in Slovenia, both now Servants of God. To these I will add two of the subjects of this book, Pope Emeritus Benedict XVI (Joseph Ratzinger) and Hans Urs von Balthasar.

In preparing this book, I want to express my deepest gratitude to Cardinal Hans Urs von Balthasar. I came in contact with the Swiss theologian as a student in 1977. Afterward, we maintained a correspondence and had many personal encounters in Basel, in Rome, in Austria, and in Slovenia when he visited our country from September 27 to 29 in 1984. I will be forever grateful that he wrote a proper foreword to my dissertation on Christian states of life. In the last paragraph he says: "Anton Štrukelj must be credited with having tactfully and carefully developed this very complicated subject that must by no means be oversimplified. His work represents the continued study of a rather neglected point of theoretical, but also practical teaching of the Church. As he has based his work on my attempts to shed light on this subject, I owe him a warm word of thanks. May this subject have further echoes and stimulate new studies and especially new and fertile practice."[1]

1. Anton Štrukelj, *Življenje iz polnosti vere: Teologija krščanskih stanov pri Hansu Ursu von Balthasarju* (Ljubljana: Družina, 1981, 1986, 1995), 5–8. German: *Leben aus der Fülle des Glaubens: Theologie der christlichen Stände bei Hans Urs von Balthasar* (Graz-Wien-Köln: Verlag Styria 2002), 7–8. (Second Edition: Ljubljana: Spes, 2015). Russian: ЖИЗЊ В ПОЛНОТЕ ВЕРЫ. Богословне чинов христианской Џеркви у Ханса Урса фон Баљтазара (Moscow: Izdatelstvo franciskancev, 2016), 3–4. Croatian: *Život iz punine vjere. Teologija kršćanskih staleža u Hansa Ursa von Balthasara* (Zagreb: Kršćanska sadašnjost, 2017), 9–13 Croatian and German Foreword.

I subsequently attended von Balthasar's funeral in Luzern on July 1, 1988, a Mass celebrated by Cardinal Joseph Ratzinger. Since then, I have prayed often at his tomb during visits to Switzerland. During this period, I was always more aware of the great significance of the theology of Adrienne von Speyr. On those trips, I have always visited her grave in Basel as well. On the occasion of the thirtieth anniversary of her death, the Community of Saint John invited me to deliver the lecture in Basel, Mariastein (an abridged version is published in this book).

Pope Benedict passed into eternal life during the production of the English version of this book. On Wednesday, January 4, 2023, I prayed several hours in St. Peter's Basilica and celebrated the holy Mass there—close to the late Pope. On Thursday, January 5, 2023, I concelebrated the funeral Mass with the Pope Francis. In the cathedral in Ljubljana at the Feast of Epiphany, January 7, there was a great Requiem Mass for Pope Benedict XVI, at which I gave the homily. The choir sang Mozart's *Requiem*. Finally, on Tuesday, March 7, 2023, I celebrated the Holy Mass and prayed direct at the Tomb of Pope Benedict XVI (in the crypt).

In addition, I translated into Slovenian his final book, with sixteen important texts of the Pope Emeritus written in the Monastery Mater Ecclesiae in the last ten years (2013 to 2023),[2] as well as an earlier work entitled *In the Beginning . . . A Catholic Understanding of the Story of Creation and the Fall.*[3]

My deepest gratitude to The Catholic University of America Press for the gracious acquisition of this modest book. My heartfelt acknowledgment to all who made this publication in English possible, particularly Fr. Joseph Fessio, SJ, who granted permission for the extensive quotations from the translations of von Balthasar, Ratzinger, and von Speyr that have appeared in English

2. Benedict XVI, *Che Cos'è Il Cristianesimo* [What is Christianity?] (Milan: Mondadori, 2023).

3. *In the Beginning . . . A Catholic Understanding of the Story of Creation and the Fall* (Grand Rapids: Eerdmans, 1995).

through his publishing house, Ignatius Press. Similar thanks to the editors of *Communio: International Review*, and indeed, to all of the editors of the various *Communio* affiliates in different countries and languages with whom I have worked over the decades.

FOREWORD TO THE GERMAN EDITION

Professor Anton Štrukelj, Professor of Dogmatics and Patristics in the theological faculty of the University of Ljubljana, began his theological career with a dissertation on Hans Urs von Balthasar's teachings about the Christian states of life ("Leben aus der Fülle des Glaubens," that is, "Life from the Fullness of the Faith"). This work has already appeared in three printings. He has remained true to this beginning. Balthasar's work is, as before, a well from which he draws new, fresh water of a contemplative, "kneeling" theology.

Štrukelj is far from being a theological eccentric. The spectrum of his work encompasses all areas of theology, from theological method, how the Trinitarian permeates all the mysteries of faith, Christology, eschatology, and anthropology, dealing especially with the view of man and woman from Balthasar's perspective. The ecumenical dimension is also constantly present in his works. Of particular note is Štrukelj's confrontation with the great Serbian Orthodox theologian Justin Popović. He devotes attention to the subject of ecclesiology. He pursues the question of the Office of Peter in one book *Ti Si Peter Skala* [You are Peter the Rock],[1] and the theology of marriage in another *Zakon in Devištvo (Marriage and Virginity)*.[2]

In addition to his own teaching and writing, Professor Štrukelj finds time to translate numerous works into Slovenian, especially those of Hans Ur von Balthasar and Joseph Cardinal Ratzinger. He also serves as secretary of the Slovenian Episcopal Conference. In all these undertakings and activities, he remains focused on the essential: moving "from a sitting to a kneeling theology." That is the source of the title of this collection of writings.

1. Anton Štrukelj, *Ti Si Peter Skala* (Ljubljana: Družina, 1996).
2. Štrukelj, *Zakon in Devištvo* (Ljubljana: Družina, 1995).

Through Balthasar, but even earlier, Štrukelj learned from his highly esteemed teacher and master, Anton Strle, that theology first springs from *pati divina*, the suffering and experiencing of the Divine, as Saint Thomas citing Dionysius the Areopagite says.

True theological knowledge shines forth when one is drawn to the truth, not only in concepts, but when it is "gracefully" incorporated in real life—when the mystery of faith is implanted in us so that it is grasped interiorly and not striven for from the exterior. That this inner view of faith, which flows from scholarly theology, nourishes and enlivens is witnessed in the work of Adrienne von Speyr. Von Balthasar was convinced that he was indebted to Speyr's enormous work to such an extent that the works of both were inseparable. Anton Štrukelj has the courage to accept this perspective and to include Adrienne von Speyr in his treatment of von Balthasar's works. He thereby testifies to the great spiritual and intellectual fruitfulness of both.

It is a sign of hope for me that one of the promising and diligent younger theologians, in a straightforward, grateful, and open way, gives himself to the school of the great masters without wanting to produce "his own approach." With this attitude, and on this path, there is the hope that theology, as praying to and worshiping One, will again become the living theology of our times.

Vienna, on the Feast of the Nativity of the Blessed Virgin Mary, September 8, 1998.

Christoph Cardinal Schönborn

FOREWORD TO THE RUSSIAN EDITION

After three generations of persecution, the Catholic Church in Russia is experiencing a rebirth. Amid that rebirth, however, there is a severe lack of theological literature, especially current works. Various ecclesiastical institutions, candidates for the priesthood, and theological students have a pressing need for them. The development of theology is of interest to other Christian confessions as well as academic and research institutes. There are also many people who inquire about theological development with regard to science and the Church.

Father Anton Štrukelj's book, *The Glory of God,*[1] closes, to some extent, the gaps in contemporary theological literature in the Russian language. This work, in the form of an anthology of treatises and articles, sets forth important aspects of the work of the famous twentieth century Swiss Cardinal, Hans Urs von Balthasar (1905–1988). The work at hand treats the questions of Christian interiority and spiritual life, as well as of theology in its wealth of meaning.

The author of this book, Father Anton Štrukelj, is a well-known theologian of our time. He is a member of the International Theological Commission of the Holy See, Professor of Dogmatic Theology and Patristics at the University of Ljubljana, and Visiting Professor of Theological Anthropology at Mary, Queen of Apostles Seminary in Saint Petersburg, Russia. He is also the author of fourteen books and nearly fifty scholarly papers.

I cherish the hope that exploring the works of great theologians like Hans Urs von Balthasar will be of great benefit not only for those who study theology or are interested in theology, but that it will be a welcome stimulus that promotes Russia's own research.

1. The EOS Publishing House edition of the book *Kneeling Theology* was published in Russia under the title *The Glory of God.*

Because it is so urgently needed and so up-to-date, I thank Father Anton Štrukelj and the Franciscan publisher for the publication of this book, *The Glory of God.* I wholeheartedly impart my blessing both to the author and to all those who read it.

Moscow, the Second of February, 1999 on the Feast of the Presentation of the Lord.

Archbishop-Metropolitan Thaddäus Kondrusiewicz

FOREWORD TO THE AMERICAN EDITION

In this English edition of his book *Kneeling Theology*, which was published in German, Italian, Polish, Russian, and Slovenian, Anton Štrukelj based his theme on the concept first developed by Hans Urs von Balthasar. This Swiss intellectual is considered one of the most important theologians of the twentieth century. Štrukelj sees his task, through a synthetic survey of questions, to seek a holistic perspective regarding the role of the theologian from his subjects, without doing a critical analysis of all their work.

The author analyzes the process and its consequences that gave rise to the religious and cultural developments of the past and the present. It is his thesis that the essence of theology should flow from holiness. He relies for his evidence on the life and work of Hans Urs von Balthasar (which includes the insights of Adrienne von Speyr, physician and mystic), Cardinal Joseph Ratzinger (Pope Benedict XVI), the Slovenian theologian (and now Servant of God) Anton Strle, and Anton Vovk—former Archbishop of Ljubljana and fearless witness of Christ and his Church—now also a Servant of God.

Štrukelj's purpose for this book is to point out that Catholic theology is best served not only by competent research and a thorough knowledge of Church tradition, but by theologians who approach their work prayerfully and on their knees.

This English language edition of *Kneeling Theology* will allow a wider circle of readers to be exposed to many current issues regarding Catholic teaching. At the same time, it will give them an opportunity to evaluate the achievements of theological science that have developed and are currently taking place in Europe. The rich theological and pastoral heritage that has been bequeathed to us by a small group of special people in this book has come about because of their scholarship and their holiness. They have, each in their own way, demonstrated what it means to do theology on their knees, and they have shared their scholarship and insights with us. We are all the richer for their witness.

Anton Štrukelj, prelate and professor of theology at the University of Ljubljana in Slovenia, was a member of the International Theological Commission and worked with Cardinal Joseph Ratzinger and other current leading theologians. Because my mother was born in Slovenia, and I have family there, I have visited the country many times over the years, and have come to know Anton Štrukelj well. I am honored to be able to count him as a friend.

Elden Francis Curtiss
Archbishop Emeritus of Omaha, Nebraska

INTRODUCTION

Servant of God Anton Strle, a Slovenian priest and theologian, was asked one day by a friend, "Why do you quote constantly from others when you write? Why do you not reveal more of your own thoughts?" This observation reminds me that Professor Strle's method greatly influenced my own way of writing and teaching. We are in good company.

Cardinal Henri de Lubac generally preferred to hide his own ideas behind thousands of quotations, especially from the Fathers of the Church. This kind of self-effacement did not detract from the personal convictions of the author but showed, by additional documentation, his own viewpoint and command of the subject. I am deeply indebted to the theologians who have taught me, those who have illuminated my own ideas and supported my efforts as a theologian: Professor Strle and the numerous good priests in Slovenia, Hans Urs von Balthasar, Cardinal Joseph Ratzinger, St. John Paul II, and many others. By being part of this theological company, I have received important support and insights, which I prefer to give directly to the reader in the form of quotations rather than interjecting my own, no doubt inferior, formulations.

The title of this book, *Kneeling Theology*, is based on a term used by Hans Urs von Balthasar. It was my privilege to have known this eminent Swiss theologian personally, "perhaps the most cultivated man of his time," according to Henri de Lubac.[1] Joseph Cardinal Ratzinger, in his funeral homily for Hans Urs von Balthasar in Luzern, July 1, 1988, made this comment: "Hans Urs von Balthasar coined the expression 'theology on its knees.'

1. Henri de Lubac, "A Witness of Christ in the Church: Hans Urs von Balthasar," in *Hans Urs von Balthasar: His Life and Work*, ed. David L. Schindler (San Francisco: Ignatius Press, 1991), 272.

He knew that theology is suspended between the abysses of adoring obedience and of humble love. He knew that theology can come into action only at the touch of the living God, which happens in prayer."[2]

What Ratzinger wrote about von Balthasar could easily be said of himself. In fact, Pope Francis wrote the following about Pope Emeritus Benedict XVI:

> Every time I read the works of Joseph Ratzinger, Benedict XVI, it becomes clear to me that he pursued "theology on his knees" and still does: on his knees, because we see that he is not only a preeminent theologian and master of the faith, but a man who really believes, really prays. We see that he is a man who embodies holiness, a man of peace, a man of God. And so he embodies in an exemplary way the essence of all priestly work. He embodies the constant relation to the Lord Jesus.[3]

Here, I draw together the work of Ratzinger, von Balthasar, and his collaborator Adrienne von Speyr, with Servant of God Archbishop Anton Vovk, and Servant of God Anton Strle, two of my fellow Slovenians who will not likely be known to English-speaking readers. My hope is to communicate how this spiritual vocation of the theologian has been and can be lived, and to show its value not only for current or aspiring theologians themselves but for the whole people of God: laity, priests, and religious.

This brief introduction develops the following points: 1) Pope Benedict as a Christian thinker and herald of Christian holiness and beauty; 2) Hans Urs von Balthasar as the proponent of "Kneeling Theology," 3) the importance of von Speyr to von Bal-

2. Joseph Ratzinger, "Homily at the Funeral Liturgy of Hans Urs von Balthasar, Luzern, July 1, 1988," in Schindler, *Hans Urs von Balthasar: His Life and Work*, 292.

3. His Holiness Pope Francis, Foreword to *Teaching and Learning the Love of God: Being a Priest Today* by Ratzinger (San Francisco: Ignatius Press, 2017), 11.

thasar and the Church, and 4) the connection of Pope Benedict XVI to the Church in Slovenia and to Anton Strle in particular.

Pope Benedict as a Christian Thinker and Herald of Christian Holiness and Beauty

The path of the life of Joseph Ratzinger, from the professor's chair to being the shepherd of souls in Rome, sharpened his appreciation of the "inner unity of theological research, theological teaching, pastoral service, and administration in the Church."[4] This is the reason he sought to draw theologians from their ivory towers into the broader pastoral life of the Church and urged them to accompany their scholarship with a life of prayer. The theologian's academic life needed to be integrated with a strong spiritual life and an appreciation for the pastoral needs of people everywhere.

When asked by Peter Seewald "What would you yourself see as specific about your theology or the way you do theology?" Cardinal Ratzinger in the interview "Salt of the Earth" answered:

> I began with the theme of the Church, and it is present in everything. Only, in dealing with the Church it was important to me, and it has become increasingly important, that the Church cannot be an end in herself but exists so that God may be seen. In that respect, I would say that I study the theme of the Church with the intention of opening a vista onto God. And in this sense God is the real central theme of my endeavors.
>
> I have never tried to create a system of my own, an individual theology. What is specific, if you want to call it that, is that I simply want to think in communion with the faith of the Church, and that means above all to think in communion with the great thinkers of the faith. The aim is not

4. Cf. Ratzinger, *Pilgrim Fellowship of Faith: The Church as Communion* (San Francisco: Ignatius Press, 2005), 17–37, and *Principles of Catholic Theology: Building Stones for a Fundamental Theology* (San Francisco: Ignatius Press, 1987), 315–31.

> an isolated theology that I draw out of myself but one that opens as widely as possible into the common intellectual pathway of the faith. For this reason, exegesis was always very important. I couldn't imagine a purely philosophical theology. The point of departure is first of all the Word. That we believe the Word of God, that we try really to get to know and understand it, and then, as I said, to think about it together with the great masters of the faith. This gives my theology a somewhat biblical character and also bears the stamp of the Fathers, especially Augustine. But it goes without saying to try not to stop with the ancient Church, but to hold fast to the great high points of thought and at the same time to bring contemporary thought into the discussion.[5]

It was obvious to his listeners and readers that Joseph Ratzinger was not only a brilliant theologian, but that he was also an excellent teacher and preacher. Two themes have emerged from his teaching and preaching that are the leitmotif of his thinking. The first is his conviction that we must serve the Church of Christ and not just ourselves, and the second, that we must be coworkers of the truth (*cooperatores veritatis*).

Yet this truth that Ratzinger prized so highly was not truth as expressed in dry, scholastic catalogs of correct propositions, but a truth full of beauty, shining with splendor. Pope Benedict XVI wrote: "I have often affirmed my conviction that the true apology of Christian faith, the most convincing demonstration of its truth against every denial, are the saints and the beauty that the faith has generated. Today, for faith to grow, we must lead ourselves and the persons we meet to encounter the saints and to enter into contact with the Beautiful."[6]

5. Ratzinger, *Salt of the Earth: Christianity and the Catholic Church at the End of the Millennium*, An Interview with Peter Seewald (San Francisco: Ignatius Press, 1997), 66.

6. Ratzinger, "The Feeling of Things, the Contemplation of Beauty," Meeting with Communion and Liberation at Rimini, Italy, August 24, 2002, available

Some years ago, Cardinal Joachim Meisner characterized Joseph Ratzinger, then the Prefect of the Congregation of the Doctrine of the Faith, a "Mozart in theology."[7] This was an apt expression considering the love that Ratzinger had of the great composer who was born in Salzburg, not far from the region in which Ratzinger was raised. And it was an apt expression for the amazing beauty and genius of the Prefect's theological work. Theological texts of his pontificate as Pope Benedict XVI reflect the splendor of language that matches the beauty of its content.

Hans Urs von Balthasar as the Proponent of "Kneeling Theology"

Pope Benedict's conviction about beauty is shared with the great Swiss theologian Hans Urs von Balthasar, "the theologian of the beautiful." This beauty does not come from the clever construction of the theologian's intellect, however, but what von Balthasar famously described as "the form of Christ."[8] Hence, the beauty of theology *is* the beauty of holiness, of explaining and showing forth the Church without spot or wrinkle as redeemed by Christ.

Ratzinger's theology drew upon the work of his friend and collaborator Hans Urs von Balthasar, who had linked theology with holiness. In an address during his visit as Pope Benedict XVI to the "Philosophical and Theological Pope Benedict XVI Insti-

at vatican.va. See also Anton Štrukelj, "Schönheit und Heiligkeit in der Theologie: Hommage an Papst Benedikt XVI aus slowenischer Sicht," in *Hommage an Papst Benedikt XVI. Aufsätze und Essays*, ed. Maximilian Heinrich Heim and Wolfgang Gottfried Buchmüller, 119–26 (Heiligenkreuz im Wienerwald: Be&Be. 2018). Anton Štrukelj, *Schönheit und Heiligkeit*. Papst Benedikt XVI zum 95 (Geburtstag: EOS Verlag Sankt Ottilien, 2021), 286 pages. Also Slovenian and Polish editions of this book.

7. Catholic News Agency, "WYD 2005 Awaits Pope 'Mozart of Theology,' Cologne's Cardinal Says," Madrid, Spain, May 13, 2005.

8. For a detailed discussion, see Matthew Levering, *The Achievement of Hans Urs von Balthasar: An Introduction to His Trilogy* (Washington, D.C.: The Catholic University of America Press, 2019), 63–80.

tute" in the renowned Cistercian Abbey Heiligenkreuz in Austria, he emphasized: "Where theology is practiced 'on bent knee,' as Hans Urs von Balthasar urged, it will prove fruitful for the Church in Austria and beyond."[9]

Von Balthasar called theology and holiness "two sisters in spirit,"[10] who belong together inseparably. This theme was of importance to him throughout his career. Notably, one finds a text "Theology and Holiness,"[11] written in 1948 when he was still a young Jesuit priest, and another written in 1987—just a year before his death—with the same title, "Theology and Holiness."[12] When, on June 23, 1984, he received the coveted Paul VI Prize from the hands of Pope John Paul II, he forcefully spoke these words: "I insist on the inseparability between theology and spirituality, their separation being the worst disaster that ever occurred in the history of the Church."[13]

This separation had been institutionalized over the course of the Church's history, in the move from monastic to scholastic theology and later in the divide between academic theologians and the structures and life of the Church. This is not to say that theology should not be rigorously scientific—Anselm, Albert the Great, and Thomas Aquinas are examples that von Balthasar gives of how theology can be both prayerful and precise. "Theology was, when pursued by men of sanctity, a theology at prayer, a kneeling

9. Benedict XVI, *Address to Heiligenkreuz Abbey*, September 9, 2007. All papal documents available at vatican.va unless otherwise noted.

10. Hans Urs von Balthasar, *Two Sisters in the Spirit: Thérèse of Lisieux and Elizabeth of the Trinity* (San Francisco: Ignatius Press, 1992).

11. Balthasar,"Theology and Sanctity" in *Explorations in Theology*, vol. I: *The Word Made Flesh* (San Francisco: Ignatius Press, 1989) , 181–209.

12. Balthasar, "Theology and Holiness," *Communio: International Catholic Review* 14 (Winter 1987): 342–50.

13. "Address of Hans Urs von Balthasar," *L'Osservatore Romano*, Weekly Edition (July 23, 1984): 7–8. Original French text: "J'insiste sur l'indivisibilité entre théologie et spiritualité, leur division étant le pire désastre survenu dans l'histoire de l'Eglise."

theology. Which is why its fruitfulness for prayer, its power to foster prayer, is so undeniable. As time went on, the 'kneeling theology' was superseded by theology at the desk."[14] Yet the necessity of working at desks—today computers—is not the end of kneeling theology. We see this in the example of Cardinal Ratzinger, both a man of prayer and the consummate German professor.

Surely, Hans Urs von Balthasar's *opus immensum* is wide-ranging not only because of its intense and profound culture, but also by his radiating force. The entire theology of Hans Urs von Balthasar is a kneeling theology because it arises from his contemplative prayer life and leads his readers into this life. His theology uses the triune God's love for his creation as its source and leads his readers into this mystery. Balthasar considers theology to be a reliable witness to the truth. As Henri de Lubac, a friend and teacher of von Balthasar, said of him: "He is theologian only to be apostle."[15] Henri de Lubac on another occasion said: "He himself is one of those men of whom he has spoken, men who devoted the work of their lives 'to the splendour of theology—theology, that devouring fire between two nights, two abysses: adoration and obedience.'"[16]

The Importance of von Speyr to von Balthasar and the Church

Cardinal Joseph Ratzinger had this to say about Christian prophecy: "I believe that it can be proven that for all the great theologians any new theological elaboration is only possible if the prophetic element has first paved the way." If it is true that behind a great theologian there is always a prophet, it is not difficult to discover the immense influence that the physician and mystic Adrienne von Speyr (1902–1967) had on the extensive work

14. Balthasar, "Theology and Sanctity," *The Word Made Flesh*, 208.

15. Henri de Lubac, "A Witness of Christ in the Church: Hans Urs von Balthasar," in *The Church: Paradox and Mystery* (Shannon, Ireland: Ecclesia Press), 115.

16. De Lubac, "A Witness of Christ in the Church," 110.

of Hans Urs von Balthasar. As Ratzinger said, "Hans Urs von Balthasar is unthinkable without Adrienne von Speyr."[17] Von Balthasar's connection to the mystic von Speyr, with whom he founded a the Community of Saint John religious society, was for him a way of unifying spirituality and his own theological work—which he called "her work" and his "two halves of one whole, with a single foundation at the center."[18]

Von Speyr was a Swiss physician, wife, writer, and theologian. Coming from a Protestant family, she converted to the Catholic Church in 1940 at the age of thirty-eight. At the Solemnity of All Saints, the theologian Hans Urs von Balthasar baptized her conditionally. Afterwards, extraordinary mystic and charismatic graces flowed. She experienced the Passion of the Lord, particularly his loneliness on the Cross and his Descent to the dead on Holy Saturday.

Von Speyr's literary legacy is outstanding, with more than sixty volumes of theology and spirituality. No wonder Pope John Paul II, during a symposium on her work in Rome (September 27–29, 1985), said of her, "May this spirituality, which Adrienne von Speyr lived with such intensity, help you to better incarnate your concern for evangelical and ecclesial life in the realities of the contemporary world."[19]

I was present at this symposium in Rome. Later, I helped in the translation of some of von Speyr's books into Slovenian. Hans Urs von Balthasar, giving his generous permission for the trans-

17. "Das Problem der christlichen Prophetie," Niels Christian Hvidt im Gespräch mit Joseph Kardinal Ratzinger [On the problem of Christian prophecy: Niels Christian Hvidt interview with Joseph Cardinal Ratzinger], *Communio: Internationale Katholische Zeitschrift* 28, no. 2 (1999): 183.

18. Peter Henrici, SJ, "A Sketch of von Balthasar's Life" in Schindler, *Hans Urs von Balthasar: His Life and Work*, 28, quoting Hans Urs von Balthasar, *Rechenschaft* (Einsiedeln: Johannes Verlag, 1965), 35.

19. Pope John Paul II, *Discorso ai partecipanti al convegno sulla personalità di Adrienne von Speyr* [Address to participants in the convention on Adrienne von Speyr] (September 28, 1985), 2.

lation of her book, *The Handmaid of the Lord*,[20] emphasized: "This is a masterpiece!" In the United States of America, fortunately, many books of Adrienne von Speyr are available. I hope to invite the readers to discover the immense richness of her deep theology, especially the inseparable unity of their double mission. Balthasar affirmed: "Adrienne is a world. Not only has she built a world community, but built it upon an extensive theology, which in its substance derives from her."[21] Balthasar considered himself an interpreter of Adrienne's charismatic insights. He says: "Perhaps my writings will be really understood only when serious attention is given to Adrienne von Speyr."[22]

The Connection of Pope Benedict XVI to the Church in Slovenia and to Anton Strle in Particular

Cardinal Ratzinger has been a great influence on theology in Slovenia; not to mention his institutional influence, when on April 7, 2006, Pope Benedict XVI reorganized the structure of the Catholic Church in Slovenia by creating three new dioceses. Evidence of his influence is the effort to translate so much of his work: already 37 books and 177 articles by Joseph Ratzinger–Pope Benedict XVI into Slovenian. [23] It was Professor Anton Strle who first introduced the writings of Joseph Ratzinger to Slovenia with the translation of his *Introduction to Christianity* in 1975.[24]

20. Adrienne von Speyr, *Magd des Herm* (Einsiedeln: Johannes Verlag, 1948). English: *Handmaid of the Lord* (San Francisco: Ignatius Press, 1985).

21. Balthasar, *Test Everything: Hold Fast to What is Good*, An Interview with Hans Urs von Balthasar by Angelo Scola (San Francisco: Ignatius Press, 1989), 88.

22. Hans Urs von Balthasar and Michael Albus, "Spirit and Fire: An Interview with Hans Urs von Balthasar," *Communio: International Catholic Review* 32 (Fall 2005): 574.

23. See the Register: *Slowenische Übersetzungen der Werke von Joseph Ratzinger–Papst Benedikt XVI* (Manuscript, 2023).

24. Joseph Ratzinger, *Einführung in das Christentum*. München: Kösel Verlag, 1968. English: *Introduction to Christianity*. San Francisco: Ignatius Press, 1990.

Cardinal Ratzinger responded to a request of Professor Strle to write the Foreword to the Slovenian translation of this book. His entire Foreword is now published also in the official edition of Joseph Ratzinger's *Collected Writings*. In the last part of it the then-Cardinal wrote:

> To my surprise, this book helped people all over the world—this was the publisher's wish and also my desire. I keep meeting unknown people who tell me that the book helped them and that it unblocked the road for them. I am pleased, therefore, that the ten languages into which the book has been translated (including Korean and Japanese) will now be joined also by Slovenian. The true aim of the book is to translate it beyond the borders of language, time, and intentions, to make people realize the unifying power that radiates forth from the person of Jesus Christ. A heartfelt thanks goes to all those who have worked hard for the success of this translation, and I hope that the book will serve the purpose for which it was written also in its Slovenian translation.—Joseph Ratzinger, Regensburg, Solemnity of the Ascension 1975.[25]

In the present book, we discuss not only Ratzinger, but the man who more than any other introduced him to Slovenia, Anton Strle. Strle published forty-five books of his own, works which reveal the holiness with which he lived. Ratzinger himself knew Strle and stands as a witness to Strle's combination of living faith and scholarship. In the July 25, 1991, Foreword to *The Selected Writings of Professor Anton Strle*, Cardinal Joseph Ratzinger said of him:

> I had the privilege of meeting Professor Strle in 1974 when we had a meeting of members of the International Theological Commission. I believe I may say the meeting with him left a strong impression on all the members of this group of

25. Joseph Ratzinger, "Vorwort zur slowenischen Ausgabe" in *Einführung in das Christentum*, Joseph Ratzinger Gesammelte Schriften [hereafter, JRGS] 4 (Freiburg: Herder, 2014), 36–37.

thirty scholars from the most varied countries of the world. Professor Strle always kept humbly in the background; he wanted only to learn and speak when he had anything truly original to say that others did not see. But it was this very modesty of stepping into the background of his own accord and giving priority only to a better understanding of the truth that drew attention to him. From his humble and benevolent personality emanated a great interior light; we felt this lean man had been pervaded through and through by contact with God. Although it was possible to see a deep ascetic life in him, this asceticism spoke of what is positive: of inner nearness to the Lord which relegated everything else to second position. This life and thinking in communion with Christ gave Professor Strle the strength of judgement and the capacity for discernment which cannot derive from mere learnedness. He had a sharp sense for what is right and what is wrong, for what purifies faith and gives it growth, and what destroys it; he knew—in one word—how to discern spirits and it was for this reason that his judgement was precious and cogent.

This is why I am very pleased that this compilation of his anthropological essays is being published. It will help make his contribution to the search for the true likeness of man become better known and more effective. The path of the Church is man, said our Holy Father [Pope John Paul II], and added that man's path is Christ. Our common question in the confusion of our time is how man should find his way. This is after all the question of how man is able to meet Christ again in our time. Professor Strle provided an important contribution to this integral anthropology in this book, which I hope will enjoy a broad readership.— Given from Rome on the Feast of Saint James the Apostle, July 25, 1991. —Joseph Cardinal Ratzinger.[26]

26. Cardinal Joseph Ratzinger, Foreword to *Božja slava—živi človek: Teološka antropologija* (*Gloria Dei—vivens homo*) by Anton Strle (Ljubljana: Družina: 1992), 5 (German) [pp. 7–8 Slovenian].

Since Anton Strle has now become a Servant of God, Ratzinger's witness has added importance. On March 6, 2017, Pope Emeritus Benedict XVI sent me a letter in which he says:

> I am very happy that the process for the beatification of the Servant of God, Professor Dr. Anton Strle, has started, and I hope it will attain soon its aim. Right in the current situation when theology sometimes leads more away from the faith instead of to the faith, it is particularly important to present to the whole of Christianity the excellent personalities of theologians in which the real essence of theology is fulfilled. . . . What I wrote in 1991 for his *Selected Writings* "*Gloria Dei—vivens homo* remains entirely my conviction now, and therefore it can be estimated as my votum in the process of beatification for the Servant of God Anton Strle.

The holiness of Anton Strle grew out of the suffering of the Slovenian Church under the Communist regime. For this reason, I have also included a chapter on Archbishop Anton Vovk, Strle's bishop when he first became a theologian, and a man who exemplified the grace under persecution that witnesses to the face of Christ, as martyrs do. Theologians today, while not neglecting great works of speculative theory, should neither neglect the lives of such witnesses as a locus for theological reflection.

Conclusion

The key for theologians to follow the path of kneeling theology is not only to look to heaven, as though revelation were beginning only now, but to look back to their forebears, the saints and Doctors, not with the goal of simply repeating the past, but to discern the face of Christ in the theological patrimony of the Church and to bring it to light today. Michael Albus, in an interview with Balthasar entitled "Spirit and Fire" asked him this question: "How do you see your own theology?" And Balthasar responded: "I consider my own theology to be like the finger of

John pointing to the fullness of revelation in Jesus Christ, which is unfolded in the immense fullness of its reception in the history of the Church, above all in the meditation of the saints. I have to say that for me, the only truly interesting theologians are the saints: from Irenaeus through Augustine to Anselm, to Bonaventure, or figures that allow the radiation of holiness to show forth, such as Dante or Newman; one could also mention Kirkegaard and Solovyov. I have actually never written because I wanted to achieve results, but in order to show individuals something that I think must be seen."[27]

The goal of this present book is to show something that I think must be seen, not only in the great saints of old, but in the ones of our time who point to them—Ratzinger and von Balthasar, along with von Speyr, and the two Servants of God from my country, Anton Vovk and Anton Strle.[28] The reader will not find the author developing his own theories but rather acting as a finger, pointing to these witnesses and through them to Christ who is both God and Word, Theos and Logos.

27. Balthasar and Albus, "Spirit and Fire," 574–75.

28. I wish this especially for readers in the United States, given the long connection between my country and yours, including Bishop Frederic Baraga, the Missionary to the Ottawa and Ojibwe indigenous peoples near Lake Superior, now the Venerable Servant of God, and the family of Archbishop Elden Curtiss, whose help on the present volume was greatly appreciated.

1

"Servants of Your Joy"

JOSEPH RATZINGER AS PRIEST, PROFESSOR, PREFECT, AND POPE

Pope Benedict XVI celebrated his 60th anniversary as priest on June 29, 2011. His ordination, and his brother Georg's, took place in Freising, Germany in 1951. These words were printed on the commemorative card for his first Mass: "We are not to dominate your faith lives. But we are coworkers in your joy (2 Cor 1:24)." "Coworkers in your joy" is also the title of Joseph Ratzinger's book of meditations on priestly spirituality.[1]

Pope Benedict XVI proclaimed and inaugurated the "Year for Priests" (2009–2010) on the 150th anniversary of the death of the Curé of Ars, Jean Marie Vianney, the patron saint of parish priests throughout the world. St. Jean Vianney often made the comment that "the priesthood is the love of the heart of Jesus."[2]

In his homily at the conclusion of the "Year for Priests" (June 11th, 2010), Pope Benedict XVI repeated the special prayer that he had printed on his 60th anniversary as priest card:

> Lord, we thank you because for our sake you opened your heart; because in your death and in your resurrection you

1. Joseph Ratzinger, "Diener eurer Freude: Meditationen über die priesterliche Spiritualität," in *Künder des Wortes und Diener eurer Freude*, JRGS 12 (Freiburg: Herder, 2010), 463–532. See Anton Štrukelj, "Duhovnik Joseph Ratzinger," *Communio: Mednarodna katoliška revija* 19 (2009): 285–319. See also Michael Karger, "'Nicht als ob wir von uns selbst etwas vermöchten' . . . Papst Benedikt XVI. im Licht seiner Primizsprüche," in *Benedikt XVI: Mit Christus für die Menschen: 60 Jahre Dienst im Weinberg des Herrn*, ed. Rudolf Voderholzer (Regensburg: Verlag Schnell & Steiner, 2011), 61–65.

2. Quoted in the *Catechism of the Catholic Church*, no. 1589.

> became the source of life. Give us life, make us live from you as our source, and grant that we too may be sources, wellsprings capable of bestowing the water of life in our time. We thank you for the grace of the priestly ministry. Lord bless us, and bless all those who in our time are thirsty and continue to seek. Amen.[3]

Pope Benedict XVI and His "Theology on the Knees"

Pope Francis, in his preface to the collection of homilies delivered by Joseph Ratzinger-Pope Benedict XVI over six decades, writes these significant words:

> Every time I read the works of Joseph Ratzinger, Benedict XVI, it becomes clear to me that he pursued theology "on his knees" and still does: on his knees, because we see that he is not only a preeminent theologian and master of the faith, but a man who really believes, really prays. We see that he is a man who embodies holiness, a man of peace, a man of God. And so he embodies in an exemplary way the essence of all priestly work.[4]

In his letter proclaiming the "Year for Priests," Benedict XVI made the point that the priest is a man who embodies "Christ's presence and . . . bears witness to his saving mercy." He himself lived this priestly activity in an exemplary way and bore witness to it. Pope Francis refers to the reoccurring theme of Pope Benedict with these words:

> As Gerhard Ludwig Cardinal Müller has so authoritatively reaffirmed, the theological work of Joseph Ratzinger—and then later of Benedict XVI—assures him a place among such

3. Pope Benedict XVI, *Homily for the Holy Mass Concluding the Year for Priests*, June 11, 2010.

4. Pope Francis, Foreword to *Teaching and Learning the Love of God: Being a Priest Today*, by Ratzinger (San Francisco: Ignatius Press, 2017), 11.

> great theologians on the Chair of Peter as Leo the Great, the saintly Pope and Doctor of the Church. With his renunciation of the active exercise of the Petrine ministry, Benedict XVI decided to place himself now entirely at the service of prayer: "The Lord is calling me, to scale the mountain, to devote myself even more to prayer and meditation. But this does not mean abandoning the Church; indeed, if God asks me this it is precisely so that I may continue to serve her with the same dedication and the same love with which I have tried to do so until now," he said in his final, moving Angelus message. From this perspective I would like to add also to the correct observation by the Prefect of the Congregation for the Doctrine of the Faith that perhaps, today in particular, as Pope Emeritus, he gives us in an especially clear way one of his greatest lessons of "theology on his knees."

Pope Francis, in his Foreword, expresses esteem for his predecessor:

> Then maybe Benedict XVI, right from *Mater Ecclesiae* convent to which he has retreated, can testify further and in an even more illuminating way to the "decisive factor," the interior center of priestly ministry that deacons, priests, and bishops must never forget: namely, the fact that the first and most important ministry is not conducting "current business" but praying for others, unceasingly, with body and soul. Just as the Pope Emeritus does today: continually immersed in God, his heart always directed toward him, like a lover who thinks at every moment of the beloved, regardless of what he is doing. So His Holiness Benedict XVI shows us with his witness what true prayer is. . . . Prayer is—as Benedict XVI says and testifies in this book—a more decisive factor: it is the intercession that the Church and the world—especially at this truly historical turning point—need today more than ever, need like bread, indeed, more than they need bread. For prayer means that one entrusts the Church to God, conscious that the Church does not belong to us but to *him* and that, precisely for this reason, he will never aban-

> don us; because prayer means entrusting the world and mankind to God. Prayer is the key that opens God's heart; the only one that succeeds in bringing God over and over again into this world of ours; and also the only one that succeeds in leading mankind and the world over and over again to God, like the prodigal son to the father who loves him so much that he is just waiting to be able to hold him again in his arms. Benedict knows that prayer is the first duty of a bishop (Acts 6:4).[5]
>
> So, true prayer is therefore accompanied by the awareness that without prayer the world loses not only its orientation, but also the true source of life: "Without a connection to God, we become like satellites that have left their orbit and then hurtle randomly into the void and not only destroy themselves but also threaten others," Joseph Ratzinger writes at one place in this book, thus offering us one of his many magnificent images.[6]

In all his books and writings, Pope Benedict XVI clearly describes and witnesses to what he considers the essence of priestly ministry. He insists that it is the mission of the priest to bring Jesus close to the people and to lead them by his words and actions to Jesus. It is the living water, the life of Jesus, for which people thirst. Only Jesus can quench their thirst and it is the priest through the living waters of baptism and the other sacraments (especially the Eucharist) who helps them come to this experience of Jesus. This is the way to human satisfaction and human fulfillment.

Living in the Light of the Easter Mystery

On Holy Saturday, April 16, 1927, Joseph Aloysius Ratzinger was born in Marktl am Inn in Upper Bavaria. On the same day he was

5. Pope Francis, Foreword, *Teaching and Learning the Love of God*, 12.
6. Pope Francis, Foreword, *Teaching and Learning the Love of God*, 12–13.

baptized at the Easter Vigil, which at that time was celebrated on Holy Saturday morning. Later he reflects on the event:

> To be the first person baptized with the new water was seen as a significant act of Providence. I have always been filled with thanksgiving for having had my life immersed in this way in the Easter mystery, since this could only be a sign of blessing. To be sure, it was not Easter Sunday but Holy Saturday, but, the more I reflect on it, the more this seems to be fitting for the nature of our human life: we are still awaiting Easter; we are not yet standing in the full light but walking toward it full of trust.[7]

In his autobiography *Milestones*, Joseph Ratzinger writes about his childhood with his family, including the difficult years under Nazism in Germany and the devastating events of World War II. He mentions that, as a teenager, he was forced to join the Hitler Youth group and later the German Army, which he eventually fled at the risk of his own life. He writes about his call to priesthood and his and his brother Georg's ordination. He recalls with joy his early pastoral ministry with people, his continuing graduate studies, and his role as professor and theologian. And he mentions with nostalgia his appointment as Archbishop of Munich-Freising in 1977.

Now let us examine some impressive events in his autobiography. We begin with some of his memories from his seminary days at Freising. Clearly, the daily celebration of the Eucharist was at the heart of his priestly formation.

The Priority of the Liturgy and Theological Study

Emerging from his seminary experience and theological studies, and his teaching in various universities, Joseph Ratzinger devel-

7. Joseph Ratzinger, *Milestones: Memoirs, 1927–1977* (San Francisco: Ignatius Press, 1998), 8.

oped certain priorities in his personal and pastoral life. The first for him was the essential role of the liturgy in the theological and pastoral life of the Church. As a cardinal, he gave a lecture entitled "Some Perspectives on Priestly Formation Today." In it he made the statement:

> One thing is clear: the daily Eucharist has to be the heart of any formation for the priesthood. The chapel must constitute the center of the seminary, and staying close to the Eucharist has to be continued and deepened by personal prayer in the presence of the Lord. The Sacrament of Penance must be, so to speak, the burning coal of purification of which the Prophet Isaiah speaks in relating the vision in which he received his vocation (6:6); it has to be this power of reconciliation by which the Lord leads us, over and over again, from all manner of division into unity.
>
> Silence belongs to the liturgy just as much as festivity. When I think back to my own years in the seminary, the moments of morning Mass with their inexhaustible freshness and purity, along with the grand liturgies celebrated with full festive splendor, remain my loveliest memories. The liturgy just by itself is beautiful; we ourselves are not the actors in it. Rather, we enter into that which is greater, that which embraces us and takes us for its own.[8]

This is a message priests, and those preparing for priesthood, need to hear today. This centrality of the Eucharist in the theology and life of Benedict XVI must become a central characteristic in the lives of priests today if they are to remain faithful to the call they have received from the Lord. This teaching is part of the patrimony of the Church and essential to its present vitality and

8. Ratzinger, "Some Perspectives on Priestly Formation Today: Keynote Address," in *The Catholic Priest as Moral Teacher and Guide: Proceedings of Symposium Held at St. Charles Borromeo Seminary, Overbrook, Pennsylvania, January 17–20, 1990* (San Francisco: Ignatius Press, 1990), 18.

fruitfulness. It must be safeguarded from any movement that would undermine the sacredness of the Eucharistic liturgy and the central role of the priest in its proper celebration. The long tradition of the centrality of the Eucharist in priestly life and ministry has been preserved from the past and must be preserved in the future as well. In his book *The Spirit of Liturgy*, Joseph Ratzinger writes: "One of the first books I read after starting my theological studies at the beginning of 1946 was Romano Guardini's first little book, *The Spirit of the Liturgy*."[9]

Joseph Ratzinger gradually came to recognize that the theology of the Fathers of the Church was essential in understanding the theology of Vatican II. Since in recent years he had been reading the Fathers of the Church, Ratzinger felt he could handle the challenge of a dissertation dedicated to the theology of Saint Augustine.

After Joseph Ratzinger finished his final examination in 1950, Professor Gottlieb Söhngen chose the following subject for his young student's doctoral dissertation: The People and the House of God in Augustine's Teaching on the Church. The prior year, in 1949, Alfred Läpple had given Ratzinger a copy of Henri de Lubac's book, *Catholicisme*, which had been masterfully translated into German by Hans Urs von Balthasar. It made a lasting impression on the young student:

> This book was for me a key reading event. It gave me not only a new and deeper connection with the thought of the Fathers but also a new way of looking at theology and faith as such. Faith had here become an interior contemplation and, precisely by thinking with the Fathers, a present reality. In this book one could detect a quiet debate going on with both liberalism and Marxism, the dramatic struggle of French Catholicism for a new penetration of the faith into

9. Ratzinger, *Theology of the Liturgy: The Sacramental Foundation of Christian Existence*, Collected Works 11 (San Francisco: Ignatius Press, 2014), 3.

> the intellectual life of our time. De Lubac was leading his readers out of a narrowly individualistic and moralistic mode of faith and into the freedom of an essentially social faith, conceived and lived as a *we*—a faith that, precisely as such and according to its nature, was also hope, affecting history as a whole, and not only the promise of a private blissfulness to individuals. I then looked around for other works by de Lubac and derived special profit from his book *Corpus Mysticum,* in which a new understanding of the unity of Church and Eucharist opened up to me beyond the insights I had already received from Pascher, Schmaus and Söhngen. Drawing on these perspectives, I could now enter into the required dialogue with Augustine, something I had already been attempting for a long time in different ways.[10]

Priestly Ordination

This is a summary, in Ratzinger's words, about his immediate preparation for ordination to priesthood and the ordination ceremony:

> The long vacation period that lasted from the end of July to the end of October was completely given over to my competition essay. But then a difficult situation came into being. At the end of October, we received ordination to the subdiaconate and to the diaconate. With this began in earnest the preparation for priestly ordination, which at that time was somewhat different from today. Now we were all together again in the seminary in Freising and were being introduced to the practical aspects of the priestly ministry; among other things, we had to be trained in homiletics and catechesis. The seriousness of this preparation demanded the whole person, without any reservation, and yet I had to try to combine it with the writing of my theme. The tolerance of the house and the consideration of my colleagues made this

10. Ratzinger, *Milestones*, 98.

difficult combination possible. My brother, who was with me on the road to the priesthood, did everything possible to relieve me of all practical tasks relating to our preparation for priestly ordination and our first Mass. My sister, who at this time was working as a secretary in a legal firm, used her free time to produce in exemplary fashion a clean copy of the manuscript, and so I was able to hand in my work by the required deadline.

I was very happy when I was finally free of such an engaging and yet burdensome task, and I could now dedicate myself completely for at least the last two months to preparing for the big step: ordination to the priesthood, which Cardinal Faulhaber would confer on us in the cathedral at Freising on the Feast of Saints Peter and Paul in 1951. We were more than forty candidates, who, at the solemn call on that radiant summer day, which I remember as the high point of my life, responded "Adsum," Here I am. We should not be superstitious; but, at the moment when the elderly archbishop laid his hands on me, a little bird—perhaps a lark—flew up from the high altar in the cathedral and trilled a little joyful song. And I could not but see in this a reassurance from on high, as if I heard the words "This is good, you are on the right way." There then followed four summer weeks that were like an unending feast. On the day of our first Holy Mass, our parish church of Saint Oswald gleamed in all its splendor, and the joy that almost palpably filled the whole place drew everyone there into the most living mode of "active participation" in the sacred event, but this did not require any external busyness. We were invited to bring the first blessing into people's homes, and everywhere we were received, even by total strangers, with a warmth and affection I had not thought possible until that day. In this way I learned firsthand how earnestly people wait for a priest, how much they long for the blessing that flows from the power of the sacrament. The point was not my own or my brother's person. What could we two young men represent all by ourselves to the many people we were now meeting? In us they

> saw persons who had been touched by Christ's mission and had been empowered to bring his nearness to men. Precisely because we ourselves were not the point, a friendly human relationship could develop very quickly.[11]

Pastoral Ministry

The following account of pastoral ministry given by the young priest:

> Made strong by the experience of these weeks, August 1951, I began my ministry as assistant pastor in the parish of the Precious Blood in Munich. The greater portion of the parish lay in a residential suburb in which intellectuals, artists, and high government officials lived; but there were also rows of houses belonging to employees and people who worked in small shops, as well as butlers and maids, who in those days belonged to the wealthier households. The rectory had been built by a famous architect. It was homey but too small, and the great number of people who came to help out in various functions often created a hectic atmosphere. But the important thing was my encounter with the pastor, good Father Blumschein, who not only said to others that a priest had to "glow" but was himself a person who glowed within. To his last breath he desired with every fiber of his being to offer priestly service. He died, in fact, bringing the sacraments to a dying person. His kindness and inner fervor for his priestly mission were what gave a special character to this rectory. What at first glance could appear to be hectic activity was in reality the expression of a continually lived readiness to serve.
>
> I surely was in need of such a model, because the load of tasks assigned to me was great. I had to give sixteen hours of religious instruction at five different levels, which obviously required much preparation. Every Sunday I had

11. *Milestones*, 99–100.

to celebrate at least two Masses and give two different sermons. Every morning I sat in the confessional from six to seven, and on Saturday afternoons for four hours. Every week there were several burials in the various cemeteries of the city. I was totally responsible for youth ministry, and to this I had to add extracurricular obligations like baptisms, weddings, and so on. Since the pastor did not spare himself, neither did I want to, nor could I spare myself. Because of my scant practical training, I had at first some difficulty with these duties. But soon the work with the children in the school, and the resulting association with their parents, became a great joy to me, and the encounter with different groups of Catholic youth also quickly generated a good feeling of community. To be sure, it also became evident how far removed the world of the life and thinking of many children was from the realities of faith and how little our religious instruction coincided with the actual lives and thinking of our families. Nor could I overlook the fact that the form of youth work, which was simply a continuation of methods developed between the two World Wars, would not be able to deal with the changing circumstances of the world we now lived in: we simply had to look for new forms. Some of the insights that came to me as I experienced these changed conditions, I gathered up some years later in my essay "The New Pagans and the Church," which at that time triggered a lively discussion.[12]

Receiving the Doctorate

In October 1952, the young priest Joseph Ratzinger was assigned to the seminary in Freising. He assumed his new duties with mixed emotions:

> My assignment to the seminary in Freising, which my superiors decided would begin on October 1, 1952, aroused various

12. *Milestones*, 100–101.

reactions in me. On the one hand, this was the solution I had desired, the one that would enable me to return to my theological work, which I loved so much. On the other hand, I suffered a great deal, especially in the first year, from the loss of all the human contacts and experiences afforded me by the pastoral ministry. In fact, I even began to think I would have done better to remain in parish work. The feeling of being needed and of accomplishing an important service had helped me to give all I could, and this gave me a joy in the priesthood that I did not experience in so direct a manner in my new assignment. I now had to give a series of lectures to the last-year students on the pastoral aspects of the sacraments, and, although the experience I could draw on was rather limited, at least it was recent and fresh in my mind. To this was added work in the cathedral—liturgical services and hours in the confessional—as well as the responsibility of a youth group started by my predecessor. Above all, I had to complete my doctorate, which at that time was no mean proposition: in each of eight subjects I had to pass a one-hour oral examination and complete a written examination, and the process culminated in an open debate for which I had to prepare theses from all theological disciplines. Especially for Father and Mother, it was a great joy when, in July 1953, I walked across the stage and received the cap as Doctor of Theology.[13]

Professor of Theology and Expert at Vatican II

In 1953, the young theologian was offered a position at the dogmatic and fundamental theology department at the Freising Higher School of Theology and Philosophy. At first, he rejected the offer in order to work on his habilitation work. (The *habilitation* is the degree that qualifies a person to hold a chair at a German university.) However, in 1954 he started to teach dogmatic theology at the Freising Higher School as the head of the depart-

13. *Milestones*, 102.

ment. He was offered a position of the head of the fundamental theology department at the Catholic Theological Faculty in 1956, but rejected the offer in order to continue to work on his habilitation. Finally, in February 21, 1957, he habilitated at the University of Munich with his work "The Theology of History in St. Bonaventure." Not long afterward, he was appointed as a private docent at the University. On January 1, 1958, Fr. Joseph Ratzinger was appointed Professor of Fundamental and Dogmatic Theology at the Freising Higher School, but by April 15, 1959, he had already started to teach at the University of Bonn as full professor of fundamental theology. His father Joseph died a few months later, on August 23, 1959.

In 1962, Cardinal Joseph Frings, Archbishop of Cologne, was a member of the Central Commission for the preparation of the Second Vatican Council. He brought Ratzinger to Rome as a theological advisor, where, after the first session, he was appointed *peritus*— an official theologian of the Council. Some of his senior colleagues referred to him as "a theological teenager" because he was only thirty-five years old at the time.[14] However, the contribution of Joseph Ratzinger to the Second Vatican Council was really very important and decisive.[15]

During his teaching career, Joseph Ratzinger taught at various prestigious universities. In 1963, he accepted the chair of dogmatic theology at the University of Münster. In the meantime, on December 16, 1963, his mother died. Then, in 1966, Joseph Ratzinger joined the Catholic theological faculty at the University of Tübingen where he was given the chair of the newly-established second department of dogmatic theology; later, he also served as dean of the faculty. He transferred to the University of Regensburg in 1969,

14. *Milestones*, 115–31. See also Norbert Trippen, "Joseph Ratzinger als Mitgestalter des II. Vatikanischen Konzils," *Communio: Internationale Katholische Zeitschrift* 35 (2006): 541–44.

15. See Ratzinger, *Zur Lehre des Zweiten Vatikanischen Konzils*, JRGS 7/1 and 7/2 (Freiburg: Herder, 2012).

where he served as chair of the department of dogmatic theology, and where, from 1976–1978, he also served as university vice-president. He had the reputation of being a popular professor. His lectures were attended by a variety of students of different ages and backgrounds and from different countries. Some of his former students are now respected theologians, intellectuals, and bishops.

Member of the International Theological Commission and Cofounder of *Communio*

In 1969, Joseph Ratzinger was appointed by Pope Paul VI to the International Theological Commission he had instituted. Ratzinger remained on the Commission until 1980. In 1972, together with Henri de Lubac, Hans Urs von Balthasar, and others, he began the international Catholic publication *Communio,* which became a leading journal of Catholic theology and culture worldwide.

Archbishop of Munich

On July 24, 1976, Cardinal Julius Döpfner, the Archbishop of Munich-Freising, died, and on March 24, 1977, Pope Paul VI appointed Joseph Ratzinger as Döpfner's successor. Three months later, the pope named the new archbishop a cardinal.

In August 1978 Cardinal Ratzinger took part in the conclave that elected John Paul I, and a few months later the conclave that elected John Paul II.[16] Then, in 1980, Pope John Paul II appointed Cardinal Ratzinger as chairman of the Synod on the Laity, and he indicated that he wanted to appoint him as Prefect of the Congregation for Catholic Education. Ratzinger respectfully declined the invitation, however, because he did not want to leave his episcopal ministry in Munich so soon after his appointment there. He was only fifty years old, one of the youngest of the German bishops, and already a cardinal.

16. See Ratzinger, *Salt of the Earth: The Church at the End of the Millennium*, An Interview with Peter Seewald (San Francisco: Ignatius Press, 1997), 59–118.

Nevertheless, his time in Munich was going to be limited. From the beginning of his various ministries in Rome, Pope John Paul II entrusted Ratzinger with a variety of responsibilities. From 1986–1992 he was president of the commission that prepared the *Catechism of the Catholic Church*, which summarized the teachings of the Church following Vatican II. The pope said of this document: "The Church now has at her disposal this new, authoritative exposition of the one and perennial apostolic faith, and it will serve as a 'valid and legitimate instrument for ecclesial communion and as a sure norm for teaching the faith, as well as a sure and authentic reference text' for preparing local catechisms."[17]

On November 6, 1998, Cardinal Ratzinger was elected Vice-Dean of the College of Cardinals, and on November 30, 2002, Dean of the College. According to official Vatican data, Ratzinger's memberships and responsibilities in the Roman Curia were the following: the Council of the Secretariat of State for Relations with States, the congregations for the Oriental Churches, for Divine Worship and the Discipline of the Sacraments, for Bishops, for the Evangelization of Peoples, for Catholic Education, for Clergy and for the Causes of the Saints, Pontifical Councils for Promoting Christian Unity, and for Culture, the Supreme Tribunal of the Apostolic Signatura, the Pontifical Commissions for Latin America, "Ecclesia Dei," for the Authentic Interpretation of the Code of Canon Law and for the Revision of the Code of Canon Law of the Oriental Churches.[18]

It is understandable that the burden of so many responsibilities weighed heavily on him. He expressed his feelings in the last chapter of his autobiography with these words:

17. Pope John Paul II, Apostolic Constitution *Fidei depositum* (October 11, 1992), 4.

18. L'Osservatore Romano, *Biography of His Holiness, Pope Benedict XVI* (2005). Available at vatican.va.

When you stand on the side of God you do not necessarily stand on the side of success. Good fortune often seems to pamper precisely the cynics. How are we to understand this? The Psalmist finds the answer by standing before God, in whose presence he grasps the ultimate insignificance of material wealth and success and recognizes what is truly necessary and what brings salvation. "*Ut iumentum factus sum apud te et ego semper tecum.*" Modern translations render the passage like this: "When my heart was bewildered . . . I was stupid and ignorant, I was like a dumb beast before you. And yet I am always with you." Augustine understood the word "beast" somewhat differently. The Latin word *iumentum* referred primarily to draft animals used for farm work in the fields, and here he sees an image of himself under the burden of his episcopal service: "A draft animal am I before you, for you, and this is precisely how I abide with you." He had chosen the life of a scholar, but God had chosen to make him into a "draft animal"—a good, sturdy ox to pull God's cart in this world. How often did he protest vehemently against all the trifles that continually blocked his path and kept him from the great spiritual and intellectual work he knew to be his deepest calling! But this is where the psalm helps him avoid all bitterness: "Yes, indeed, I have become a draft animal, a beast of burden, an ox—and yet this is just the way in which I am with you, serving you, just the way in which you keep me in your hand." Just as the draft animal is closest to the farmer, doing his work for him, so is Augustine closest to God precisely through such humble service, completely within God's hand, completely his instrument. He could not be closer to his Lord or be more important to him. The laden bear that took the place of Saint Corbinian's horse, or rather donkey—the bear that became his donkey against its will: Is this not an image of what I should do and of what I am? "A beast of burden have I become for you, and this is just the way for me to remain wholly yours and always abide with you."

> What else could I say in detail about my years as a bishop? It is said of Corbinian that, once in Rome, he again released the bear to its freedom. The legend is not concerned about whether it went up into the Abruzzi or returned to the Alps. In the meantime, I have carried my load to Rome and have now been wandering the streets of the Eternal City for a long time. I do not know when I will be released, but one thing I do know: that the exclamation applies to me too: "I have become your donkey, and in just this way am I with you."[19]

Following this brief presentation of the life and work of Joseph Ratzinger up to the time of his election as pope, we now turn to his theological reflections regarding the ordained priesthood.

Priests in Difficult Period after Vatican II

The period following Vatican II was a difficult time for priests. The traditional understanding of the ordained priest defined by the Council of Trent was reiterated by Vatican II with new insights and deeper scriptural references. This led to a great deal of speculation and unrest during the postconciliar era. This resulted in unprecedented numbers of men leaving priesthood, and a sharp decline in priestly vocations. The issues were not so much the result of theological confusion about the meaning of priesthood, but the way it was to be lived in the modern world. The decline would not have been so rapid if the theological foundations of priestly ministry had not been discredited by certain progressive priests and by a secular culture that discouraged men from exploring priesthood according to the mind of the Church.

In 1968 Cardinal Ratzinger published a paper entitled "The Question Concerning the Meaning of Priestly Ministry."[20] The fol-

19. Ratzinger, *Milestones*, 155–56.

20. Ratzinger, "Zur Frage nach dem Sinn des priesterlichen Dienstes," *Geist und Leben* 41 (1968): 347–76. Reprinted in JRGS 12, 350–86.

lowing year he wrote an article entitled "Priestly Ministry: A Search for its Meaning."[21] In 1970 he published a scholarly text, *Priestly Ministry*,[22] and in 1972 he led a discussion about "Sacrifice, Sacrament and Priesthood in the Development of the Church."[23] This same year, he led a conference in Regensburg for the 100th anniversary of the seminary there on "The Priest as Mediator and Minister of Christ in the Light of the Message of the New Testament."[24]

As a key issue in the Catholic-Protestant dispute over tradition and apostolic succession, Ratzinger published "Holy Orders (*Ordo*) as the Sacramental Expression of the Principle of Tradition."[25] In the discussion about the possibility of ordaining women as priests, Ratzinger (while serving as Archbishop of Munich) published an article in a 1977 Italian edition of *L'Osservatore Romano* entitled "Is the priesthood of Men an offence of the rights of Women?"[26] In the

21. Ratzinger, "Der Priester im Umbruch der Zeit," *KIBI* 49 (1969): 251–54. Reprinted in JRGS 12, 387–401. English: *Priestly Ministry: A Search for Its Meaning* (New York: Sentinel Press, 1971).

22. Ratzinger, "Il ministero sacerdotale," *L'Osservatore Romano* 110 (28.5.1970): 3 and 8. Reprinted as "Das priesterliche Amt," in JRGS 12, 402–7.

23. Ratzinger, "Opfer, Sakrament und Priestertum in der Entwicklung der Kirche," *Catholica* 26 (1972): 108–25. Reprinted in JRGS 12, 83–106; English: "Sacrifice, Sacrament and Priesthood in the Development of the Church," in *Principles of Catholic Theology. Building Stones for a Fundamental Theology* (San Francisco: Ignatius Press, 1987), 250–67.

24. Ratzinger, "Der Priester als Mittler und Diener Christi im Licht der neutestamentlichen Botschaft, in 100 Jahre Priesterseminar in St. Jakob zu Regensburg 1872–1972" in *Theologische Prinzipienlehre. Bausteine zur Fundamentaltheologie* (München: Wewel, 1982), 281–99. Reprinted in JRGS 12, 107–28. English: "The Priest as Mediator and Minister of Christ in the Light of Message of the New Testament," in *Principles of Catholic Theology*, 267–84.

25. Ratzinger, "Das Weihesakrament (Ordo) als sakramentaler Ausdruck des Prinzips Überlieferung," in *Theologische Prinzipienlehre*, 251–63. JRGS 12, 70–84. English: "Holy Orders (Ordo) as the Sacramental Expression of the Principle of Tradition," in *Principles of Catholic Theology*, 239–50.

26. Ratzinger, "Il sacerdozio dell'uomo: Un'offesa ai diritti della donna?" *L'Osservatore Romano* 117 (26.3.1977). Reprinted in JRGS 12, 129–38.

same year he discussed "the celibacy of Catholic priests."[27] He paid special attention to the formation of priests: "Some Perspectives on Priestly Formation Today."[28]

Cardinal Joseph Ratzinger gave an important lecture on the nature of priesthood "Biblical Foundation of Priesthood" delivered in Latin during the opening session of the Bishops' Synod in Rome in 1990.[29] As Prefect of the Congregation for the Doctrine of the Faith, Cardinal Ratzinger published several explanations concerning the apostolic letter of Pope John Paul II, "Ordinatio Sacerdotalis" issued in 1994.[30] Ratzinger gave a lecture "The Ministry and Life of Priests" during the International Symposium for priests organized by the Vatican Congregation for the Clergy on the occasion of the 30th anniversary of the promulgation of *Presbyterorum Ordinis*, December 7, 1965.[31]

In addition to Cardinal Ratzinger's treatises regarding priestly ministry, he gave many sermons on this same subject. A number of them were published in collections, such as: *Ministers*

27. Ratzinger, "Zum Zölibat der katholischen Priester," *Stimmen der Zeit* 195 (1978): 781–83. Reprinted in JRGS 12, 154–58.

28. Ratzinger, "Perspektiven der Priesterausbildung heute," in *Unser Auftrag: Besinnung auf den priesterlichen Dienst*, ed. J. Ratzinger, P. W. Scheele, and Karl Hillenbrand (Würzburg: Echter, 1990), 11–38; new edition: "Bereitung zum priesterlichen Dienst," in *Ein neues Lied für den Herrn: Christusglaube und Liturgie in der Gegenwart* (Freiburg: Herder, 2007), 216–36; JRGS 12, 432–50. English: "Some Perspectives on Priestly Formation Today: Keynote Address," in *The Catholic Priest as Moral Teacher and Guide* (San Francisco: Ignatius Press, 1990), 1–20.

29. Ratzinger, "Vom Wesen des Priestertums," in JRGS 12, 33–50; English: "Biblical Foundations of Priesthood," *Communio: International Catholic Review* 17, no. 4 (Winter 1990): 617–27.

30. La lettera Apostolica "Ordinatio Sacerdotalis," *La civiltà cattolica* 145 (1994): 61–72. See Ratzinger, "Grenzen kirchlicher Vollmacht: Das neue Dokument von Papst Johannes Paul II; zur Frage der Frauenordination," *Communio: Internationale Katholische Zeitschrift* 23, no. 4 (1994): 337–45. Reprinted in JRGS 12, 139–53.

31. Ratzinger, "Il ministero e la vita dei presbiteri," in *Congr. pro Clericis*. Sacrum ministerium II (1996) 7–21. (Das Werk: B_1007).

of Your Joy,[32] all of them a treasure of the author's deep spirituality. The catalog of his essays is extensive. Recently, a collection of his homilies spanning six decades was published as *Teaching and Learning the Love of God. Being Priest Today*.[33] This collection offers deep insights, both historical and theological, on the meaning of the ministry and witness of Catholic priests. The Cardinal's extensive writing on the theology of the Sacrament of Holy Orders, including his books on liturgy and the sacraments, especially the Eucharist, his writing about church music, preaching, and ecumenism which involves the priesthood—all this underlies Joseph Ratzinger's profound understanding and extensive scholarship regarding ordained priesthood in the Church. The bibliography covering the literary-theological works of Cardinal Ratzinger prior to his election as Pope, total 445 pages of titles of publications translated into thirty different languages.[34] His collected writings, *Joseph Ratzinger, Gesammelte Schriften*, were published in sixteen volumes which gave his readers an insight into the extent of his academic, pastoral, and scientific mind and heart.[35]

Biblical Foundations of Priesthood

At the end of a lecture given in Latin during the October 1, 1990, opening session of the Synod of Bishops in Rome, Cardinal Ratzinger focused on certain conclusions regarding priestly ministry which need to be heard today. These are his words:

32. Ratzinger, *Diener eurer Freude: Meditationen über priesterliche Spiritualität* (Freiburg: Herder, 1988, 2006). Reprinted in JRGS 12, 463–532. English: *Ministers of Your Joy: Scriptural Meditations on Priestly Spirituality* (Slough, U.K.: St. Paul Publications, 1989).

33. Ratzinger, *Teaching and Learning the Love of God: Being Priest Today; Selected Writings*, with a foreword by Pope Francis and an introduction by Gerhard Cardinal Müller (San Francisco: Ignatius Press, 2017).

34. Ratzinger, *Das Werk: Veröffentlichungen bis zur Papstwahl. Hrgb. vom Schülerkreis*, ed. Vinzenz Pfnür (Augsburg: Sankt Ulrich Verlag, 2009).

35. Some volumes are double, requiring two books to print.

We have seen that the New Testament priesthood inaugurated with the apostles has a thoroughly Christological structure: it signifies the incorporation of man into the mission of Jesus Christ. Accordingly, the essential foundation of priestly ministry is a deep personal bond to Jesus Christ. Everything hinges on this bond, and the heart of all preparation for the priesthood and of all continuing priestly formation must be an introduction to it. The priest must be a man who knows Jesus intimately, who has encountered him and has learned to love him. For this reason, the priest must be above all a man of prayer, a truly "spiritual" man. Without a strong spiritual substance, he cannot long endure in his ministry. Christ must also teach him that the main purpose of his life is not self-realization and success. He must learn that he is not in the business of building himself an interesting or comfortable life, or of setting up for himself a community of admirers and devotees but is working for another One and that it is He who truly matters. This is initially opposed to the natural emphasis of our existence, but with time it proves that precisely this process in which the self becomes inconsequential is what truly liberates.

He who acts on Christ's behalf knows that it is always the case that one sows and another reaps. He does not need to bother incessantly about himself; he leaves the outcome to the Lord and does his own part without anxiety, free and cheerful because he is hidden within, in the whole. If priests today so often feel overworked, tired, and frustrated, the blame lies with a strained pursuit of results. Faith becomes a burdensome piece of baggage that the priest just barely manages to keep dragging along, whereas it should be a wing that bears us aloft.

Participation in Christ's love for men, in his will to save and help them, grows of itself out of intimate communion with him. . . . But whoever has discovered Christ from inside and knows him firsthand also discovers that this relationship alone bestows meaning on everything else and transforms even difficulties into graces. Only such joy in Christ can also give joy for ministry and make it bear fruit.

He who loves desires to know. Therefore, true love of Christ also expresses itself in the wish to know him ever better and to know everything that pertains to him. If love of Christ necessarily becomes love of men, it follows that education in Christ must include education in the natural virtues of humanity. If loving Christ implies getting to know him, it follows that the willingness to undertake committed and careful study is a sign of the seriousness of one's vocation and of the earnest inward search for intimacy with him. Training in faith is training in true humanity. It is also to learn the reason of faith. Because Christ is never alone but came in order to unite the world in his Body, love for the Church becomes an additional component: we do not seek a Christ whom we have invented, for only in the real communion of the Church do we encounter the real Christ. And once again the depth and seriousness of one's relation to the Lord himself is revealed in the ready willingness to love the Church, to live together with her and to serve Christ in her.

I would like to conclude by citing a text from Pope Saint Gregory the Great, in which he uses images of the Old Testament to describe the essential connection between interior life and ministry that we have mentioned here: "What else are holy men but rivers that . . . water the parched earth? Yet they would . . . dry up . . . if they . . . did not return to the place where they began their course. That is, if they do not abide in the interiority of the heart and do not bind themselves fast with chains of longing in love for the Creator . . . their tongue withers up. But out of love they constantly return to this inner sanctuary, and what they . . . pour out . . . in public they draw from the well . . . of love. By loving they learn what they proclaim in teaching" (*In Ezechielem I*, hom. 5, 16: PL 76:828 B).[36]

36. Ratzinger, "Biblical Foundations of Priesthood," 626–27.

Ratzinger's Perspective Regarding Priestly Formation

For Cardinal Ratzinger, good priestly formation was fundamental in renewing Church life. These are his words: "To my mind, the fashioning of seminaries into centers where students receive a qualitatively excellent spiritual formation while deepening theological instruction imparted in the classroom is a paramount task of the present hour."[37]

Priestly formation needs to be holistic, involving every aspect of a seminarian's life—human development, academic formation, pastoral training, and above all else, spiritual formation. The seminarian needs to be formed, according to the words of Saint Peter: "As living stones, let yourselves be built into a spiritual house, a holy priesthood to offer spiritual sacrifices pleasing to God through Jesus Christ" (1 Pt 2:5). Although these words of Peter were first used as catechetical instruction for those preparing for baptism, they were applicable in a special way for those preparing for priestly ordination. It is essential for the seminarian to recognize the power of baptism as a necessary prerequisite in order to live the life of Christ in building up the community of believers. But what could be more important in a seminary than young men, through the power of their baptism that fosters their growth in discipleship, gradually becoming part of the living Church?

Ratzinger asks the question,

> Why should we have a seminary? How should the formation of priests proceed today? In our Scripture text, we find first of all a reference to the building of a spiritual house out of living stones. *House* in the biblical sense of the term denotes not so much a building of stones but kith and kin, the family. . . . The baptized who are originally strangers to one another are to become one family, God's family. This is a process that ought to find concrete application in the seminary so that the

37. Ratzinger, *The Nature and Mission of Theology* (San Francisco: Ignatius Press, 1995), 128.

future priest develops the ability in his parish, or wherever he may be, to bring people together into the family, into the community of God's house. To be sure, there is still the qualification *spiritual* house. . . . Here the word *spiritual* is derived from the Holy Spirit and from his creative power, without which nothing is real at all. A spiritual house built by the Holy Spirit is first and foremost the truly real house. The belonging to one another that stems from the Holy Spirit reaches deeper and is stronger and more lively than the simple kinship of blood. All those who have been touched by the Holy Spirit are brought together, stand in closer solidarity than any other kind of relationship could establish . . .

Now it should be noted that the reference to building in our passage appears in the *passive*: as living stones, let yourselves be built into a spiritual house. In accordance with our urge to be doing something, we completely transpose these words into the active: to build the kingdom of God, to build the Church, to build a new society, etcetera. The New Testament views our role in another way. The builder is God himself or the Holy Spirit. We are the stones; the building, as far as we are concerned, is a "being built" . . . If we want to be the house, each one of us has to take upon himself the destiny of being well prepared. In order to be of use for the house, we have to let ourselves be properly formed for the place where we are needed. The one who wishes to be part of the whole vast array and become a stone set in it has to allow himself to be united to the whole. He can no longer simply do or act as the thought occurs to him and it seems the thing to do. He can no longer simply go where he wants. He has to accept the fact that it is another who girds him and leads him where he would not go (cf. Jn 21:18). In John's Gospel, we find still another figure: the vine that has to produce fruit must be pruned; it has to allow itself to be clipped. The process of bearing greater fruit is experienced only by accepting the pain of being pruned, purified (Jn 15:2).[38]

38. Ratzinger, "Some Perspectives on Priestly Formation Today," 1–20.

This formation plan justifies the hardships of purification and guarantees that it is truly purification and not destruction. A person grows into this kind of priest when he seeks to acquire "everything that is true, noble, good, pure, worthy of love, and honorable, everything virtuous and worthy of praise" (Phil 4:8). A person becomes ready for priestly ministry when he becomes true to himself.

An Education in Proper Living as a Human Being

The first aspect on priestly formation concerns the education in proper living as a human being. These are the words of Ratzinger:

> The formation of priests has to offer more than a professional training: an education in proper living as a human being. Furthermore, it has first and foremost to provide for the acquiring of those fundamental virtues without which no family can long remain united. This is so important for the priest because not only must he be ready to live together with the family of his presbyterate, his local Church and the Church universal, but his task, over and above this, is to bring and hold together in the community of faith those who are strangers to one another by reason of origin, education, temperament, and the circumstances of life. He has to lead people to reconciliation, to be able to forgive and to forget, to forbearance and magnanimity. He has to help each bear with the other in his otherness, to have patience with the other, and to exhibit in proper balance trust and prudence, discretion and openness, and much more besides. He must be ready before all else to stand by people in their tribulations: both in physical sufferings and in the disappointments, adversities, and worries of which no one is spared. How should he do all this if he himself has not learned it first of all? To be able to accept and endure suffering is one of the basic requirements for human happiness; when this is not learned, life is bound to fail. Being provoked with everyone and everything dries up the soil of the soul, so to

speak, and makes it a wasteland. Formerly we used to speak of the mastery of pain in connection with asceticism. This word is no longer used today; we come nearer to its meaning when we translate it from the Greek into English: "training." Everyone knows that there can be no success without training and its corresponding mastery of the self. For every possible art today people train themselves with zeal and concentration, and thus peaks of achievement are attainable in many areas that in former times would have been unthinkable. But why does it seem so farfetched to be in training for real, genuine living? To practice the art of renunciation, of self-mastery, of inner freedom from our addictions?[39]

Among the many things that might be said here, I would like to raise one point in particular: *to educate in the truth*. The truth often makes people uncomfortable; it is probably the strictest of teachers in the process of learning unselfishness and real freedom.

A person becomes right for the building when he becomes true. When this goal is achieved, the seminary becomes a home. Without this common path it would be no more than a collection of student rooms whose occupants ultimately remain each on his own. Being prepared to be purified even guarantees that such a house will have its share of humor and cheerfulness. Without it the atmosphere becomes chiefly one of griping and complaints against everyone, including oneself. In such an atmosphere, the days are gray and joy cannot grow because it does not have the sunshine it needs to ripen.[40]

Servants of Your Joy

If preparation for the priesthood is essentially at its heart a liturgical training, then a seminary needs to be a house wherein a wide-ranging cultural formation is provided:

39. "Some Perspectives on Priestly Formation Today," 5.
40. "Some Perspectives on Priestly Formation Today," 8–9.

> music, literature, and the arts delight the human spirit; all these have an important place in seminary formation. Seminarians have various gifts, and the good thing is that in one seminary many diverse gifts can be brought together in one community for the benefit of all. No one person can do everything, but this is not an excuse for a seminarian to remove himself from cultural activity. In the liturgy, we touch the Beautiful itself; we touch eternal life. From the liturgy, joy should radiate through the house; in it the problems of the day can again and again be transformed and overcome. When the liturgy is at the center of our life, the words of the Apostle apply to us: "Rejoice, again I say rejoice . . . the Lord is near" (Phil 4:4). It is only from the heart of the liturgy that we can understand what is meant when the Apostle Paul defines the priest of the New Covenant as "the servant of your joy" (2 Cor 1:24).[41]

Practically speaking, this means that in the study of theology the intellectual and the spiritual dimensions are inseparable from each other. Cardinal Ratzinger is convinced that "rational education, training in methodical work, is an indispensable element on the path to the priesthood. One who loves wants to learn. He can never know enough about the one he loves. Concern for learning is thus an inner demand of love. . . . A piety that tries to evade this ends up with just feeling. Building without the truth is a kind of spiritual self-abuse to which we may not succumb."[42]

In addition to his statement that "one who loves wants to learn," Cardinal Ratzinger made this statement in one of his homilies about a new book by Pope John Paul II:

> in which he tells about his years as a young priest and then describes what an experience it was for him to discover the love of young people and to recognize the beauty of their

41. "Some Perspectives on Priestly Formation Today," 19.
42. "Some Perspectives on Priestly Formation Today," 12–13.

love. And how he recognized that the priest's task is to teach people to love. To love love and to teach them to love. For, indeed, we must learn it. After all, love does not consist only in the first great moment of being swept away. Love consists precisely in the patience of accepting one another, of becoming ever closer to one another from within. It consists in the fidelity of putting up with one another; it consists in walking together. Love, like the Gospel, is not sugar water, not comfortable, but, rather, a great challenge and, for this very reason, the purification and transformation and healing of our life, which leads us into the big picture.

Teaching and learning love. That is the real task of someone who speaks about God. And this is what we need most, for if we do not become loving in the right way, we separate ourselves from God and from ourselves, and life becomes dark and pointless.[43]

To Be a Witness and Not a Messenger with a Telegram

In Joseph Ratzinger's words:

> The priesthood that stands at the service of the Incarnate Word has to make God's Word present in its unadulterated purity and its everlasting reality. It is essential that the priest of the New Covenant does not present just any personal philosophy of life that he thinks good or has read about, but the Word that has been entrusted to our faithful hands and that we may not tamper with, as Paul states forcefully and clearly in the Second Letter to the Corinthians (2:17). Here we find ourselves before the challenging responsibility to which the priest must set himself; behind it the breadth and depth of what priestly formation and training mean become clear. As a priest, I may not present my personal ideas for I am sent by Another, and that alone gives importance to my

43. Ratzinger, *Teaching and Learning the Love of God: Being a Priest Today*, 317–18.

message. "We are ambassadors for Christ, and God it is who is appealing through us. We beg you in Christ's name: be reconciled with God!" (2 Cor 5:20). It is this statement of Paul that remains the true definition of what is the fundamental form and mission of priestly existence in the Church of the New Covenant. I have to deliver the Word of Another and that means first of all: I have to come to know it; I have to have understood it; it must become my own.

This proclamation, however, requires much more than the attitude of a messenger with a telegram who faithfully delivers strange words that mean nothing to him. I have to hand on the Word of Another in the first person, in a quite personal way and so appropriate it to myself that it becomes my own word. For this message does not require a telegrapher but a witness. While a person usually forms his thought and then looks for the right word, the reverse is true here: the Word goes before him. He puts himself at its disposal and gives himself to the Word.[44]

The Fruitfulness of Celibacy

The priesthood demands a departure from bourgeois existence; it has to incorporate within itself in a methodical way this losing of one's self. The Church's joining of celibacy to the priesthood brings out these considerations: celibacy stands in starkest contradiction to the normal fulfillment of life. When a man accepts it interiorly, he cannot look upon the priesthood as one professional attainment among others. Instead, he must somehow assent to the renunciation of his own life's aspirations and allow himself to be girded and led where he really would rather not go. Before entering into such a decision, the Word of the Lord has to be heard and reflected upon: "If one of you intends to build a tower, would he not first sit down and reckon the cost to see if he had means enough to complete it?" (Lk 14:28). No one

44. Ratzinger, "Some Perspectives on Priestly Formation Today," 10–11.

can choose the priesthood for himself to fulfill his own life. A basic requirement for the priesthood is a careful discernment of whether I am responding to the Lord's call or am only looking for self-fulfillment. The requirement to keep in vital contact with him remains constant all along the path. For if we turn our glance from him, what happened to Peter when he met Jesus walking on the water will surely happen to us. Only the look of the Lord can overpower gravity, but he really can do it. We remain sinners. But when he takes hold of us, the waters of the deep lose their power.[45]

In this context, Cardinal Ratzinger refers to the phrase used by the celebrant in the First Eucharistic prayer (the Roman Canon), "*nobis quoque peccatoribus* (also to us sinners)." He calls upon those who have gone ahead of him, beginning with John the Baptist along with him seven male martyrs and seven holy women and virgins, to continue their support for the living community of the faithful. It is significant that this Eucharistic prayer calls upon the names of holy women in its prayer for priests. This reminds us of Ratzinger's comments that the concept of celibacy comes from the words of Christ:

> Priestly celibacy has nothing to do with misogyny. Nor does it mean having no association with women. The process of a priest's interior growth depends quite essentially upon his finding a proper relationship with women; he needs the support given by mothers, virgins, career women, widows, who accept his special calling and accompany him in it with a selfless, pure feminine goodness and concern.[46]

In an interview with Peter Seewald titled "Salt of the Earth," Cardinal Ratzinger stated that the teaching of the Church concerning priestly celibacy comes from Christ himself,

45. "Some Perspectives on Priestly Formation Today," 16.
46. "Some Perspectives on Priestly Formation Today," 17.

> There are, Christ says, those who give up marriage for the sake of the kingdom of heaven and bear testimony to the kingdom of heaven with their whole existence. Very early on the Church came to the conviction that to be a priest means to give this testimony to the kingdom of heaven. In this regard, it could fall back analogously to an Old Testament parallel of another nature. Israel marches into the land. Each of the eleven tribes gets its land, its territory. Only the tribe of Levi, the priestly tribe, doesn't get an inheritance; its inheritance is God alone. This means in practical terms that its members live on the cult offerings and not, like the other tribes, from the cultivation of land. The essential point is that they have no property. In Psalm 16 we read, "You are my assigned portion; I have drawn you as my lot; God is my land." This figure, that is, the fact that in the Old Testament the priestly tribe is landless and, as it were, lives on God—and thereby also really bears witness to him was later translated, on the basis of Jesus' words, to this: "the land where the priest lives is God."[47]

If I have children, then I continue to live in them; it's a sort of immortality through posterity. For this reason, the ultimate condition of life is to have posterity and thereby to remain in the land of the living. Again, the words of Ratzinger:

> The renunciation of marriage and family is thus to be understood in terms of this vision: I renounce what, humanly speaking, is not only the most normal but also the most important thing. I forego bringing forth further life on the tree of life, and I live in the faith that my land is really God—and so I make it easier for others, also, to believe that there is a kingdom of heaven. I bear witness to Jesus Christ, to the Gospel, not only with words, but also with this specific mode of existence, and I place my life in this form at his disposal.

47. Ratzinger, *Salt of the Earth*, 194.

> In this sense, celibacy has a christological and an apostolic meaning at the same time. The point is not simply to save time—so I then have a little bit more time at my disposal because I am not a father of a family. That would be too primitive and pragmatic a way to see things. The point is really an existence that stakes everything on God and leaves out precisely the one thing that normally makes a human existence fulfilled with a promising future.[48]

Celibacy is a special way of life that evolved early in the Church based on good biblical grounds. These are the words of Ratzinger:

> It is not a dogma. It is a form of life that has grown up in the Church and that naturally always brings with it the danger of a fall. When one aims so high, there are failures. . . . The poorer an age is in faith, the more frequent the falls. People need to get straight in their minds that times of crisis for celibacy are always times of crisis for marriage as well. For, as a matter of fact, today we are experiencing not only violations of celibacy; marriage itself is becoming increasingly fragile as the basis of our society.
>
> The candidate for the priesthood has to recognize the faith as a force in his life, and he must know that he can live celibacy only in faith. Then celibacy can also become again a testimony that says something to people and that also gives them the courage to marry. The two institutions are interconnected. If fidelity in the one is no longer possible, the other no longer exists: one fidelity sustains the other. . . . In both cases the question of a definitive life decision is at the center of one's own personality.[49]

The Church Lives by Abiding with Christ and Standing by Him

As a conclusion to the teaching of Cardinal Ratzinger about priestly ministry and formation of priests is the following homily

48. *Salt of the Earth*, 195.
49. *Salt of the Earth*, 196–97.

he delivered at the silver episcopal jubilee of Cardinal Meisner and his Auxiliary bishops at Cologne, Germany in 2000. It is based on the Gospel reading from St. John (15:1–8):

> Dear Cardinal Meisner! Dear Auxiliary Bishops Dick and Plöger! Dear brothers and sisters in the Lord! The liturgy of this Easter Sunday, on which we observe with grateful joy the silver episcopal jubilee of Cardinal Meisner, Auxiliary Bishop Dick, and Auxiliary Bishop Plöger, places before us one of the great images for the mystery of Christ that the Gospel of John gives us, bread—for the exquisite character of creation, for the festivity and the joy that it provides. It immediately became an image of election, of the story of the love that God seeks with mankind, and thus an image of the People of God.
>
> The grapevine is smaller than the other trees, the teachers in Israel used to say; but by its fruit it surpasses them all. Thus, the grapevine became an image for Christ, an image for the unity between Christ and the Church, an image for the unity of Creator and creation, an image of the promise: God is everything to everyone (1 Cor 15:28). And, of course, in this the Eucharistic mystery shines through, which the Lord gives us himself as the fruit of the vine, gives us the sacred wine of his love, of his life.
>
> *Standing by Christ*
>
> All the great themes of the faith—creation, Christ, Church, sacrament—are intertwined in this image, which thus becomes also a parable for the priestly ministry in being with Christ and for Christ, in standing up in the Church and for the Church, in going toward his kingdom. Therefore, on this day it is addressed in a particular way to you, dear confreres, who today are looking back on twenty-five years of episcopal activity in the Church of God.
>
> If you read the Gospel (Jn 15:1–8) carefully, you can tell that it is constructed like a fugue with three themes that intertwine more and more and thus interpret the message

of the grapevine: abiding—pruning—fruit—these are the three basic terms of this parable; just in the eight verses of the Gospel reading the word "abide" occurs six times, and so in it we heard the basic theme that Jesus intended to present to us with this image—the basic theme that is developed and deepened in the two other accompanying themes.

"Abiding" therefore is the first basic term that stands in front of us like a signpost for us and also for the priestly ministry: only the one who abides lives with the grapevine and stays alive. "Abiding"—that is certainly not one of the favorite words of our time. Quite the contrary—what counts is change, things that are new and different, mobility that does not let itself be pinned down but is able to detach itself quickly from former things and to turn to changed circumstances.

And yet: without abiding, there is no growth; without connection, there is no progress. Where there is no connection, there are only torn-off branches that are doomed to wither and belong to the world of the dead, even though they still appear ever so strong and alive. The Church lives by abiding with Christ, standing by him, even if that does not seem modern. "Do you too want to leave me?" the Lord asks us. And you, dear brothers, answered along with Peter: "Lord, to whom should we go? You alone have the words of eternal life" (Jn 6:67–68). We stand by you; we do not let the winds of the moment bend us and drive us away. You are the root that supports and gives life. You, O Lord, said: "No one will snatch from my hand those whom my Father has given to me" (Jn 10:28–29). Therefore, we ask you, Lord, let us not be snatched from your hand. Let not the faithful whom you have entrusted to us be snatched from your hands. Let not the wolves tear to pieces your sheep, who after all are your flock. . . .

"Abiding"—dear Cardinal Joachim, in difficult times in the German Democratic Republic you experienced what that means: abiding. You did not bow to the dictatorship. You made no false compromises, for you knew: only Christ abides. And if we abide with him, even in adverse winds, then we stand aright. And in doing so, you also had in view the other, the ecclesial dimension of this abiding. Peter spoke the word about abiding, and we pronounce it with him. Another part of abiding in the grapevine is precisely abiding in the great communion of saints, for whose cohesiveness Peter stands.

Ministry of Pruning

When we read the acts of the martyrs of the century that has just passed, we repeatedly encounter this: knowledge about the great communion of the Church, knowledge about Peter as the seal of unity supported people in the confusion: it was for them a signpost pointing to where the whole grapevine is and a sign that all the parts of the grapevine belong to one another. Only in the whole, in the one grapevine, do we also abide with Christ.

Since you came to the West, your witness of standing firm and abiding assumed other forms that demanded no less of the courage of humility. A saying of Saint Ambrose comes to mind; he had to fight quite similar battles: "Since the Church has been living under Christian emperors, she has no doubt grown in power and wealth, but has become weaker in moral strength" (*In Luc* IX, 32). How true that is today, too! "Abiding" is not something static and comfortable. Part of abiding is the ongoing service of pruning. Today in this connection, we find it very easy to mouth the remark about the "*Ecclesia semper reformanda*" [The Church must always be reformed] because we are always thinking about others and about the structures that are to be changed, especially far away in Rome. But pruning means, in reality, something very personal and, if we understand it correctly, shifts us directly to the body.

Here a remark that Saint Augustine made in his sermons on the Psalms comes to mind; in it we can hear the autobiographical element, the retrospective view of his own life: "Before such people enlist in God's service, they enjoy delightful freedom in the world, like grapes or olives hanging there. . . . Any who approach God's service must know that they have come to the winepresses. They will be bruised, trampled, and squeezed, not so that they may perish in this world, but to ensure that they trickle down into God's storage vats" (*Exposition of Psalm* 83, 1).

You too, dear brothers, in the twenty-five years of your episcopal ministry, have certainly had in abundance this experience of being bruised and trampled. Otherwise, we cannot become mature wine. This applies to all of us, priests, bishops, and laity, each in his own way. In order for ripe fruit to develop, rain, storms, and sunshine are necessary. And in order for the fruit to serve its purpose, we have to go through the winepress of suffering, whether we like it or not.

Christ himself went ahead of us: on the Cross, as God's sacred cluster, he allowed himself to be pressed, and so he offers himself to us down through the ages in the Eucharistic chalice as the wine of God's love. And again and again Eucharist comes about only by gathering and pressing the grapes, through their fermentation and maturation, in which the whole Church must become good wine and thus one with Christ, the grapevine that supports and enlivens us all.

With the saying about pruning, the third leitmotif of this Gospel has now been introduced: the theme of the fruit for which the grapevine is intended. The parable silently contrasts the grapevine that puts forth leaves only and the grapevine that is pruned and thus bears fruit. A Church that produces many papers but no vocations of persons who give themselves entirely to the Lord is a grapevine that puts forth leaves but no grapes. Papers pass away; words resound.

Faith Becomes Love

Structures become outdated—but the Lord looks for fruit that lasts. God does not want dead, artificial things that ultimately are thrown away: he wants living things, life. The grapevine is Christ; along with him the grapevine is his Church, the People of God, which grows on its pilgrimage through the ages. But the remark once made by the Jewish philosopher of religion Philo of Alexandria— a contemporary of Jesus—still applies also: "The soul is the most sacred vineyard" (*Somn Il*, 172f.). The Lord waits for the grapevine to set down roots in the soul and, through all the prunings, to bring forth the fruit of faith, hope, and love.

He waits for men who make themselves available, not just for a more or less long-term experiment, but entirely and unconditionally with their life, full-time, who also allow him to lead them where they actually did not want to go. He waits for our Yes—that is the real fruit for which he created us.

When faith becomes the force that supports a person and the person relies entirely on God, then faith automatically becomes love. The great figures of faith—from Paul via Francis of Assisi down to Maximilian Kolbe and Mother Teresa—show us this. Where faith deteriorates, love also grows cold and selfishness increases. However, when Christ dwells in our souls, his love is enkindled there, too, and the face of the earth is renewed through the love in which God himself enters into this world.

"You crown the year with your bounty," it says in Psalm 65:11. Dear brothers, twenty-five years of episcopal ministry are a sort of harvest festival of thanksgiving. In looking back on these twenty-five years, with all their toils and their blessings, we sense it: Yes, you crown the years of ministry with your goodness. On this retrospective day, the Church of Cologne thanks you, the Church of God thanks you, and the Lord himself thanks you for your fidelity in abiding, for your patience in the maturing processes, and for the fruit that you bring him.

With you, we all thank God for the gift of fidelity, for perseverance with the Lord and for the joy of faith that you pass on in the midst of all tribulation. And we pray to the good Lord that he will grant you again and again the crown

> of his goodness. We ask him to help you to keep going, so that your ministry, too, might continue to be blessed and to produce abundant fruit unto eternal life.[50]

In Chapter 2 of *Salt of the Earth*, Ratzinger returns to where he began.

> I began with the theme of the Church, and it is present in everything. Only, in dealing with the Church it was important to me, and it has become increasingly important, that the Church cannot be an end in herself but exist so that God may be seen. In that respect I would say that I study the theme of the Church with the intention of opening a vista onto God. And in this sense God is the real central theme of my endeavors.
>
> I have never tried to create a system of my own, an individual theology. What is specific, if you want to call it that, is that I simply want to think in communion with the faith of the Church, and that means above all to think in communion with the great thinkers of the faith. The aim is not an isolated theology that I draw out of myself but one that opens as widely as possible into the common intellectual pathway of the faith. For this reason exegesis was always very important. I couldn't imagine a purely philosophical theology. The point of departure is first of all the word. That we believe the word of God, that we try really to get to know and understand it, and then, as I said, to think it together with the great masters of the faith. This gives my theology a somewhat biblical character and also bears the stamp of the Fathers, especially Augustine. But it goes without saying that try not to stop with the ancient Church but to hold fast to the great high points of thought and at the same time to bring contemporary thought into the discussion.[51]

50. Ratzinger, *Teaching and Learning the Love of God*, 336–42.
51. Ratzinger, *Salt of the Earth*, 66.

2

"Coworkers of the Truth"

THE ECCLESIAL VOCATION OF THE THEOLOGIAN IN THE LIGHT OF POPE BENEDICT XVI

Because of their connection with Christ, every Christian, every priest, should become a well-spring which gives life to others. Consequently, we should be able and willing to offer life-giving water to a parched and thirsty world. This should be the urgent duty of theologians in the service of Christ and his Church: to be coworkers in proclaiming the truth.

Joseph Ratzinger: Life in the Church and Living Theology

The abbot of the Cistercian Abbey Heiligenkreuz in Vienna, P. Maximilian Heinrich Heim, wrote a thoughtful book entitled *Joseph Ratzinger: Life in the Church and Living Theology,* the theological thought and pastoral work of Pope Benedict XVI. The Pope wrote the preface for this important work.[1]

To understand the ecclesial foundation of the theologian Joseph Ratzinger, it is important to know the scientific background which roots him in the contemporary world. That his theological mind developed from extensive study of many disciplines is evident in his various autobiographical publications.[2]

1. Maximilian Heinrich Heim, *Joseph Ratzinger: Life in the Church and Living Theology; Fundamentals of Ecclesiology with Reference to* Lumen Gentium, with foreword by Joseph Ratzinger (San Francisco: Ignatius Press, 2007).

2. Joseph Ratzinger, *Salt of the Earth: The Church at the End of the Millennium,* An Interview with Peter Seewald (San Francisco: Ignatius Press, 1997); Ratzinger, *God and the World: Believing and Living in Our Time,* A Conversation with Peter Seewald (San Francisco: Ignatius Press, 2002); Ratzinger, *Milestones: Memoirs, 1927–1977* (San Francisco: Ignatius Press, 1998).

And even after he became Pope, Ratzinger continued his scholarly research as evident by the publication of his books on Jesus of Nazareth.[3]

For Cardinal Joseph Ratzinger, the Church is the transtemporal subject of faith, a subject that is rooted in the trinitarian mystery and testifies to its identity along with its origin in Christ.

> Belief in the Trinity is *communio*; to believe in the Trinity means to become *communio*. Historically, this means that the "I" of the creed-formulations is a collective "I", the "I" of the believing Church, to which the individual "I" belongs as long as one believes. In other words, the "I" of the credo embraces the transition from the individual "I" to the ecclesial "I." In the case of the subject, the "I" of the Church is a structural precondition of the creed: this utters itself (has meaning) only in the *communio* of the Church; the oneness of the believing subject is the necessary counterpart and consequence of the known "object," of that "Other" who is known by faith and who thereby ceases to be merely the "Other."[4]

This means that an individual does not believe because of his own resources, but rather, as Ratzinger stresses, because of the faith of the Church that he embraces, always "along with the whole Church."[5] Because the "I" of the believer exists only as a result of the "we," the profession of the triune God in the ecclesial

3. Ratzinger, *Jesus von Nazareth: Beiträge zur Christologie*, JRGS 6/1 (Freiburg: Herder, 2013).

4. Ratzinger, *Principles of Catholic Theology: Building Stones for a Fundamental Theology* (San Francisco: Ignatius Press, 1987), 23. Cf. Ratzinger, "Die Dimensionen des Problems: These I-VIII. Kommentar von Joseph Ratzinger" in *Die Einheit des Glaubens und der theologische Pluralismus*, ed. Internationale Theologenkommision (Einsiedeln: Johannes Verlag, 1973), 17–51, especially 36–42.

5. Ratzinger, "Die Dimensionen des Problems," 36. Cf. Heim, *Joseph Ratzinger*, 147–50.

communio constitutes the faith of the Church, with which personal faith is then bound up.[6] The subject that holds everything together is the Church, and this is true also in relation to the articles of faith, for without her these would be only a more or less lengthy "catalogue of things to be believed; within and by the Church, they are made one."[7] With this premise, Ratzinger addressed the central article of faith, the Eucharist. For the Church

> came into existence because someone lived and suffered his word; by reason of his death, his word is understood as the word par excellence, as the meaning of all being, as logos. In the solemn remembrance of the Church, the central mystery of salvation, namely, the death and Resurrection of the Lord, is present and mightily effective.[8]

This saving event, this paschal mystery, which simultaneously universalizes and personalizes and into which the individual enters through the Church, is for Ratzinger the most fascinating thing about being a Catholic:

> That I, living within this great communion, can know that I am in communion with all the living and the dead; and that I also find in it a certainty about the essence of my life—namely, God who has turned to me—on which I can found my life, with which I can live and die.[9]

This is the reason Cardinal Joseph Ratzinger emphasizes the importance of "identification with the Church." The individual Christian is able to believe by sharing the faith of the whole Church. The basic core of this faith is a very simple act: it is a question of "sharing in the basic decision of Jesus Christ through a

6. Ratzinger, *Principles of Catholic Theology*, 26–27.
7. *Principles of Catholic Theology*, 23–24.
8. *Principles of Catholic Theology*, 26.
9. Ratzinger, *Salt of the Earth*, 21.

participation in the basic decision of the Church."[10] The Christian loves the Church and fosters affection for her: "*Sentire cum Ecclesia*." A man of the Church "believes together with the Church."[11]

> By its very nature, faith is believing communion with the whole Church. The "I believe" of the Creed refers, not to some private "I," but rather to the corporate "I" of the Church. Faith is possible in the measure that I become one with this corporate "I," which does not abolish my own "I" but broadens it out and, in this way, brings it to itself for the first time.[12]

When Peter Seewald asked, "What would you yourself see as specific about your theology or the way you do theology?" Cardinal Ratzinger answered:

> I began with the theme of the Church, and it is present in everything. Only, in dealing with the Church it was important to me, and it has become increasingly important, that the Church can not be an end in herself but exist so that God may be seen. In that respect I would say that I study the theme of the Church with the intention of opening a vista onto God. And in this sense God is the real central theme of my endeavors.
>
> I have never tried to create a system of my own, an individual theology. What is specific, if you want to call it that, is that I simply want to think in communion with the faith of the Church, and that means above all to think in communion with the great thinkers of the faith. The aim is not an isolated theology that I draw out of myself but one that opens

10. Ratzinger, "Identification with the Church," in *Living with the Church*, ed. Joseph Ratzinger and Karl Lehmann (Chicago: Franciscan Herald Press, 1978), 27.

11. Ratzinger, "Die Dimensionen des Problems," 36.

12. Ratzinger, *The Nature and Mission of Theology: Essays to Orient Theology in Today's Debates* (San Francisco: Ignatius Press, 1995), 94.

> as widely as possible into the common intellectual pathway of the faith. For this reason exegesis was always very important. I couldn't imagine a purely philosophical theology. The point of departure is first of all the word. That we believe the word of God, that we try really to get to know and understand it, and then, as I said, to think it together with the great masters of the faith. This gives my theology a somewhat biblical character and also bears the stamp of the Fathers, especially Augustine. But it goes without saying that try not to stop with the ancient Church but to hold fast to the great high points of thought and at the same time to bring contemporary thought into the discussion.[13]

The role of the Church in Christianity is at the heart of Joseph Ratzinger's theology. As Pope, he recognized his "actual vocation in being a professor." The path of his life, from the professor's chair to being the shepherd of souls in Rome, sharpened his appreciation of the "inner unity of theological research, theological teaching, pastoral service, and administration in the Church." This is the reason he sought to draw theologians from their ivory towers into the broader pastoral life of the Church. He urged them to accompany their scholarship with a life of prayer—to integrate their academic life with a strong spiritual life and an appreciation for the pastoral needs of people everywhere.

Ratzinger understood that theology as a discipline "belongs in the university and within the wide-ranging dialogue of sciences, not merely as a historical discipline and one of the human sciences, but precisely as theology, as inquiry into the rationality of faith."[14]

At the same time, theology must be something other than religious studies. It is more than a "methodical arrangement of

13. Ratzinger, *Salt of the Earth*, 66.

14. Pope Benedict XVI, *Apostolic Journey to München, Altötting, and Regensburg: Meeting with the Representatives of Science in the Aula Magna of the University of Regensburg*, September 12, 2006.

reflections on the issues of religion because it arises from the answer that was not found by ourselves." The task of theology is to understand the word that God has given the human family. This is the reason that even the simplest of believers, even those who do not understand the reasons, cannot be without the theology that underlies their faith. Theological research basic to theological development, if it is to remain Catholic, must always respect the teaching of the Church. It requires not only "scientific competence, but also, and in no small measure, the spirit of faith and humility of a person who knows that the living and true God infinitely surpasses all human capacities."[15]

The Nature and Mission of Theology

What is theology? Is it only the word of God interpreted by human minds, or must there also be the inspiration of grace? For Christians, theological study means unraveling the data that the Church has from the Scriptures and the lived experience of the Church. It flows from the blending of biblical faith and Greek rationality which is the basis for historical Christianity. Theology "is based on the assumption, accepted by faith, that what is believed, that is, theology's own foundation, is reasonable—is, indeed, reason itself. Hence the essential part of faith is that it seeks to understand its foundation and its contents, and precisely this enterprise is what we call theology. More precisely, we speak of theology when the enterprise is carried on in an orderly fashion and according to commonly recognised, well-founded rules that we term methodology."[16]

15. See Stefan von Kempis, "Theologie" in *Benedikt XVI.—das Lexikon: Von Ablass bis Zölibat* (Leipzig: Edition Radio Vatikan/Benno Verlag, 2007), 232–34. Cf. Ratzinger, *Pilgrim Fellowship of Faith: The Church as Communion* (San Francisco: Ignatius Press, 2005), 17–37; *Principles of Catholic Theology*, 315–31.

16. Ratzinger, *Church, Ecumenism, and Politics: New Endeavors in Ecclesiology* (San Francisco: Ignatius Press, 2008), 150. JRGS 8/1 and 8/2 (Freiburg:

Faith and reason are not opposed. Faith that does not lead to knowledge about God is empty, and reason that undermines faith limits the explanation for causality in the universe and human life. In the foreword to his book *The Nature and Mission of Theology*, Cardinal Ratzinger writes:

> Theology and theologians have become a common and at the same time controversial topic of discussion in the Church, indeed, in Western society in general. . . . In this situation, the dialogue concerning theology and the clarification of its methods, its mission and its limits have become urgent. Individual sections of this book were occasioned by the challenges of this dialogue. They do not form a systematic treatise on theology, a project which my professional obligations unfortunately do not permit me to undertake. Rather, the pieces assembled here represent so many preliminary approaches to the subject from diverse points of view. I hope that precisely in their openness to further development these first efforts can help the nature of the theologian's work in today's circumstances to be better understood as well as to sustain it in its essential task: to serve the knowledge of the truth of revelation and, in so doing, unity in the Church.[17]

In the chapter titled "The Spiritual Basis and Ecclesial Identity of Theology," Cardinal Ratzinger wrote:

> If the Church and her authority constitute a factor alien to scientific scholarship, then both theology and the Church are in equal danger. In fact, a church without theology impoverishes and a churchless theology melts away into caprice. For this reason, the question of the intrinsic connection between

Herder, 2010). See also Cardinal Kurt Koch, *Das Geheimnis des Senfkorns: Grundzüge des theologischen Denkens von Papst Benedikt XVI*, Ratzinger-Studien 3 (Regensburg: Verlag Friedrich Pustet, 2010).

17. Ratzinger, *The Nature and Mission of Theology*, 7–9.

> Church and theology must be thought through from the ground up and given an unambiguous resolution; not in order to demarcate spheres of interest, or to maintain power or eliminate it, but for the sake of the rectitude of theology and ultimately of our faith itself.[18]

Ratzinger seeks to explain the foundations of faith, the inner connection between the Church and theology. Since there are many ways to show this connection, the Cardinal points out certain theologians who were able to make this connection, each in his own way: Romano Guardini, Erik Peterson, Karl Barth, and Heinrich Schlier. They helped form the ecclesiology that connected theology to Church life.[19]

In order to understand correctly the ecclesial character of the theologian, Cardinal Ratzinger wrote about "the new subject as the precondition and foundation of all theology." He refers to a sentence in the letter to the Galatians in which St. Paul describes the distinctive elements of Christianity as a personal experience which reinvigorates the Christian life but at the same time presents an objective reality: "It is no longer I who lives, but Christ who lives in me" (Gal 2:20). This affirmation is at the end of a brief spiritual autobiography which Paul shares with his readers. Ratzinger writes:

> This inner event is at one and the same time wholly personal and wholly objective. It is an individual experience in the highest degree, yet it declares what the essence of Christianity is for everyone. . . . The point is that conversion in the Pauline sense is something much more radical than, say, the revision of a few opinions and attitudes. It is a death-event. In other words, it is an exchange of the old subject

18. *The Nature and Mission of Theology*, 48.

19. *The Nature and Mission of Theology*, 45–50. Among the French-speaking theologians, Louis Bouyer should be added to the list as a figure of equal importance.

> for another. The "I" ceases to be an autonomous subject standing in itself. It is snatched away from itself and fitted into a new subject. The "I" is not simply submerged, but it must really release its grip on itself in order to receive itself anew in and together with a greater "I."[20]

The exchange of subjects includes a passive element, which Paul rightly characterizes as death, in the sense of receiving a share in the event of the Cross. It can come to someone only from the outside, from another person. The "I no longer live" does not describe a private mystical experience but rather defines the essence of baptism. What takes place is a sacramental event, hence, an event involving the Church. There is a passive element in Paul's words which he characterizes as death, in the sense of sharing in the event of the Cross. "I no longer live" does not describe a private mystical experience but rather defines the essence of Baptism. What takes place is a sacramental event which involves the Church. The passive side of becoming a Christian (dying to one's self) calls for the action of the Church which calls the new Christian into the life of the Church, into the body of Christ. This is the reason the new Christian is called to "put on Christ" (Rom 13:14), to be clothed with Christ within the context of the Christian community.

This is the reason for Ratzinger's insistence that theology must necessarily presuppose faith. These are his words:

> This implies that theology is based upon a new beginning in thought which is not the product of our own reflection but has its origin in the encounter with a Word which always precedes us. We call the act of accepting this new beginning "conversion." Because there is no theology without faith, there can be no theology without conversion. Conversion can take many forms. It need not always be an instantaneous event, as it was in the case of Augus-

20. *The Nature and Mission of Theology*, 50–51.

tine or Pascal, Newman or Guardini. In one form or another, however, the convert must consciously pronounce in his own name a Yes to this new beginning and really turn from the "I" to the "no-longer-I." It is thus immediately obvious that the opportunity for creative theology increases the more that faith becomes real, personal experience; the more that conversion acquires interior certainty thanks to a painful process of transformation; the more that it is recognized as the indispensable means of penetrating into the truth of one's own being. This is why in every age the path to faith can take its bearings by converts; it explains why they in particular can help us to recognize the reason for the hope that is in us (cf. 1 Pet 3:15) and to bear witness to it. The connection between faith and theology is not, therefore, some sort of sentimental or pietistic twaddle but is a direct consequence of the logic of the thing and is corroborated by the whole of history. Athanasius is inconceivable without Anthony, the father of monasticism, and the latter's new experience of Christ; Augustine is likewise unthinkable without his passionate journey to a radical Christian life. Moreover, Bonaventure and the Franciscan theology of the thirteenth century would have been impossible without imposing a new representation of Christ in the figure of Saint Francis of Assisi, nor could Thomas Aquinas have existed without Dominic's breakthrough to the gospel and to evangelization. One could continue in this vein along the whole course of history. Pure rationality is not itself sufficient to bring forth great Christian theology.[21]

Ecclesial Vocation of the Theologian

On May 4, 1990, the Congregation for the Doctrine of the Faith published an instruction on the "ecclesial vocation of the theologian" which touched off a passionate debate in the academic

21. *The Nature and Mission of Theology*, 57–58.

community.[22] As Prefect for the Congregation, Cardinal Joseph Ratzinger presented the document during a press conference with these words:

> The significance of the theologian and of theology for the whole community of believers became evident in a new way at the Second Vatican Council. Before the Council, it had been usual to consider theology as a pursuit reserved to a small circle of clerics, as an elitist and abstract affair which could hardly lay claim to the interest of the Church at large. The new mode of seeing and expressing the faith which prevailed at the Council was the fruit of the dramatic, and until then practically unnoticed, history of a new theological sensibility which had made its debut after the First World War in conjunction with new spiritual movements. . . . The liturgical movement, the biblical and ecumenical movements, finally, a strong Marian movement shaped a new spiritual climate favorable to the growth of a new theology, which later bore fruit for the whole Church at the Second Vatican Council. The bishops themselves were surprised by the bounty of a theology which in part was still unfamiliar to them and willingly took the theologians as teachers and guides into hitherto virgin territory, even though the final decisions regarding what could be adopted as an official expression of the Council and, therefore, of the Church herself, remained in the hands of the Fathers.[23]

Cardinal Ratzinger went on to explain:

> After the Council, the dynamic of this development continued apace. Theologians increasingly felt themselves to be the true teachers of the Church and even of the bishops. Moreover, since the Council, they had been discovered by

22. Congregation for the Doctrine of the Faith, Instruction *Donum Veritatis: On the Ecclesial Vocation of the Theologian* (May 24, 1990).

23. *The Nature and Mission of Theology*, 101–2.

the mass media and had captured their interest. The Magisterium of the Holy See now appeared in the public eye to be the last holdover of a failed authoritarianism. The impression was that the insistent claim to competence on the part of a nonacademic authority threatened to keep thought under tutelage, whereas in reality the path to knowledge could not be prescribed by authority but rather depended solely upon the force of argument. In these circumstances, it has become necessary to reflect anew on the position of theology and of the theologian as well as on their relationship to the Magisterium. Such a reflection would attempt to understand both theology and the Magisterium in accord with their inner logic and, in so doing, would contribute not only to peace in the Church but, above all, to a correct way of relating faith and reason. It is this task which the Instruction tries to serve.[24]

. . .

For this reason, the Instruction places the subject of theology within the broad horizon of the question of man's capacity for truth and of his true freedom. The Christian faith is not a pastime, and the Church is not one club among others of a similar or even of a different sort. Rather, faith responds to the primordial question of man regarding his origin and goal. It bears on those basic problems which Kant characterized as the essential core of philosophy: What can I know? What may I hope for? What is man? In other words, faith has to do with truth, and only if man is capable of truth can it also be said that he is called to freedom.

The first item in the alphabet of faith is the statement: In the beginning was the Word. Faith reveals to us that eternal reason is the ground of all things or, put in other terms, that things are reasonable from the ground up. Faith does not aim to offer man *some sort of* psychotherapy; its psychotherapy is the truth. This is what makes it universal and by

24. *The Nature and Mission of Theology*, 102.

nature missionary. It is also the reason why faith is intrinsically "*quærens intellectum*," as the Fathers say, that is, in search of understanding. Understanding, hence, rational engagement with the priorly given Word, is a constitutive principle of the Christian faith, which of necessity spawns theology. This trait, moreover, distinguishes the Christian faith from all other religions, even from a purely historical point of view. Theology is a specifically Christian phenomenon which follows from the structure of this faith.[25]

Ratzinger pointed out that the instruction he was presenting

treats of the task of the theologian in this broad context and thereby manifests plainly the greatness of his mission. A striking feature of the division of the text is that it does not begin with the Magisterium but with the truth, which it presents as a gift of God to his people. The truth of faith, in fact, is not bestowed upon the isolated individual, for God has willed instead to build history and community with it. It has its place in a common subject: the people of God, the Church. The vocation of the theologian is presented next, and the Magisterium and the mutual relation of the two are discussed only afterward. This implies two things:

a. Theology is not simply and exclusively an ancillary function of the Magisterium: It is not limited to gathering arguments for a priori magisterial decisions. If that were so, the Magisterium and theology would draw perilously close to an ideology whose sole interest is the acquisition and preservation of power. Theology has a specific origin of its own. The document, borrowing from Saint Bonaventure, designates two roots of theology in the Church. The first is the dynamism toward truth and understanding inherent in the faith; the second is the dynamism of love, which desires to know the beloved more intimately. Correspondingly, there are two directions in theology, which, however, continually

25. *The Nature and Mission of Theology*, 103.

cross and recross each other. The first, more outwardly moving direction, devotes its efforts to dialogue with every reasonable search for truth; the second, which moves predominantly inward, strives to fathom the inner logic and depth of the faith.

b. The document treats the ecclesial mission of the theologian, not in the context of the dualism Magisterium-theology, but rather in the framework of the triangular relationship defined by the people of God, understood as the bearer of the *sensus fidei* and the common locus of all faith, the Magisterium and theology. The development of dogma in the last 150 years is a clear index of how closely these three elements hang together: the dogmas of 1854, 1870 and 1950 became possible because the *sensus fidei* had discovered them, while the Magisterium and theology followed its lead and tried slowly to catch up with it.

This is already a statement of the essentially ecclesial identity of theology. Theology is never simply the private idea of one theologian. If it were, it could count for little, for as a private idea it would sink rapidly into insignificance. On the contrary, the Church, as a living subject which endures amid the changes of history, is the vital milieu of the theologian; the Church preserves faith's experiences with God. Theology can remain historically relevant only if it acknowledges this living environment, inserts itself into it and attains an inner participation in it. It follows that the Church is not an organization which the theologian must regard as alien and extrinsic to thought. Insofar as the Church is a corporate subject which transcends the narrowness of individuals, she is the condition which makes theological activity possible. It is thus evident that two things are essential for the theologian. First, the methodological rigor which is part and parcel of the business of scholarship; in this regard, the document refers to philosophy, the historical disciplines and the human sciences as privileged partners of the theologian. But he also has need of inner participation in the organic structure of the Church; he needs that faith which is prayer, contemplation and life. Only in this symphony does theology come into being.

This also makes for an organic understanding of the Magisterium. We said that the Church enters into the nature of theology. But the Church is more than an exterior organization of believers only if she has her own voice. Faith precedes theology; theology is the quest to understand the Word which, not having been devised by us, elicits the utmost effort from our thought but is never engulfed by it. This Word which precedes theological research is the measure of theology and requires its own organ—the Magisterium, which Christ committed to the apostles and, through them, to their successors. I do not wish to discuss in detail here how the document explains the relationship between the Magisterium and theology. Under the title 'reciprocal collaboration', it sets forth the task proper to each and explains how they ought to live and work together. The priority of faith, which lends the Magisterium authority and a final right of decision, does not obliterate the independence of theological research but guarantees it a solid basis. The document does not conceal the fact that there can be tensions even under the most favorable circumstances. These tensions, however, can be productive, provided that each side sustains them in the recognition that its function is intrinsically ordered to that of the other. The text also presents the various forms of binding authority which correspond to the grades of the Magisterium. It states—perhaps for the first time with such candor—that there are magisterial decisions which cannot be the final word on a given matter as such but, despite the permanent value of their principles, are chiefly also a signal for pastoral prudence, a sort of provisional policy. Their kernel remains valid, but the particulars determined by circumstances can stand in need of correction.[26]

26. *The Nature and Mission of Theology*, 104–6.

At the conclusion of his presentation, Cardinal Joseph Ratzinger made the point that

> The Instruction was published in the hope that the distinction between constructive kinds of tension and a perverse and unacceptable form of antithesis between theology and the Magisterium will help to relax the strained atmosphere in the Church. The Church needs a sound theology. Theology needs the living voice of the Magisterium.[27]

It was the intention of the Prefect to demonstrate with clarity the role of those entrusted with the teaching office in the Church as it related to the church's Magisterium. He was clarifying the nature and purpose of theology. These are his words:

> The task of the teaching office is, not to oppose thinking, but to ensure that the authority of the answer that was bestowed on us has its say and, thus, to make room for the truth itself to enter. To be given such a task is exciting and dangerous. It requires the humility of submission, of listening and obeying. It is a matter, not of putting your own ideas into effect, but of keeping a place for what the Other has to say, that Other without whose ever-present Word all else drops into the void. The teaching office, properly understood, must be a humble service undertaken to ensure that true theology remains possible and that the answers may thus be heard without which we cannot live aright.[28]

In one of his earlier publications, *Dogma and Preaching*, Joseph Ratzinger explained the foundations for the authentic announcement of revealed truth. Engaging the question, "How can we apply Christian doctrine to daily life?," his response was:

27. *The Nature and Mission of Theology*, 107.
28. Ratzinger, *Pilgrim Fellowship of Faith*, 37.

> The path from dogma to preaching has become very difficult. There are no longer any patterns of thought and assumptions that carry the content of dogma into everyday life; it is too much to demand of the individual preacher, however, that he himself should figure out each time the entire path from the doctrinal formula to its core and from there back to contemporary language. Should we not instead leave out dogma entirely? With such a radical cure, which appears to many today to be the only way out, preaching becomes speaking in one's own name and loses all objective interest whatsoever. . . . The inner tension of preaching depends on the objective arch spanning and upheld by the pillars: Dogma—Scripture—Church—Today; not one of them can be taken away without the whole thing eventually collapsing.[29]

It was obvious to his listeners and readers that Joseph Ratzinger was not only a brilliant theologian but that he was also an excellent teacher and preacher. Two themes emerged from his teaching and preaching that are the leitmotif of his thinking. The first was his conviction that we must serve the Church of Christ and not just ourselves, and the second was that we must be coworkers of the truth (*cooperatores veritatis*).

29. Ratzinger, *Dogma and Preaching: Applying Christian Doctrine to Daily Life* (San Francisco: Ignatius Press, 2011), 7.

3

From a Sitting to a Kneeling Theology

THEOLOGY AND HOLINESS IN HANS URS VON BALTHASAR

One of the strong influences in the development of Ratzinger's theology came from Hans Urs von Balthasar who had linked theology with holiness. The great Swiss theologian considered theology and holiness to be "two sisters in spirit"[1] who belong together inseparably. Von Balthasar was able to demonstrate the original unity of these two sisters. In an earlier text written in 1948, "Theology and Sanctity,"[2] he had emphasized the connection between theology and holiness. Then in 1987, with the same title, "Theology and Holiness,"[3] he continued to develop this theme. When he received the coveted Pope Paul VI Award from the hands of Pope John Paul II, on June 23, 1984, he forcefully spoke these words: "I insist on the inseparability between theology and spirituality, their separation being the worst disaster that ever occurred in the history of the Church."[4] These are his words:

> Most Holy Father, Eminent Cardinals, Mr. President of the Paul VI Institute, Reverend Fathers, Ladies, Gentlemen, Dear Friends!

1. Hans Urs von Balthasar, *Two Sisters in the Spirit: Thérèse of Lisieux and Elizabeth of the Trinity* (San Francisco: Ignatius Press, 1992).

2. Balthasar, "Theology and Sanctity," in *Explorations in Theology*, vol. I, *The Word Made Flesh* (San Francisco: Ignatius Press, 1989), 181–209.

3. Balthasar, "Theology and Holiness," *Communio: International Review* 14, no. 4 (1987): 342–50.

4. Balthasar, "Address of Hans Urs von Balthasar," *L'Ossevatore Romano*, Weekly Edition (23 July 1984): 7–8. Original French address: "J'insiste sur l'indivisibilité entre théologie et spiritualité, leur division étant le pire désastre survenu dans l'histoire de l'Eglise."

First of all, Most Holy Father, I wish to thank you for your kindness. You gladly consented to hand over to me this prize awarded by the Paul VI Institute, which is dedicated to the person, to the work, and to the epoch of this Pope of deeply venerated and very dear memory.

By means of this award, Mr. President and your Council, you have wished to honor the work I have attempted to accomplish for our Holy Church. Permit me to describe for you in a few words how I conceive this work which has been initiated rather than terminated. In what appears to me to be important in this work, I would like to distinguish three stages, of which the first is for me by far the most important.

On my ordination card, which shows the beloved disciple in the embrace of Jesus, I had the following three words inscribed: *Benedixit, fregit, deditque*. The breaking, of which I already had a presentiment, took place in fact when I was obliged, in obedience to a formal order of Saint Ignatius, to leave—much against my will—my spiritual home, the Society of Jesus, in order to realize a kind of extension of his ideal in the world. It was then that Saint John was shown to us as the ideal companion of Jesus, the only disciple who followed him to the very end. The one who best understood that all ecclesial obedience is based on that of the Son, who by it reveals trinitarian love. The one for whom the light must penetrate the very depths of darkness. The one to whom the Crucified entrusts his Mother, the spotless Church, the one also whose Gospel of love culminates in an apotheosis of Peter. Peter must make profession of his greater love and receive the announcement of his own crucifixion, in order to be able to succeed the Good Shepherd. John, then, is the one who—while keeping himself in the background—unites Mary and Peter. He has been given as an ideal to our Institute (of three branches: priests, men, women). This Institute, still in process of formation, intends then to be catholic in the widest and most theological sense of the term.

This is why, in the second place, I have attempted to make as concrete as possible the meaning of catholicity by the translation of what, in the great theological tradition, seemed to me should be known and assimilated by Christians of today. I began with the Apostolic Fathers, Irenaeus, Origen, Gregory of Nyssa, Maximus, Augustine, proceeded through the Middle Ages with Anselm, Bonaventure, St Thomas and the great English and Flemish mystics, to arrive by way of Dante, Catherine of Siena, John of the Cross, Berullius, Pascal at our own day: with Thérèse of Lisieux, Madeleine Delbrêl, Claudel, Péguy, Bernanos, Cardinal de Lubac (10 vol.), Adrienne von Speyr (60 vol.). To make known the greatest and the most spiritual among our brothers and sisters: this appeared to me to be in the spirit of the one who is called, without qualification, "the theologian."

This brings me, in the third place, to my own poor books, too numerous alas, regarding which I would like only to point out three trends.

1. After bringing out the unique character of Christ as compared with all the religions and thus demonstrating that all philosophical anthropology can culminate only in the light of the perfect man, the Son of God, who allows us to transcend our mortal birth in a new birth to the immortal trinitarian life, I insist on the inseparability between theology and spirituality, their separation being the worst disaster that ever occurred in the history of the Church.

2. Likewise, there is a strict unity among all theological treatises. No Christology without the Trinity and vice versa, nor without history of salvation from the faith of Abraham to the Church; no Incarnation of the Lord without the Cross and the Resurrection. One must react then against the fragmentation that believes itself to be scientific, and against all spiritualism of neoplatonic tendency, even that found in the most sublime mystical doctrine.

3. It seems necessary for me to insist on the theology of the Evangelical Counsels and to show that they contain nothing of a flight from the world because through them one dedicates oneself to the salvation of the world in the wake of Christ and of his eucharistic self-giving. Thérèse of

> Lisieux understood this marvelously. All of this, as you can see, brings us back to the idea of our Institute, to that Ignatian openness towards the world which has no other point of departure than the Cross, origin of all fecundity, the Cross from which Christ founded the first virginal nucleus of his Church: "Woman, behold your son," and "my well-loved son, behold your Mother," conduct her to the center of my Church whose unity I have entrusted to Peter.[5]

The entire *opus immensum* of Hans Urs von Balthasar testifies to his radical conviction and endeavor to once again link together theology and holiness, dogmatics and spirituality.[6] This short presentation should expose this important issue, according to the title of one of his books: *The Whole in the Fragment*.[7]

Holy Theologians: "The Pillars of the Church"

Great theologians were always saints and "pillars of the Church;" they were "theological existences." "In short, these pillars of the Church were complete personalities: What they taught, they lived with such directness, so naively, we might say, that the subsequent separation of theology and spirituality was quite unknown to them."[8]

The following paragraphs demonstrate the determination of the author to link academic theology with spiritual life.

5. Balthasar, "Address of Hans Urs von Balthasar," 7–8.

6. See Jutta Konda, *Das Verhältnis von Theologie und Heiligkeit im Werk von Hans Urs von Balthasar* (Würzburg: Echter, 1991); Antonio Sicari, OCD, "Hans Urs von Balthasar: Theology and Holiness," in *Hans Urs von Balthasar: His Life and Work*, edited by David L. Schindler (San Francisco: Ignatius Press, 1991), 121–32; Elio Guerriero, *Hans Urs von Balthasar: Eine Monographie* (Freiburg: Johannes Verlag Einsiedeln, 1993).

7. Balthasar, *The Whole in the Fragment: Aspects of the Theology of History*, 2nd ed. (San Francisco: Ignatius Press, 1990).

8. Balthasar, "Theology and Sanctity," in *The Word Made Flesh*, 182–83. Cf. Balthasar, "Revelation and the Beautiful," in *The Word Made Flesh*, 95–126; Balthasar, *Theo-Drama: Theological Dramatic Theory*, vol. III, *Dramatis Personae: Persons in Christ* (San Francisco: Ignatius Press, 1992), 263–82.

In the whole history of Catholic theology, there is hardly anything that is less noticed, yet more deserving of notice, than the fact that, since the great period of Scholasticism, there have been few theologians who were saints. We mean here by 'theologian' one whose office and vocation is to expound revelation in its fullness, and therefore whose work centers on dogmatic theology. If we consider the history of theology up to the time of the great Scholastics, we are struck by the fact that the great saints, those who not only achieved an exemplary purity of life, but who also had received from God a definite mission in the Church, were, mostly, great theologians. They were "pillars of the Church" by vocation channels of her life: their own lives reproduced the fullness of the Church's teaching, and their teaching the fullness of the Church's life.[9]

It was by virtue of this unity of knowledge and life that the great teachers of the Church were able, as was required by their special office, to be true lights and pastors of the Church. . . . It is not surprising, therefore, to find that, in the early centuries, the offices of teacher and of pastor (in the sense of Ephesians 4 and 1 Corinthians 12) were normally conjoined. Irenaeus, Cyprian, Athanasius, the two Cyrils, Basil, Gregory Nazianzen, Gregory of Nyssa, Epiphanius, Theodore of Mopsuestia, Chrysostom, Theodoret, Hilary, Ambrose, Augustine, Fulgentius, Isidore—all were bishops, not to mention the two great popes, Leo and Gregory. Among the great doctors, exceptions to this rule were the two Alexandrians, Jerome, Maximus and John of Damascus; but these representatives of the monastic and ascetical life bring out still more clearly the union of doctrine and life. The same may be said, too, of most of the bishops and teachers mentioned above, who were either monks themselves or were closely associated with monasticism and promoters of it.[10]

9. "Theology and Sanctity," in *The Word Made Flesh*, 181.
10. "Theology and Sanctity," in *The Word Made Flesh*, 182.

This notion of "theology and sanctity" is illuminatingly corroborated and, as it were, canonized by that mysterious writer who, next to Augustine, did most to form the theology of the Middle Ages and even of modern theology: namely, the Areopagite. It is through the writings of Denis that the *de jure* identification of bishop, saint, and teacher of the Church was most effectively impressed on theology, and this has been received as part of the gospel tradition.

> The early medieval thinkers in the West, under the aegis of Augustine, did not depart from this basic concept. Anselm, himself abbot, bishop and doctor of the Church, knew no other canon of truth than the unity of knowledge and life. The same may be said of Bede, Bernard and Peter Damian. But as theology increasingly took on a 'scholastic' form, and Aristotelianism burst in like an elemental force, the naive unity hitherto accepted was gravely shaken. No one would think of denying that the gain in clarity, insight, and mastery of the entire field was enormous. More resoundingly than in the time of the Fathers, who, almost as a matter of course, achieved eminence in the schools of antiquity, was the jubilation over the *spolia Aegyptiorum* repeated. The mood which fastened on Christian thinkers was like the intoxication of victors after a battle, at the sight of booty far beyond their expectations.[11]

The booty in this case, however, was primarily philosophical, and only indirectly theological. Philosophy began to emerge as a special discipline alongside theology.

> The great Scholastic period of Albert, Bonaventure and Thomas was peculiarly fitted for theology to irradiate and transfigure the self-subsisting science of nature, raising it to the plane of the sacred, and so to impart to the secular sciences a real Christian ethos, one affecting the whole outlook of the scientific investigator.[12]

11. "Theology and Sanctity," in *The Word Made Flesh*, 184–85.
12. "Theology and Sanctity," in *The Word Made Flesh*, 185–86.

The Separation between Theology and Holiness

The divorce between theology and sanctity gradually became more pervasive.

> All the Church's theology is rooted in the period that stretches from the apostles into the Middle Ages, when the great theologians were also saints. Then the life and doctrine, orthopraxy and orthodoxy were wedded; the one fertilized the other, and they brought forth much fruit. In modern times, theology and sanctity became divorced, to the great harm of both.[13]

Thomas is succeeded by the fall into nominalism,

> which for the first time allows an irreconcilable opposition to arise between (scholastic) theology and spirituality (*devotio moderna*, Erasmus). The Reformation will seek an escape from this opposition; and yet this tension becomes fruitful once more as the Franciscans and the Preaching Friars, each in a different way, attempt to master the whole arch of theology. . . . Nevertheless, the two pillars on which this arch rests have developed too far apart from each other for the arch to be safely placed. Thus, the neoscholasticism of the Counter-Reformation becomes the classic era of the separation between theoretical and affective theology: on the one hand a dry process of distinction, no longer borne and justified by the object, and on the other hand, a spiritual theology which is no longer nourished by the center of revelation.[14]

Prayerful theology, or "kneeling theology," does not mean "affective theology" as opposed to theology properly so called, and strictly scientific. "'Scientific' theology became more and

13. Balthasar, *Two Sisters in the Spirit*, 26.

14. Balthasar, *Convergences: To the Source of Christian Mystery* (San Francisco: Ignatius Press, 1983), 34.

more divorced from prayer, and so lost the accent and tone with which one should speak of what is holy, while 'affective' theology, as it became increasingly empty, often degenerated into unctuous, platitudinous piety."[15]

In the following epoch, there was the disappearance of the "complete" theologian in the sense of patristic theology, in which the theologian is also a saint.

> The Fathers found straightaway the appropriate dogmatic clothing for their very personal experience; everything became objective, and all the subjective conditions, experiences, fears, strivings, the "shock" in a word, were made to serve a fuller understanding of the content of revelation, to orchestrate its great themes. Every form of spirituality, of mysticism, was seen as serving a function in the Church. Like sanctity itself, they were above all tasks within the Church.[16]

So, a new science of "Christian life" was born. In the *devotio moderna* there were, of course, also the saints. In fact, John of the Cross was a doctor, not of dogmatic but of mystical theology. Among the spirituals, some simply found food for their devotion in contemplating the gospel, without reference to their other studies. Theology and sanctity have become, as it were, each a world of its own, with hardly any point of contact, and so the saints and spiritual writers are more and more ignored by theologians.

> The saints, intimidated by the conceptual entanglements drawn round the gospel truth, no longer dare to collaborate in the necessary work of exposition of doctrine, or think themselves qualified to do so. They leave dogma to the prosaic word of School and become—lyrical poets.[17]

15. Balthasar, "Theology and Sanctity," in *The Word Made Flesh*, 208.
16. "Theology and Sanctity," in *The Word Made Flesh*, 190.
17. "Theology and Sanctity," in *The Word Made Flesh*, 192.

Consider the doctrinal wealth drawn from the writings of the Areopagite—not without reason the most commented on of all the mystics—in comparison with that yielded by even the greatest of the moderns, John of the Cross. And then compare, if you can bring yourself to do so, the nourishment offered by a modern theological manual for a life of holiness with that contained in any patristic commentary on Scripture. The impoverishment brought about by the divorce between the two spheres is all too plain; it has sapped the vital force of the Church of today and the credibility of her preaching of eternal truth. This impoverishment is felt considerably more strongly by those who have to preach to the modern pagans than by professors in their seminary lecture rooms. It is the former who look round for some example of the conjunction of wisdom and holiness. They long to discover the living organism of the Church's doctrine, rather than a strange anatomical dissection: on the one hand, the bones without the flesh, "traditional theology"; on the other, the flesh without bones, that very pious literature that serves up a compound of asceticism, mysticism, spirituality and rhetoric, a porridge that, in the end, becomes indigestible through lack of substance. Only the two together (corresponding to the prototype of revelation in Scripture) constitute the unique "form" capable of being "seen" in the light of faith by the believer, a unique testimony, invisible to the world, and a "scandal" to it.[18]

Saints as a Living Theology

We cannot hope to recover this unity except by making a serious reassessment of the nature of theology. The content of dogmatic theology is revelation itself, which it aims to understand in a living faith, and to set forth by the application of reason animated and illuminated by faith and love. Dogmatic theology has its center precisely where revelation has its center—just as faith, the

18. "Theology and Sanctity," in *The Word Made Flesh*, 192–93.

basic act on which rests the work of exposition, has its center at the very heart of revelation. "This is what the saints are fully aware of. They never at any moment leave their center in Christ. They give themselves to their work in the world, while 'praying at all times' and 'doing all to the glory of God' (1 Tm 5:17; 1 Cor 10:31). When they philosophize, they do so as Christians, which means as believers, as theologians."[19] The great Christian thinkers are living examples: the more intense their sense of God and his holiness, the more fervent their language. And this simply means that their thought is a function of their faith.

In the view of Balthasar a true theology exists in an excellent way in the life of the saints. Their theology as a whole "exists only in the act of hearing and obeying, under the word and en route to carrying out the word, proclaiming it and giving it back to God in prayer."[20] The prayer "means to be free and to be still in the presence of God, to wait patiently for the understanding, 'worshipping by loving and loving by worshipping with all one's powers'. . . . If I am able to understand, then I say thank you, if not, I bow my head in reverence."[21]

The lived experience of the Church is that theological knowledge begins and achieves its fulfillment in prayer. The lives and teachings of the saints have been the best commentary on the Gospel. As Balthasar remarks, "the life of the saints is theology in practice."[22] The saints "sit with Mary at the feet of Jesus, hearing from his own mouth the words of revelation. They want to know what the Lord says to them, and nothing else."[23] "Their one desire is to be receptive, men of prayer in other words. Their theology is

19. "Theology and Sanctity," in *The Word Made Flesh*, 195.

20. Balthasar, "Summa Summarum," in *Explorations in Theology*, vol. III, *Creator Spirit* (San Francisco: Ignatius Press, 1993), 371.

21. Balthasar, *The Glory of the Lord: A Theological Aesthetics*, vol. II, *Studies in Theological Style: Clerical Styles* (San Francisco: Ignatius Press, 1984), 216.

22. "Theology and Sanctity," in *The Word Made Flesh*, 204.

23. "Theology and Sanctity," in *The Word Made Flesh*, 205.

essentially an act of adoration and prayer."[24] Prayer is the realistic attitude in which the mystery must be approached. This attitude, which is that of prayer, is never superseded or outdistanced by the attitude demanded by knowledge. Knowledge must never be separated from the attitude of prayer with which it began.

> Prayerful theology does not mean "affective theology" as opposed to theology properly so called, and strictly scientific. The antithesis is merely superficial, and invalidated by the exact, and very often abstract studies of Anselm and Albert, not to mention Thomas. Theology must always be conducted with rigorous precision.[25]

The theology of the saints was always born in prayer and enriched by prayer. A Christian always stands in need of interior illumination, which is a gift of the Holy Spirit whose light compels man to fall on his knees in worship. Balthasar quotes the words of Markus Barth: "Theology is the kind of thing that does not work without prayer." And again: "If theology is not prayer, if it does not come from prayer and lead to prayer, it is worthless."[26] This is the reason both Ratzinger and Balthasar agree that nothing is worthy of theological reflection unless it is subject to prayer. St. Bernard of Clairvaux was clear about this need, "there is no theology without prayer." Balthasar agreed with Bernard and lists other great defenders of kneeling theology as well:

> There can be no doubt that it was prayer in the Fathers, in Augustine, Bede, and Anselm and in the flowering monastic theology of the twelfth century up to Bonaventure, and then again in the other great thinkers of modern times, Pascal, Kierkegaard, and Newman. For these writers it was always

24. "Theology and Sanctity," in *The Word Made Flesh*, 206.
25. "Theology and Sanctity," in *The Word Made Flesh*, 207.
26. Balthasar, *Theo-Logic*, vol. III, *The Spirit of Truth* (San Francisco: Ignatius Press, 2005), 358 and 365.

> a "confessing theology." The "rational" theology, which did not begin with Thomas but always had to be put forward by the Fathers incidentally, so to speak, in order to defend the faith against heresy and which consists in illuminating and ordering faith's inner textual unity (*sapientis est ordinare*), can be nothing other than an indispensable preliminary to a praying and confessing theology.[27]

Entirely persuaded of the inseparability of "the two sisters"—theology and sanctity—Hans Urs von Balthasar coined the famous expression "*kneeling theology*":

> Theology was, when pursued by men of sanctity, a theology at prayer, a kneeling theology. Which is why its fruitfulness for prayer, its power to foster prayer, is so undeniable. As time went on, the 'kneeling theology' was superseded by theology at the desk.[28]

Sanctity as the Essence of Theology

In order to extricate Christian theology from an increasingly sterile, rationalistic, and strictly academic environment, Balthasar reflected on the essence of theology that is born from faith and prayer. In his article entitled "Theology and Holiness" (1987) he states that "theology earns its name only as the unity of sanctity and the witness born in the life of the Church."[29] Therefore, Jesus Christ, in speaking of his Father (Jn 1:18) uses the original language of God about God (theo-logia). It is only from this primary foundation that Christian theology is possible. Real theological progress can only come from deep springs, and not only from the younger springs of the Bible but also from a renewed study of patristic theology. To this point, Balthasar quotes Irenaeus:

27. Balthasar, *The Spirit of Truth*, 365.
28. Balthasar, "Theology and Sanctity," in *The Word Made Flesh*, 208.
29. Balthasar, "Theology and Holiness," *Communio*, 341–50.

> "It is from the Church that we have received the faith and carefully guard it. For, like a treasure deposited in a precious vessel, it ceaselessly regains its youth by the work of the Holy Spirit. And in doing so, it rejuvenates the very vessel that contains it."[30]

The basic rule for Church renewal in every age is "renewal from the source"[31] which means a renewal that comes from solitude and prayer and a holy life.[32] This basic rule learned from saints refers back to its source—to God's revelation of Himself, especially in his Son made man, Jesus Christ.

> The saints are the most important commentary on the Gospel because they are living interpretations of the Word made flesh. They provide us with access to the sound waves, when they are not heard by the human ear, are not able to be perceived; and so, for one who is deaf, even when the sound is beautiful music, he cannot hear it. Theology without prayer falls on deaf ears.[33]

If spirituality is the yeast of theology, then only saints are able to produce a living theology. This is the reason saints are so important in the life of the Church. Hans Urs von Balthasar draws attention to this vital role of saints in developing the life of the Church:

> For theologians, they are rather a new interpretation of revelation: they bring out the scarcely suspected treasures in the

30. Irenaeus, *Adversus Haereses* III, 24, 1, quoted in Balthasar, "Young until Death," in *Explorations in Theology*, vol. V, *Man Is Created* (San Francisco: Ignatius Press, 2014), 223.

31. This is the title of Balthasar's monograph *Romano Guardini: Reform from the Source* (San Francisco: Ignatius Press, 2010).

32. Balthasar, "Loneliness in the Church," in *Explorations in Theology*, vol. IV, *Spirit and Institution* (San Francisco: Ignatius Press, 1995), 261–98.

33. Balthasar, "Zugänge zu Christus," in *Wer ist Jesus Christus*, ed. J. Sauer (Freiburg-Basel-Wien: Herder, 1977), 9–25, at 21.

> deposit of faith. Even when the saints have not been theologians, nor themselves very learned, their sheer existence proves to be a theological manifestation that contains most fruitful and opportune doctrine, the directions of the Holy Spirit addressed to the whole Church and not to be neglected by any of her members.[34]

The Church's theology needs to be an explanatory meditation on the profession of faith before it can be understood by the faithful and then be shared with others. Therefore, theology must have its foundation in the Holy Spirit and his gifts in order to move minds and hearts.

Balthasar, following the great saints in the Church's theological tradition, makes the claim that: "Lovers are the ones who know most about God; the theologian must listen to them."[35] This is the agenda of Balthasar—he bends his ear to the saints—he listens to them and makes them known. Consequently, much of his writing refers to the saints. Only those theologians who are holy interest him. Balthasar, who gives the saints priority in publications, often claimed

> that the history of theology proves this statement: Only those theologies became vitally effective in history which bore their spirituality not as an addition but within themselves, which embodied it in their innermost being.[36]

The Witnessing Power of Holy Theology

Only the existence of saints who manifest the gift of the Spirit are able to convince the world about the truth of the Gospel. This was a theme in the teaching of Cardinal Henri de Lubac: "The proud

34. Balthasar, *Two Sisters in the Spirit*, 25.

35. Balthasar, *Love Alone is Credible* (San Francisco: Ignatius Press, 2004), 12.

36. Balthasar, *Convergences: To the Source of Christian Mystery*, 44.

spirits who never prayed and who today pass for torchbearers of culture vanish, with regularity, after a few years and are replaced by others."[37]

The main evidence of a holy life is obedience to the divine calling which imitates the suffering of Christ in his abandonment by his Father and his descent into darkness. This means being obedient to the Church, even when it is represented by unworthy leaders. The saint is called to strengthen and revitalize Church life. Real saints are never on an ego trip—they seek only the will of God and not the realization of their own ideas and plans. "The saints are always obedient but not docile, *obéissant, non dociles.*"[38]

Balthasar argued unconditionally for the inalienability of theology and holiness as evidenced by his comments regarding true theology. In his article entitled "Theology and Holiness," he demonstrated the inner connection between the mission of the Church and the testimony of holy lives. "Theology can be nothing other [than] a form in which Christians who have been sent forth bear witness to their faith in Christ who himself is 'the true witness' (Rv 1:5) to the One who sent him." To be able to bear witness in this way, the disciples of Christ need to be sanctified for their mission to proclaim the truth. Balthasar calls this "sanctification for the mission," the way Christians need to be sanctified for the mission of proclaiming the truth. "'Sanctification for the mission' is sought explicitly by Christ for his disciples. . . . Everyone who counts himself a member of the Church of Christ must in his particular way be both saint and witness."[39] The whole, unspoiled truth of revelation must be clearly and forcefully declared:

37. Henri de Lubac, "A Witness of Christ in the Church: Hans Urs von Balthasar," in *The Church: Paradox and Mystery* (Shannon, Ireland: Ecclesia Press, 1969), 112.

38. Balthasar, *Bernanos: An Ecclesial Existence* (San Francisco: Ignatius Press, 1996), 589.

39. *Bernanos*, 344–45.

> It is absolutely impossible that one bears witness, evangelizes, catechizes, preaches or by selecting according to one's own whim some part of the whole truth, on the pretext that the audience cannot take more, that some part does not concern them or is no longer relevant. Such witness would be mistaken: for every essential element of the Christian truth belongs necessarily to the integrity of the whole. If one essential element or another is eliminated, then the whole will certainly lose clarity and credibility. . . . A witness who criticizes that to which he must bear witness is in his self-contradiction no longer witness at all.[40]

A theologian must be ready to give his very life for Christ. This is what Balthasar calls "a serious case" making this assertion. This is "the best criterion, because it forces us to face the Christian truth that our readiness to die for Christ is the only adequate response we can make to his willing sacrifice of himself out of love for us."[41]

"*The Moment of Christian Witness,* with its allusion to blood-witness, was nothing but a danger signal: the situation of the Church today is bloody earnest!"[42] The prognosis Hans Urs von Balthasar gives us is significant today considering the present situation of the Church worldwide. He writes:

> The solution to which some openly and shamelessly invite us in these difficulties is that of pluralism of opinion within the substance of dogma. . . . The form of the Catholic Church would thereby be completely assimilated to that of Protestantism. . . . But what she would then need in order to master such a superhuman task would not be merely theologians (that too), but, in plain terms, saints. Not mere

40. *Bernanos*, 345.

41. Balthasar, *The Moment of Christian Witness* (San Francisco: Ignatius Press, 1994), 99.

42. *The Moment of Christian Witness*, 152.

> decrees, much less the institution of new study commissions, but saintly figures to serve as beacons by which we can find our bearings.[43]

The Church must be grounded in Christological holiness. The words of Balthasar: "Real, empirical Church was and is also today the Church of saints."[44]

> *The Church of saints* forms the full content and thereby the canon of ecclesial existence; but the canon of holiness is not left to the arbitrary discovery and legislation of Christians but is established by the Spirit in the Church for every epoch in a way that is often very unexpected. It is here that necessary transpositions take place centrally.[45]
>
> The Church has received the promise of objective sanctity. . . . But this in no way eliminates the obligatory vocation to subjective and personal sanctity, which is indeed the ultimate reason for her whole institutional and objective side. The office of the priest is for the sake of the community; the wellsprings of grace, the sacraments, are there for those who receive them; the word of God is there for its hearers. And the nearer a man is placed to the Church's springs of objective sanctity, whether as a priest or member of an order or as a custodian of some sacramental grace, the stricter is his obligation to conform to and prepare himself for that objective sanctity that he administers and preserves.[46]

But the reverse is also true. Subjectively, sanctity is identified with love that prefers God and fellow men rather than loving only one's self—and this means love for the community of the Church is a priority. "Love seeks not its own" (1 Cor 13:5). The words of Balthasar:

43. *The Moment of Christian Witness*, 153–54.
44. Balthasar, "Loneliness in the Church," 289.
45. Balthasar, "Truth and Life," in *Creator Spirit*, 276–77.
46. Balthasar, *Two Sisters in Spirit*, 19.

> A sanctity that sought its own and made self its aim would be a self-contradiction. . . . The mission that each individual receives contains within itself the form of sanctity that has been granted to him and is required of him. In following that mission, he fulfills his appropriate capacity for sanctity. This sanctity is essentially social and outside the arbitrary disposition of any individual. For each Christian, God has an idea that fixes his place within the membership of the Church; this idea is unique and personal, embodying for each his appropriate sanctity.[47]

For Balthasar, "Holiness is more than an example, a pattern, it is an immediate source of the fruitfulness of God's life for the Church and humanity."[48]

Throughout the Church's history there have been many examples of missions that are personal and social in nature, exercised by both men and women, some with an official mandate and some without, some that have been public and some private, the majority invisible. But as Balthasar writes:

> Behind the great ones, those exhibited to our gaze, are those no less far-reaching. Such are the missions of penance, of prayer, of charity, of suffering, which remain unknown or, once known, have now been forgotten. All these are included in the symbolic figure of one hundred and forty-four thousand mentioned in Revelation.[49]

Cardinal Henri de Lubac, a friend and teacher of Balthasar, said of him:

> He himself is one of those men of whom he has spoken, men who devoted the work of their lives "to the splendor of the-

47. *Two Sisters in Spirit*, 20.

48. Balthasar, "Vom Ordensstand," in *Die grossen Ordensregeln*, 7th ed. (Freiburg: Johannes Verlag Einsiedeln, 1994), 7.

49. Balthasar, *Persons in Christ*, 280.

> ology—theology, that devouring fire between two nights, two abysses: adoration and obedience."[50]

The entire theology of Hans Urs von Balthasar is a kneeling theology because it arises from his contemplative prayer life and leads his readers into this life. His theology uses the triune God's love for his creation as its source and leads his readers into this mystery. Balthasar considers theology to be a reliable witness to the truth. As Henri de Lubac observed of him: "He is theologian only to be apostle."[51]

50. De Lubac, "A Witness of Christ in the Church," 110.
51. De Lubac, "A Witness of Christ in the Church," 115.

4

"Beauty Will Save the World"

THE CHRISTIAN MESSAGE ABOUT BEAUTY ACCORDING TO POPE BENEDICT XVI AND HANS URS VON BALTHASAR

> Is there anyone who does not know Dostoyevsky's often quoted sentence: "The Beautiful will save us"? However, people usually forget that Dostoyevsky is referring here to the redeeming Beauty of Christ. We must learn to see Him. If we know Him, not only in words, but if we are struck by the arrow of his paradoxical beauty, then we will truly know him, and know him not only because we have heard others speak about him. Then we will have found the beauty of Truth, of the Truth that redeems. Nothing can bring us into close contact with the beauty of Christ himself other than the world of beauty created by faith and light that shines out from the faces of the saints, through whom his own light becomes visible.[1]

With these words, Pope Benedict XVI invites us to think about beauty. And what is beauty? First, let us examine the relationship between earthly beauty and the revealed glory of God. Then we will consider the theology of beauty according to Joseph Ratzinger and Hans Urs von Balthasar.

Earthly Beauty and Divine Glory

First, we begin with a brief philosophical and theological overview. Philosophy speaks of the four transcendentals that charac-

1. Joseph Ratzinger, "The Feeling of Things, the Contemplation of Beauty": Message of His Eminence Card. Joseph Ratzinger to the Communion and Liberation (CL) Meeting at Rimini (August 24–30, 2002). Available at vatican.va.

terize every being: one (*unum*), good (*bonum*), true (*verum*) and beautiful (*pulchrum*).

In his last "retrospective,"[2] Hans Urs von Balthasar summarizes these transcendentals:

> Man exists only in dialogue with his neighbor. The infant is brought to consciousness of himself only by love, by the smile of his mother. In that encounter, the horizon of all unlimited being opens itself for him, revealing four things to him: (1) that he is *one* in love with the mother, even being other than his mother, therefore all being is *one*; (2) that love is *good*, therefore all being is *good*; (3) that that love is *true*, therefore all being is *true*; and (4) that that love evokes *joy*, therefore all being is *beautiful*.[3]

Balthasar goes on: "The One, the Good, the True and the Beautiful, these are what we call the transcendental attributes of Being, because they surpass all the limits of essences and are coextensive with Being."[4]

Hans Urs von Balthasar, in his article "Earthly Beauty and Divine Glory," gives the following definition of beauty and glory:

> Beauty, along with unity, truth and greatness, is one of the so-called transcendental qualities of all beings and, as such, of "being" itself. However, it must be immediately added that all created beings are merely analogs of the absolute divine being and that the "difference" between the two is greater than the "similarity" (Fourth Lateran Council, DS 806). What is called the "beauty" of a created being is in consonance with the sublime attrib-

2. Hans Urs von Balthasar, *My Work: In Retrospect* (San Francisco: Ignatius Press, 1993), 111–19.

3. *My Work*, 114.

4. *My Work*, 115.

ute of the Divine Being that is known as "glory" (*kābōd*, *doxa*, *gloria*).[5]

Every being is defined by these four transcendental properties:

Whatever is said about this, it is essential to recognize that no adequate conceptual statements can be made about the transcendental categories of being. But as we necessarily think in concepts and have to give expression to these, we can come closer to the meaning of unity, truth, goodness and beauty only through roundabout, convergent thinking. These qualities are not unknown to us, because they are present—even though in varying degrees and appearances—in all that exists; but they cannot be expressed by limiting "definitions" because "being," as such, transcends all specific "definitions." Nevertheless, that these qualities are a trustworthy basis of all our judgments is evident from the fact that we can measure offenses against their "essence": we define "lying" as an offense against truth, "malice" against goodness, "fragments" versus unity, "ugliness" and "trash" against beauty. Since the transcendentals penetrate all being, it follows that they are not delimited from each other but penetrate each other. Thus, there is an element of "goodness" in "beauty," in "truth," and so on.[6]

From the foregoing, both the affinity and the (greater) difference between earthly beauty and divine glory become evident. Earthly beauty always appears limited in a finite being or through harmonious coordination of finite entities, while God, viewed as the absolute Being and as infinite reality—both aspects of the sole Eternal Life—shines in other, all-transcending and all-pervading indivisible glory.[7]

5. Balthasar, "Earthly Beauty and Divine Glory," *Communio: International Catholic Review* 10, no. 3 (1983): 202–6, at 202.

6. "Earthly Beauty and Divine Glory," 202–3.

7. "Earthly Beauty and Divine Glory," 203.

In his great work *The Glory of the Lord: A Theological Aesthetics*, Hans Urs von Balthasar writes:

> As the last *transcendentale*, the beautiful guards the others and sets the seal on them: there is nothing true or good, in the long term, without the light of grace of that which is freely bestowed. And a Christianity which went along with modernity and subscribed merely to the true (faith as a system of correct propositions) or merely to the good (faith as that which is most useful and healthy for the subject) would be a Christianity knocked down from its own heights. But when saints interpreted their existence in the light of God's greater glory, they were always the guardians of the beautiful.[8]

Joseph Ratzinger: "Mozart in Theology"

Some years ago, Cardinal Joachim Meisner called Joseph Ratzinger, then Prefect of the Congregation of the Doctrine of the Faith, a "Mozart in theology." This was an apt expression considering the love that Ratzinger had of the great composer who had been his neighbor in Salzburg. And it was an apt expression for the amazing beauty and genius of the Prefect's theological work. Theological texts of Pope Benedict XVI reflect the linguistic beauty that matches the beauty of their content.

Pope Benedict XVI, in an address following a concert organized by the Vatican to celebrate his 80th birthday (on April 16th of 2007), made these comments:

> I am convinced that music—and here I am thinking in particular of the great Mozart . . . —really is the universal language of beauty which can bring together all people of good will on earth and get them to lift their gaze on high and open

8. Balthasar, *The Glory of the Lord: A Theological Aesthetics*, vol. IV, *The Realm of Metaphysics in Antiquity* (San Francisco: Ignatius Press, 1989), 38–39.

themselves to the Absolute Good and Beauty whose ultimate source is God himself. In looking back over my life, I thank God for placing music beside me, as it were, as a travelling companion that has offered me comfort and joy. I also thank the people who, from the very first years of my childhood, brought me close to this source of inspiration and serenity. I thank those who combine music and prayer in harmonious praise of God and his works: they help us glorify the Creator and Redeemer of the world, which is the marvelous work of his hands.[9]

Divine Beauty

Joseph Ratzinger had an amazing insight into the beauty of Christ as revealed in the Scriptures. These are his words:

> Every year, in the Liturgy of the Hours for the Season of Lent, I am struck anew by a paradox in the Vespers for Monday of the Second Week of the Psalter. Here, side by side, are two antiphons, one for the Season of Lent, the other for Holy Week. Both introduce Psalm 44 [45], but they present strikingly contradictory interpretations. The Psalm describes the wedding of the King, his beauty, his virtues, his mission, and then becomes an exaltation of his bride. In the Season of Lent, Psalm 44 is framed by the same antiphon used for the rest of the year. The third verse of the Psalm says: "You are the fairest of the children of men, and grace is poured upon your lips." Naturally, the Church reads this psalm as a poetic-prophetic representation of Christ's spousal relationship with his Church. She recognizes Christ as the fairest of men, the grace poured upon his lips points to the inner beauty of his words, the glory of his proclamation. So it is not merely the external beauty of the Redeemer's appearance that is glorified: rather, the beauty of Truth appears in him, the beauty

9. Benedict XVI, *Address of His Holiness Benedict XVI after the Concert for His 80th Birthday*, April 16, 2009.

> of God himself who draws us to himself and, at the same time captures us with the wound of Love, the holy passion (eros), that enables us to go forth together, with and in the Church, his Bride, to meet the Love who calls us. On Monday of Holy Week, however, the Church changes the antiphon and invites us to interpret the Psalm in the light of Is 53:2: "*He had neither beauty, no majesty, nothing to attract our eyes, no grace to make us delight in him.*" How can we reconcile this? The appearance of the "fairest of the children of men" is so wretched that no one desires to look at him. Pilate presented him to the crowd saying: "Ecce homo! Behold the man!," to rouse sympathy for the crushed and battered Man, in whom no external beauty remained.[10]

Pope Benedict XVI had great insight into the teaching of St. Augustine. These are his words:

> Augustine, who in his youth wrote a book *On the Beautiful and the Harmonious [De pulchro et apto]* and who appreciated beauty in words, in music, in the figurative arts, had a keen appreciation of this paradox and realized that in this regard, the great Greek philosophy of the beautiful was not simply rejected but rather, dramatically called into question and what the beautiful might be, what beauty might mean, would have to be debated anew and suffered. Referring to the paradox contained in these texts, he spoke of the contrasting blasts of "two trumpets," produced by the same breath, the same Spirit. He knew that a paradox is a contrast and not a contradiction. Both quotes come from the same Spirit who inspires all Scripture, but sounds different notes in it. It is in this way that he sets us before the totality of true Beauty, of Truth itself.
>
> The prophet Isaiah raised a question that interested the Fathers of the Church whether or not the Messiah would be concerned about beauty. Implicit in their inquiry was a more

10. Ratzinger, "The Feeling of Things."

radical question about whether beauty is true or whether it is ugliness that ultimately leads to a deeper truth about reality. Whoever believes in a God who manifests himself in the awful appearance of Christ crucified, who would show his love for them "to the end" (John 13:1)—such a believer, even if he knows that beauty is truth and truth is beauty, is willing to learn by the suffering of Christ that beauty also embraces pain and even the darkness of death. To accept suffering and death as Jesus is the only way to understand the full meaning and underlying truth about beauty.

This awareness that beauty has something to do with pain was recognized even in early Greek culture. For example, in Plato's *Phaedrus* the author contemplates the encounter with beauty as a salutary emotional shock that causes man to leave his protective shell and sparks his "enthusiasm" by attracting him to reality outside himself. Man, says Plato, has lost the original perfection in which he was conceived. So he now searches perennially for his primitive form. Nostalgia and longing impel him to pursue this quest. Beauty prevents him from being content with his present situation. This causes him to suffer. In a platonic sense we could say that the arrow of nostalgia pierces his heart, and this wound, if he is honest with himself, develops into wings for himself that lift him upwards towards the transcendental.

In a 14th century book titled *The Life of Christ* by the Byzantine scholar Nicholas Cabasilas, we find that Plato's earlier experience of nostalgia (as outlined in the previous paragraph) is transformed by the Christian experience of Jesus and his teaching. Cabasilas writes:

> When men have a longing so great that it surpasses human nature and eagerly desire and are able to accomplish things beyond human thought, it is the Bridegroom who has smitten them with this longing. It is he who has sent a ray of his beauty into their eyes. The greatness of the wound already shows the arrow which has struck home, the longing indicates who has inflicted the wound. (cf. *The Life in Christ*, the Second Book, 15).

> What is beautiful tends to wound us because it summons man to face his final destiny beyond his present status. Beauty surfaces a need to really understand its cause and nature and purpose which results in knowledge. This is what Plato meant by the arrow of nostalgia piercing the heart—that beauty causes man to seek its cause and the reality of its impact on him. This is the reason that the beauty of Christ and his person and teaching result in being struck and overcome by the beauty of Christ is a more real, more profound knowledge than mere rational deduction. Of course we must not underrate the importance of theological reflection, of exact and precise theological thought; it remains absolutely necessary. We must rediscover this form of knowledge; it is a pressing need of our time. (ibid.)[11]

Then Cardinal Ratzinger refers to his friend Balthasar:

> Starting with this concept, Hans Urs von Balthasar built his *Opus magnum* of Theological Aesthetics. Many of its details have passed into theological work, while his fundamental approach, in truth the essential element of the whole work, has not been so readily accepted. Of course, this is not just, or principally, a theological problem, but a problem of pastoral life that has to foster the human person's encounter with the beauty of faith. All too often arguments fall on deaf ears because in our world too many contradictory arguments compete with one another, so much so that we are spontaneously reminded of the medieval theologians' description of reason, claiming that it "has a wax nose": in other words, it can be pointed in any direction, if one is clever enough. Everything makes sense, is so convincing, whom should we trust?[12]

11. Ratzinger, "The Feeling of Things."
12. Ratzinger, "The Feeling of Things."

Hans Urs von Balthasar: The Theologian of the Beautiful

Elio Guerriero described Hans Urs von Balthasar as "the theologian of beautiful" and wrote a comprehensive monograph about him.[13] Michael Albus in an interview with Balthasar entitled "Spirit and Fire" asks him this question: "How do you see your own theology?"

And Balthasar responds:

> I consider my own theology to be like the finger of John pointing to the fullness of revelation in Jesus Christ, which is unfolded in the immense fullness of its reception in the history of the Church, above all in the meditation of the saints. I have to say that for me the only truly interesting theologians are the saints: from Irenaeus through Augustine to Anselm, to Bonaventure, or figures that allow the radiation of holiness to show forth, such as Dante or Newman; one could also mention Kierkegaard and Solovyov. I have actually never written because I wanted to achieve results, but in order to show individuals something that I think must be seen. Yesterday I read a sentence from Goethe that I would like to share with you: "In our time no one should keep silent or give in. One must speak and do something. Not in order to be victorious, but in order to remain at one's post. Whether one is with the majority or the minority makes no difference at all."[14]

Glory Surpasses Beauty

Hans Urs von Balthasar says in the same conversation:

> In my aesthetics I completed a long journey through worldly-aesthetic categories (in the first volume) that could

13. Elio Guerriero, *Hans Urs von Balthasar: Eine Monographie* (Freiburg: Johannes Verlag Einsiedeln, 1993).

14. Hans Urs von Balthasar and Michael Albus, "Spirit and Fire: An Interview with Hans Urs von Balthasar," *Communio: International Catholic Review* 32, no. 3 (2005): 573–93, at 574–75.

> help us to understand something theological. However, I then moved more and more to the biblical and specifically Christian; namely, to the *kābōd*, the glory of God that is not aesthetics but God Himself in his appearance. My concern was a teaching on the "perception" (*aisthesis*) of what is Christian in the world in general. What man perceives, however, is the truth, the glory of the poor love of God. Something of this glory radiates upon the Church, as it is clear in Paul.[15]

It is important to say that glory surpasses beauty. The Bible, in describing God's glory, tries to express its sublimity and uniqueness. It is significant that the word "*kābōd*" did not originally call forth the idea of radiant light (as do the Greek "*doxa*" and the Latin "*gloria*"), but indicated the importance of the person, his distinction, his honor, as well as his spiritual radiance, from which then the sensible radiance is derived. Heinrich Schlier, therefore, would translate *doxa* as "radiance of power."

> God did not intend to aggrandize his 'wholly other' glory in its appearance to men, but rather diminished it—fulfilling the prophecy that the Servant of God will have no "form nor comeliness" (Is, 53:2), Jesus took upon himself the blemish of the world's sin, to 'take it away,' so that the inconceivable, unfathomable glory of the absolute (triune) love may shine in the world and in its history. In the insolvable paradox of rejection by mankind (the cross) and vindication by God (resurrection) the divine kābōd illumines like lightning, once for all, definitively, eschatologically, that is, unsurpassably. Paul cannot cease pointing to this paradox in the glory that was manifested in Christ, and which from then on also becomes the basic sign of a witness to Christ, in whom God 'imprints' his 'image.' When John finally dares to state that God is love, for him this cannot be separated even for a moment from the Father's sacrifice of the Son as

15. Balthasar and Albus, "Spirit and Fire," 576.

> a substitutionary atonement, dying for the sinner; and in no other way is the Holy Spirit of God given to a Christian in the world than by this spirit of self-gift.[16]

A Theological Aesthetics could be described as a "section on the beauty of God and his revelation."[17] Balthasar started with this work, which is rightly judged as a great work, after long preparation.[18] After this long preparation, seven volumes of Herrlichkeit (*The Glory of the Lord)* were published in German between the years 1961–1969.[19] Almost a decade was needed to produce the theology of beauty, "which has been conceived and born under the constellation of the *kalon* (beautiful) and of *charis* (grace)."[20]

In the first volume Hans Urs von Balthasar says in a nutshell:

> The word with which we embark on this first volume of a series of theological studies is a word with which the philosophical person does not begin, but rather concludes. It is a word that has never possessed a permanent place or an authentic voice in the concert of the exact sciences, and, when it *is* chosen as a subject for discussion, appears to betray in him who chooses it an idle amateur among such very busy experts. It is, finally, a word from which religion, and theology in particular, have taken their leave and distanced themselves in modern times by a vigorous drawing of the boundaries. In short, this word is untimely in three different senses, and bearing it as one's treasure will not win

16. Balthasar, "Earthly Beauty and Divine Glory," 204–5.

17. Balthasar, *The Glory of the Lord: A Theological Aesthetics*, vol. I, *Seeing the Form* (San Francisco: Ignatius Press, 2009), 55. Originally published by T&T Clark, 1982.

18. Peter Henrici, "Erster Blick auf Hans Urs von Balthasar," *Hans Urs von Balthasar: Gestalt und Werk*, ed. Karl Lehmann and Walter Kasper (Cologne: Communio, 1989), 42; cf. Peter Henrici, *Hans Urs von Balthasar: Aspekte seiner Sendung* (Freiburg: Johannes Verlag Einsiedeln, 2008).

19. See Anton Strle, *Teologi za prihodnost* [Theologians for the future], (Ljubljana: Družina, 1998), 7–59.

20. Balthasar, *Seeing the Form*, 10.

> one anyone's favors; one rather risks finding oneself outside everyone's camp. Yet if the philosopher cannot begin with this word, but can at best conclude with it (always assuming that he has not forgotten it under way), should not the Christian for this very reason perhaps take it as *his* first word? . . . Beauty is the word that shall be our first. Beauty is the last thing which the thinking intellect dares to approach, since only it dances as an uncontained splendor around the double constellation of the true and the good and their inseparable relations to one another. Beauty is the disinterested one, without which the ancient world refused to understand itself, a word which both imperceptibly and yet unmistakably has bid farewell to our new world, a world of interests, leaving it to its own avarice and sadness. No longer loved or fostered by religion, beauty is lifted from its face which threatens to become incomprehensible to man. We no longer dare to believe in beauty and we make of it a mere appearance in order the more easily to dispose of it. Our situation today shows that beauty demands for itself at least as much courage and decision as do truth and goodness, and she will not allow herself to be separated and banned from her two sisters without taking them along with herself in an act of mysterious vengeance.[21]

The Church needs beauty, by which the quality of what it believes becomes visible. And again, Hans Urs von Balthasar leads us to this truth when he writes:

> In the world without beauty—even if people cannot dispense with the word and constantly have it on the tip of their tongues in order to abuse it—in a world which is perhaps not wholly without beauty, but which can no longer see it or reckon with it: in such a world the good also loses its attractiveness, the self-evidence of why it must be carried out. Man stands before the good and asks himself why *it*

21. *Seeing the Form*, 17–18.

must be done and not rather its alternative, evil. For this, too, is a possibility and even the more exciting one: Why not investigate Satan's depths? In a world that no longer has enough confidence in itself to affirm the beautiful, the proofs of the truth have lost their cogency.[22]

Conclusion: The Liberating Truth

Joseph Ratzinger adds:

> A beauty that is deceptive and false, a dazzling beauty that does not bring human beings out of themselves to open them to the ecstasy of rising to the heights, but indeed locks them entirely into themselves, such beauty does not reawaken a longing for the Ineffable, readiness for sacrifice, the abandonment of self, but instead stirs up the desire, the will for power, possession and pleasure. It is that type of experience of beauty of which Genesis speaks in the account of the Original Sin. Eve saw that the fruit of the tree was "beautiful" to eat and was "*delightful to the eyes.*" The beautiful, as she experienced it, aroused in her a desire for possession, making her, as it were, turn in upon herself. Who would not recognize, for example, in modern advertising, the images made with supreme skill that are created to tempt human beings irresistibly, to make them grab things and seek the passing satisfaction rather than be open to others. So it is that modern Christian art is caught between two negative influences (as perhaps it always was): on the one hand, it must oppose the cult of the ugly which maintains that everything beautiful is deceptive and represents only that which is crude, low and vulgar and only this reality is true; on the other hand, Christian art must counter a deceptive beauty that tends to diminish human life rather than enhancing it which is also false.[23]

22. *Seeing the Form*, 19.
23. Ratzinger, "The Feeling of Things."

Christian art, in fact, faces a difficult task. Joseph Ratzinger addresses this issue of artistic renditions, especially images as they relate to liturgy, in his important 1999 book, *The Spirit of the Liturgy*. He outlines the basic principles for Catholic liturgy and asked this question:

> But what does it mean practically? Art cannot be "produced," as one contracts out and produces technical equipment. It is always a gift. Inspiration is not something one can choose for oneself. It has to be received, otherwise it is not there. One cannot bring about a renewal of art in faith by money or through commissions. Before all things it requires the gift of a new kind of seeing. And so it would be worth our while to regain a faith that sees. Wherever that exists, art finds its proper expression.[24]

After this analysis of what constitutes proper Christian art, Pope Benedict XVI reaches this conclusion:

> I have often affirmed my conviction that the true apology of Christian faith, the most convincing demonstration of its truth against every denial, are the saints, and the beauty that the faith has generated. Today, for faith to grow, we must lead ourselves and the persons we meet to encounter the saints and to enter into contact with the Beautiful.[25]

24. Ratzinger, *Theology of Liturgy*, Collected Works 11 (San Francisco: Ignatius Press, 2014), 83.

25. Ratzinger, "The Feeling of Things." See also Anton Štrukelj, "Schönheit und Heiligkeit in der TheologieL Hommage an Papst Benedikt XVI aus slowenischer Sicht," in *Hommage an Papst Benedikt XVI: Aufsätze und Essays*, ed. Maximilian Heinrich Heim and Wolfgang Gottfried Buchmüller (Heiligenkreuz im Wienerwald: Be&Be, 2018), 119–26.

5

Hans Urs von Balthasar and Adrienne von Speyr

THE UNITY OF TWO WORKS

"The Church, expert in humanity, has a perennial interest in whatever concerns men and women. . . . The Church, enlightened by faith in Jesus Christ, speaks of *active collaboration* between the sexes precisely in the recognition of the difference between man and woman."[1] This affirmation of the Congregation for the Doctrine of the Faith in the *Letter on the Collaboration of Men and Women in the Church and in the World* (signed by Cardinal Joseph Ratzinger) is an appropriate introduction to our topic.

If it is true that behind a great theologian there is always a prophet, it is not difficult to discover the immense influence that the physician and mystic Adrienne von Speyr (1902–1967) had on the extensive work of Hans Urs von Balthasar. The immense quantity (and quality) of his theological work is based primarily on Adrienne's prophetic experiences. As early as 1955, Balthasar emphasized her influence. The work of Adrienne von Speyr "corresponds in themes and tone to those of my own books."[2] The inseparable unity of their work together was made clear by Balthasar in his book, *Our Task*, which resulted in a symposium on Adrienne von Speyr called by Pope John Paul II in Rome September 27th–29th, 1983. Balthasar had written in his book by way of introduction that "This book has one chief aim: to prevent any

1. Congregation for the Doctrine of the Faith, *Letter to the Bishops of the Catholic Church on the Collaboration of Men and Women in the Church and in the World* (May 31, 2004), 1 and 4.

2. Balthasar, *My Work: In Retrospect* (San Francisco: Ignatius Press, 1993), 19.

attempt being made after my death to separate my work from that of Adrienne von Speyr. It will show that in no respect is this possible, as regards both theology and the developing community."[3] The fruitfulness of this collaboration between Balthasar and Speyr gave evidence of the special relationship these two great minds and hearts had together.

Double Mission and the Unity of Their Works

It is appropriate to describe the collaboration of Balthasar and Speyr as a "double mission" undertaken together. Amid a variety of missions in the Church, there are some that are individual and others that are double which complement each other, often as "two halves of the moon."[4] "The model for this is the Crucified Lord bringing together Mary and John to form the virginal first cell of the Church. (Adrienne often returns to them.) Replicas of it include the collaboration of St. John of the Cross and St. Teresa, St. John Eudes and Marie des Vallées, and St. Francis de Sales and St. Jane Frances de Chantal."[5] This collaboration was the

3. Balthasar, *Our Task: A Report and a Plan* (San Francisco: Ignatius Press, 1994), 13.

4. *Our Task*, 16. See Johann G. Roten SM, "The Two Halves of the Moon: Marian Anthropological Dimension in the Common Mission of Adrienne von Speyr and Hans Urs von Balthasar," in *Hans Urs von Balthasar: His Life and Work* (San Francisco: Ignatius Press, 1991), 65–86; Peter Henrici, "Hans Urs von Balthasar: A Sketch of His Life," in Schindler, *Hans Urs von Balthasar: His Life and Work*, 7–43; Elio Guerriero, *Hans Urs von Balthasar: Eine Monographie* (Freiburg: Johannes Verlag Einsiedeln, 1993); Thomas Krenski, "Mit Handbuchwissen wäre Adriennes Theologie nicht aufzufangen gewesen: Hans Urs von Balthasar und Adrienne von Speyr," Lecture in Mainz, June 11, 2005; Jacques Servais, "Per una valutazione dell'influsso di Adrienne von Speyr su Hans Urs von Balthasar," *Rivista Teologica di Lugano* 6, no. 1 (2001): 67–89; Rino Fisichella, "Hans Urs von Balthasar e Adrienne von Speyr: L'inseparabilità delle due opere," *Communio: Rivista Internazionale di Teologia e Cultura* 156 (1997): 61–74. See also Balthasar, Foreword to *Heilige Zeichen*, by Egon Kapellari (Graz-Wien-Köln: Verlag Styria, 1987), 7–10.

5. Balthasar, *Our Task*, 16–17.

result of their common interests and insights. In Balthasar, Adrienne was looking for an asylum, actually "the place of the community where God's will was supposed to be revealed."[6] This became a common cause for both of them because of the community that they were part of (the Church) whose many missions are interwoven. "Truth means 'sounding together.' Truth is symphonic. Symphony sounds. Not in unison, but what is far more beautiful—in symphony. Even the eternal Truth is symphonic."[7] Balthasar, with his musical background, considered his role in this symphony of ideas as one who presents the original score. "Even if nothing in my work were original (and that would not surprise me), there would still remain the passion to hand on what has been preserved to others (because it is unfamiliar to so many), together with the order to do this; for missions more than personal qualities are what individualize the Christian."[8] As mediator of Adrienne's divine inspiration, Balthasar believed his task was to discern critically whether or not what she experienced corresponded to the Creed of the Church, to Tradition.

Hans Urs von Balthasar was asked by Angelo Scola to describe the complementary nature of his work with Adrienne von Speyr. He replied:

> Adrienne is a world. Not only has she built a world community, but built it upon an extensive theology, which in its substance derives from her. All I attempted to do was gather it up and embed it in a space, such as the theology of the Fathers, that of the Middle Ages and the modern age, with which I was fairly familiar. My contribution consisted in providing a comprehensive theological horizon, so that all that was new and valid in her thought would not be watered

6. Quoted in Adrienne von Speyr, *Erde und Himmel: Ein Tagebuch* II (Einsiedeln: Johannes Verlag, 1975), 86, no. 1319.

7. Balthasar, *Truth is Symphonic: Aspects of Christian Pluralism* (San Francisco: Ignatius Press: 1987), 7–9.

8. Balthasar, *My Work*, 19–20.

down or falsified, but be given space to unfold. With a mere textbook-theology one could not have captured Adrienne's work; it required a knowledge of the great tradition to realize that her original propositions in no way contradicted it.

The Holy Spirit may suddenly illuminate parts of revelation that have always been there, but have not been sufficiently reflected upon. The history of the Church confirms it. Before Saint Francis, no one had thought so deeply about the poverty of Christ. This poverty is not a secondary consideration but a new access to the center. Before Augustine, many had spoken of the love of God, but none did it in as penetrating a manner as he. Before Ignatius, no one had grasped Christ's obedience to the Father in quite so central way. Correspondingly, aspects exist in Adrienne's work that have not been as expressly discovered in revelation before. But once examined carefully, one realizes that they "work."

A case in point is her reflection on prayer in the triune God: prayer not only, as one had always understood, as something that ascends from man to God, but, more profoundly, what descends from God to man, permitting a participation in the inner-trinitarian prayer of God. In God himself lie the archetypes of all our modes of prayer. Within the trinitarian life God worships God, God may petition God; in thanksgiving one may recognize how the One God, within the Trinity, can make a choice, form a decision. The Holy Spirit, who is poured into our hearts, who searches the depth of God, is given to us too, elevating us into the sphere of inner-trinitarian prayer. This is but one of many instances in which Adrienne first astonishes, and then, on further reflection, brings joy. I believe the Church will gradually have to adopt substantial parts of her doctrine and, perhaps, wonder why these beautiful and enriching things have not been recognized earlier. But the Holy Spirit distributes his gifts when he wills.[9]

9. Balthasar with Angelo Scola, *Test Everything: Hold Fast to What is Good* (San Francisco: Ignatius Press, 1989), 88–89.

Hans Urs von Balthasar was convinced that God Himself inspired the insights that Speyr received and gave them their direction. He was also sure that the charismatic graces she received were authentic. This meant that there was a certain cohesion between Adrienne's visions and Balthasar's own objective interpretations.[10] So there was a certain correspondence between Adrienne's visions and Balthasar's own objective interpretation. Balthasar wrote:

> God calls often two by two those whom he has chosen so that there are no longer two persons with separate vocations, but "two in one vocation." Such unions can have the same necessity and urgency as the call itself. What has been written about the union established by God in the natural order, can also be said of them: "What therefore God has joined together, let no man put asunder" (Mt 19:6).[11]

"Two in One Call"

Balthasar paid special attention to the saints and wrote many monographs about them. Adrienne had an unusual relationship with the saints. She describes their prayer life and their openness to God. Balthasar had a decided interest and commitment to the unified mission he had with Speyr. As a writer and publisher, he emphasized with Speyr the mission of many saints. These are his words:

10. It would be wrong to label the great theologian as "gullible" compared to the visionary experience of Adrienne. Quite the opposite! He himself says: "No one will ever know how much tangible evidence of the supernatural truth I have received. It's as if we wanted to whip up the truth with a cudgel. The cloud of witnesses, the real rain of evidence poured on me from all sides. From the outside, it seemed like a risk, what I was doing or would do. But not for a moment from the inside. Everything in advance was worn by an incredible grace, and only in few instances it was difficult to withstand. I never had a slightest doubt" (quoted in Adrienne von Speyr: *Erde und Himmel II*, 200, no. 1579).

11. Balthasar, *The Christian State of Life* (San Francisco: Ignatius Press, 1983), 450.

> In our case, the plan was that we should collaborate intensively on a common external work. The long period of preparation (for Adrienne, from 1902 to 1940) was meant to make us ready for the complementary task. This involved two things. First, there was the great difference between our two parts. For Adrienne, there was the seemingly endless quest for Catholic truth, the medical profession, and the experience of marriage. For me, there was an education—first in all literary, then philosophical and theological—which was intended to give me a knowledge of the spiritual tradition of the Church, within which I could situate what was special and new about Adrienne's insights. Secondly, there was an affinity or association between us enabling what was different to become complementary.[12]

The fruit of this collaboration, the unity created by their united mission, was the establishment of the secular institute *Johannesgemeinschaft,* The Community of Saint John. Balthasar has this to say about their work: "Her work and mine are neither psychologically nor philologically to be separated: two halves of a single whole, which has as its center a unique foundation."[13]

Balthasar affirms in his retrospective on 1955 that secular institutes are

> beyond doubt the unifying midpoint of the Church; they constitute the link between the lay state and the life of the vows and show not only the existential unity of the Church but also her perennial and most "up-to-date" mission in the world. About this nucleus my activities as author, editor and publisher are gathered in concentric circles. My goal has been to order the treasures of revelation, of Church theology and spirituality critically around this center, bound as much to the past as to the future. This task involves,

12. Balthasar, *Our Task*, 17.
13. Balthasar, *My Work*, 89.

> above all, the administration of the vast literary estate of Adrienne von Speyr.[14]

Balthasar considers himself an interpreter of Adrienne's charismatic insights. He says: "Perhaps my writings will be really understood only when serious attention is given to Adrienne von Speyr."[15]

Even though Speyr's contributions have yet to be fully recognized, it is clear that the writings of Balthasar indicate that the unique and original work of Adrienne will be eventually fully appreciated. Balthasar's words "Over the years she would help to correct the proofs of my books, which after 1941 were greatly influenced by her wealth of ideas."[16] Speyr was given complete freedom by Balthasar to express her ideas, with the originality of her theological insights. This, combined with Balthasar's profound knowledge, produced an amazing harmony of two great minds and hearts with one call, one united mission.

At the center of the combined work of Balthasar and Speyr was the secular institute, the Community of Saint John. As early as 1955 Balthasar wrote: "All this would remain mere literary chatter were it not at the service of, and obedient to, an ecclesial action that has been assigned to me, which I myself have not chosen. This is the center; everything else, even if developed earlier, has been placed around it."[17]

It was in 1975 that Balthasar asserted his primary intention and purpose of this work:

> The activity of being a writer remains and will always remain, in the working-out of my life, a secondary function, something *faute de mieux*. At its center there is a completely

14. *My Work*, 58.

15. Balthasar and Michael Albus, "Spirit and Fire: An Interview with Hans Urs von Balthasar," *Communio: International Catholic Review* 32 (Fall 2005): 574.

16. Balthasar, *Our Task*, 59.

17. Balthasar, *My Work*, 43.

> different interest: the task of renewing the Church through the formation of new communities that unite the radical Christian life of conformity to the evangelical counsels of Jesus with existence in the midst of the world, whether by practicing secular profession or through the ministerial priesthood to give new life to living communities. All my activity as a writer is subordinated to this task.[18]

In order to emphasize the primary purpose of this work, Balthasar continued to stress the complementary role of Adrienne von Speyr. He writes,

> to remove the impression that in the books that I have mentioned, and others, I have simply expounded my own convictions. The greater part of so much of what I have written is a translation of what is present in more immediate, less technical, fashion in the powerful work of Adrienne von Speyr, of which only a part has been published.[19]
>
> The richness contained there will only be recognized in more mature times. Then it will be seen how strongly the intuition of this woman has influenced my books—*Heart of the World,*[20] *The God Question and Modern Man,*[21] *Theologie der drei Tage* [Theology of three days][22]—and various other books, which essentially are only a theological transcription of so much learned directly from her. This is an assertion that can only be verified at a later date.[23]

18. *My Work*, 95.
19. *My Work*, 105.
20. *Heart of the World* (San Francisco: Ignatius Press, 1979). German: *Das Herz der Welt* (Zürich: Verlag der Arche, 1944).
21. *The God Question and Modern Man* (New York: Seabury Press, 1967). German: *Die Gottesfrage des heutigen Menschen* (Vienna: Verlag Herold, 1955).
22. *Mysterium paschale: The Mystery of Easter* (San Francisco: Ignatius Press, 1995). German: *Theologie der drei Tage* (Einsiedeln: Benzinger, 1969).
23. *My Work*, 106–7.

Common Theological Work

The Protestant Adrienne (Kaegi-) von Speyr became a convert to the Catholic faith on the feast of All Saints in 1940. These are Balthasar's words:

> Immediately, the visions, first of all Marian and Ignatian, began and soon thereafter also the dictations of the Gospel according to John: at night the content of a passage was shown to her, and on the following day she dictated—about half an hour a day, later during the holidays more; occasionally we have worked on two or even three books at the same time: the dictations always went with sterner and steeper experiences of suffering, states of complete abandonment of God (she called it "being in a dump"), which had for me an unexpected climax on Holy Saturday, whose theology was unveiled by her—probably for the first time in the history of theology—with astonishing abundance and precision, year after year, so that of course the mystery of this conclusion of the Passion was always preserved.[24]

Very soon after her conversion in 1940, Adrienne received many promptings about founding a new community. These are Balthasar's comments:

> Soon afterward she said to me: "God is always looking for people who at the decisive moment will not be afraid." The first thing she was told that she could expect was suffering (in which a God-given anxiety would play a key role). She would be asked relentlessly whether she was ready, in all seriousness, to give up everything. But just before the first real experience of the Passion in Holy Week 1941, as she said in a letter (March 30, 1941), Mary appeared to her. "She

24. Balthasar, "Adrienne von Speyr (1902–1967): Die Miterfahrung der Passion und Gottverlassenheit," in *Frauen des Glaubens*, ed. Paul Imhof (Würzburg: Echter, 1985), 267–77, at 272.

advised me to devote myself to young women. So many vocations can be found there in embryo which should be helped to develop." From now on she begins to consider "the possibility of a new community."[25]

It was now that for the first time she got to know the supernatural world in all its dimensions—from heaven to hell. Numerous promises were made, and equally numerous miraculous healings took place at her hands. The theological mission in the stricter sense would begin (with the dictations on St. John's Gospel in May 1944), only when she had been sufficiently initiated into the mysteries of the Passion and the new life flows from it. But chronologically, the community she was called to found came first. In July 1941 she presented the basic idea to me.[26]

Adrienne's preoccupation with the community she had been asked to found (she now usually called it "the Child") became more and more intensive. From holidays (July 1941) she writes: "My prime time belongs to the Child, in the sense that a lot of things are now being quietly examined, reflected on, and somehow prayed over." She began to make notes about them. A few days later she sees Mary in front of her '(not a vision, but really there, *en chair et en os* [in flesh and bone], with the Child on her arm.' She sees houses, large and small, "full of life and work." A. is prompted to new reflections and notes, which she proposes to show me.[27]

She prayed constantly for the "Child" and learned a great deal about it. She also prayed for my "inadequacy," so that I would be able to cooperate properly. And more than anything else, she wanted to "teach" the "Child" "the spirit of penance"[28]

In the following months, A. suffered much for priests. The idea came up, albeit indistinctly, that we should have

25. Balthasar, *Our Task*, 47.
26. *Our Task*, 47–48.
27. *Our Task*, 49.
28. *Our Task*, 50–51.

> a task in relation to the clergy. . . . The next few months overflowed with terrifying visions. A. went through all the horrors of the war. She had to experience the psychological state of the tortured and starving, of people burned to death, and of the tortures. She saw scenes of the Passion and practiced excessive penance; overwhelmed by what she had seen, A. sometimes forgot the limits I had imposed to her.[29]
>
> After Easter 1944 Adrienne was shown how important prayer would be in the new community. "In addition to obligatory prayer, space should be provided for personal prayer. This is even more important for women than for men." To her horror she was shown what she would look like if she no longer prayed. "She saw herself wrapped up in activism and externals: the shell, the dead skin of her earlier life. Christians who stop praying are hard to save."[30]

In May 1944 Adrienne began her comments on St. John's Gospel and continued them through that year. In the spring of 1954 she experienced a vision, along with the Blessed Mother and her child, of some priests that would be connected with a community that did not yet exist. Then, on August 5th of that year, in Estavayer, the foundation of the new community took place. The responsibility that Balthasar felt for the new community became the cause of the most difficult decision he ever had to make, to leave the Society of Jesus. These are his words, "It was only after I had left that it became increasingly evident that a men's branch should be founded in addition to the one for women."[31]

Some extracts from Adrienne's letters help clarify her relationship with Balthasar, who was often away giving lectures and retreats. Since she did not always understand many of her experi-

29. *Our Task*, 51–52.
30. *Our Task*, 54.
31. *Our Task*, 56.

ences and visions, she submitted them to Balthasar for his interpretation. These are her words: "You see, you always give my experiences such a beautiful meaning. You understand them much better than I do. Your guidance really does make the experience meaningful and grace-filled."[32]

Adrienne's letters made it clear that the two missions, hers and Balthasar's, were bound together as one. "The letters emphasize very strongly that our two missions from now on are bound together into one."[33] She expressed her gratitude to Balthasar in almost all her letters. And her last words as she was dying were these: "Thank you, thank you, thank you." She was grateful to the Lord for her conversion and the graces that flowed from it. And she was grateful for her friendship with Balthasar. She wrote that "there are moments when I can clearly see that the two of us are being allowed to serve as instruments, to serve totally, and yet that means supreme happiness, albeit touched with pain."[34]

The Integration of Two Works since 1940

In his book *Our Task*, Balthasar describes

> the spiritual part played by Adrienne in what I have written since I first met her. This is not an easy task. The views and projects I brought with me are so interconnected with what came from her that the two can never be neatly separated. Still, certain things are clear. . . . I have explained how Adrienne's experiences bolstered my chief interests (in St. Irenaeus, Origen, St. Gregory of Nyssa, and St. Maximus the Confessor), answered unresolved questions, and confirmed the correctness of what I was trying to do.[35]

32. *Our Task*, 83.
33. *Our Task*, 86.
34. *Our Task*, 88–89.
35. *Our Task*, 95.
36. *Heart of the World* (San Francisco: Ignatius Press, 1979). German: *Das Herz der Welt* (Zürich: Verlag der Arche, 1944).

> *The Heart of the World*, written in 1943,[36] is the first direct echo of my involvement with Adrienne's Pascal experiences—the Eastertide and eucharistic experiences as well as those of Good Friday and Holy Saturday. The lyrical, hymn-like style of the book is not appropriate to her own, which was always plain and down-to-earth. It is a sign of my enthusiasm and sense of wonder at these privileged insights into the mystery of Christ in all its fullness. More seen here is repeated later in more objective form. The chapter on the descent into hell is directly dependent on Adrienne's Holy Saturday experiences.[37]
>
> *Der Laie und der Ordensstand* [The layman and the religious state][38] is the first and rather inadequate prospectus for what will be described below as Adrienne's and my most important concern: a community for women and men who live and work in the world but at the same time follow the evangelical counsels.[39]

Balthasar's book *Thérèse of Lisieux: The Story of a Mission* (1950) would not have come about without Adrienne's theology of mission.[40] This is also true of *The Christian State of Life* (1954).[41] These are his words:

> Adrienne's doggedly maintained opinion about the "two states" (marriage and the counsels—there is no third way) also left its mark on the study. The final version tries to situate the priestly office among the states of Christian life and

37. *Our Task*, 96.

38. *Der Laie und der Ordensstand* (Einsiedeln: Johannes Verlag, 1948). Revised edition with additional essays in English as *The Laity and the Life of the Counsels: The Church's Mission in the World* (San Francisco: Ignatius Press, 2003).

39. Balthasar, *Our Task*, 97.

40. *Thérèse of Lisieux: Story of a Mission* (New York: Sheed and Ward, 1954). German: *Thérèse von Lisieux: Geschichte einer Sendung* (Olten: Hegner-Bücherei im Summa-Verlag, 1950).

41. *The Christian State of Life* (San Francisco: Ignatius Press, 1983). German: *Christlicher Stand*, 2nd ed. (Einsiedeln: Johannes Verlag, 1981).

> thus, like Adrienne, to demonstrate convergence between the priesthood and the life of the counsels.[42]

The work of Adrienne von Speyr also entitled *The Christian State of Life* (1956) contained the same theological ideas as those of Balthasar.[43]

Balthasar wrote many works about theology of ministry, especially regarding priestly spirituality.[44] These writings prioritized the theology of celibacy, and the evangelical counsels in general, for diocesan clergy, without trying to turn parish priests into religious priests.[45]

Hans Urs von Balthasar's book *A Theology of History* (1950),[46] like the collection of his essays titled *The Whole in the Fragment: Aspects of the Theology of History* (1963),[47] contains much of his own work, but, as he said, "However the consistent centering on Christ, especially the doctrine of the 'Forty Days,' the idea of the universalizing of the Christ-event by the Holy Spirit, and the doctrine of mission and the Christian tradition are clearly inspired by Adrienne."[48]

42. Balthasar, *Our Task*, 99. See Hans Urs von Balthasar, Foreword to *Leben aus der Fülle des Glaubens: Theologie der christlichen Stände bei Hans Urs von Balthasar*, by Anton Štrukelj (Graz-Wien-Köln: Verlag Styria, 2002); 2nd ed. Ljubljana 2015; Russian translation Moscow 2016; Croatian translation Zagreb 2017. This book was written as a dissertation in the Slovenian language and published in Ljubljana in 1981, 1986, 1995. I am indebted to Dr. Hans Urs von Balthasar for his initiative as well as for the generous help and precious advice for this dissertation. Moreover, I am cordially grateful for his foreword to my dissertation.

43. Speyr, *The Christian State of Life* (San Francisco: Ignatius Press, 1983). German: *Der Christlicher Stand* (Einsiedeln: Johannes Verlag, 1956).

44. Balthasar, *Priestly Spirituality* (San Francisco: Ignatius Press, 2013).

45. See Balthasar, *Our Task*, 113.

46. *A Theology of History* (San Francisco: Ignatius Press, 1994). German: *Theologie der Geschichte: Ein Grundriss*, new edition (Einsiedeln: Johannes Verlag, 1959).

47. *The Whole in the Fragment: Aspects of the Theology of History*, 2nd ed (San Francisco: Ignatius Press, 1990). German: *Das Ganze im Fragment: Aspekte der Geschichtstheologie* (Einsiedeln: Benziger Verlag, 1963).

48. *Our Task*, 99–100.

Balthasar's book, *The Theology of Karl Barth: Exposition and Interpretation* (1951) is the fruit of numerous conversations with the Swiss theologian.[49] (Adrienne indicated that she supported these talks with intensive prayer and penance.) Her influence was quite evident in Balthasar's books *The Christian and Anxiety* (1951), *Razing the Bastions* (1952), *Engagement with God* (1971), *Katholisch: Aspekte des Mysteriums* [Catholic: Aspects of the mysteries] (1975), and particularly in the section of the *Word Made Flesh* entitled "Theology and Sanctity" which was originally published in 1948.[50] Closely connected with the issues raised are his books on the French author George Bernanos (1954) and German poet Reinhold Schneider (1953).[51] Balthasar wrote an important commentary to *Summa Theologiae* 2a–2ae, qq. 171–82 (1954), which comprises the gifts of the Holy Spirit and the active and contemplative lives.[52]

49. *The Theology of Karl Barth: Exposition and Interpretation* (San Francisco: Ignatius Press, 1992). German: *Karl Barth: Darstellung und Deutung Seiner*, 4th ed. (Einsiedeln: Johannes Verlag, 1976).

50. See *Our Task*, 102–3. Respectively: *The Christian and Anxiety* (San Francisco: Ignatius Press, 2000), German: *Der Christ und die Angst*, 6th ed. (Einsiedeln: Johannes Verlag, 1989); *Razing the Bastions* (San Francisco: Ignatius Press, 1993), German: *Schleifung der Bastionen*, 5th ed. (Einsiedeln: Johannes Verlag, 1989); *Engagement with God* (San Francisco: Ignatius Press, 2008), German: *In Gottes Einsatz leben*, 2nd ed. (Einsiedeln: Johannes Verlag, 1972); *In the Fullness of the Faith: On the Centrality of the Distinctively Catholic* (San Francisco: Ignatius Press, 1988), German: *Katholisch: Aspekte des Mysteriums* (Einsiedeln: Johannes Verlag, 1975); "Theology and Sanctity," in *Explorations in Theology*, vol. I, *The Word Made Flesh* (San Francisco: Ignatius Press, 1989), 181–209. German: *Verbum Caro* (Einsiedeln: Johannes Verlag, 1960).

51. Respectively, *Bernanos: An Ecclesial Existence* (San Francisco: Ignatius Press, 1996), German: *Gelebte Kirche: Bernanos*, 3rd ed. (Einsiedeln: Johannes Verlag, 1988); *Tragedy under Grace: Reinhold Schneider on the Experience of the West* (San Francisco: Ignatius Press, 1997), German: *Nochmals Reinhold Schneider* [new ed. of *Reinhold Schneider: Sein Weg und sein Werk*] (Einsiedeln: Johannes Verlag, 1991).

52. *Thomas und die Charismatik: Kommentar zu Thomas von Aquin, Summa Theologica Quaestiones II-II 171–182, besondere Gnadengaben und die zwei Wege menschlichen Lebens*, new ed. (Freiburg: Johannes Verlag Einsiedeln, 1996).

While Balthasar always had the teaching and example of the Fathers of the Church as the background for his work, his immediate source of inspiration was Adrienne's scriptural exegesis which was nothing more than her ability to hear and contemplate God's Word. An example of her insights is evident in Balthasar's book on contemplative prayer (1955) which was built on the biblical foundation that came from contemplation on the words of Scripture.[53] This was also true of his commentary on the letters to the Thessalonians and the pastoral epistles (1955).[54]

Some of his minor works have many features that go back more or less directly to Adrienne: *Convergences* (1969), *Truth Is Symphonic* (1972), *Elucidations* (1971), *New Elucidations* (1979), *A Short Primer for Unsettled Laymen* (1980), and *Christen sind einfältig* [Christians are simple] (1983).[55] The unity of the two's works blending into one is apparent in the important trilogy of Balthasar begun in 1960. The first part, the theological aesthetics titled *The Glory of the Lord* (1961–1969), examines the idea of the "wonder" of being, with the focus on the Johannine understanding of glory as uniting both the Cross and the Resurrection of Jesus. In this paschal glory, the triune God shines forth in a unique but clear way. Much

53. *Prayer* (San Francisco: Ignatius Press, 1986); German: *Das betrachtende Gebet* (Einsiedeln: Johannes Verlag, 1955).

54. *Pastoralbriefe des Heiligen Paulus: Fur das betrachtende Gebet erschlossen*, 2nd ed. (Einsiedeln: Johannes Verlag, 1992).

55. See Balthasar, *Our Task*, 105–7. Respectively, *Convergences: To the Source of Christian Mystery* (San Francisco: Ignatius Press, 1983), German: *Einfaltungen: Auf dem Wege christlicher Einigung*, 3rd ed. (Einsiedeln: Johannes Verlag, 1987); *Truth Is Symphonic: Aspects of Christian Pluralism* (San Francisco: Ignatius Press, 1987), German: *Die Wahrheit ist symphonisch: Aspekte des christlichen Pluralismus* (Einsiedeln: Johannes Verlag, 1972); *Elucidations* (San Francisco: Ignatius Press, 1998), German: *Klarstellungen: Zur Prüfung der Geister*, 4th ed. (Einsiedeln: Johannes Verlag, 1978); *New Elucidations* (San Francisco: Ignatius Press, 1986), German: *Neue Klarstellungen*, 2nd ed. (Einsiedeln: Johannes Verlag, 1995); *A Short Primer for Unsettled Laymen* (San Francisco: Ignatius Press, 1985), German: *Kleine Fibel für unversicherte Laien*, 3rd ed. (Einsiedeln: Johannes Verlag, 1989); *Christen sind einfältig* (Einsiedeln: Johannes Verlag, 1983).

of Balthasar's works are the fruit of his theological study, but as he pointed out,

> everything leads into a theology of the Cross which is in perfect conformity to Adrienne's. At this point mention should be made of the short programmatic work *Love Alone is Credible* (1963).[56] Only Adrienne's Christology, which gets beyond every kind of *apokatastasis* doctrine, can justify this daring title.[57]

Balthasar emphasizes the importance of aesthetics in relating to the theological concept of the beautiful. He attributes this emphasis to Adrienne:

> Without knowing anything about aesthetics, Adrienne, in her brilliant little book, *Light and the Images: Elements of Contemplation* (1955),[58] works along the same lines and, in the process, has given us one of the most concentrated accounts of Christian contemplation ever written. It expels all Neo-Platonizing hostility to images, and it does so in the name of the images created for us by God, but above all in the name of him whom creation images, God's incarnate Son. We cannot get beyond his bodiliness, because it is the very means by which all the light of God's love is communicated to us.[59]

The second part of Balthasar's trilogy *Theo-Drama* (1973–1983) is based, first of all, on the concept of mission. Secondly, it is concerned with the confrontation that takes place between the finite freedom of creatures and infinite divine freedom.

56. *Love Alone is Credible* (San Francisco: Ignatius Press, 2004); German: *Glaubhaft ist nur Liebe* (Einsiedeln: Johannes Verlag, 1963).

57. Balthasar, *Our Task*, 109.

58. *Light and the Images: Elements of Contemplation* (San Francisco: Ignatius Press, 2004); German: *Das Licht und die Bilder: Elemente der Kontemplation*, 2nd ed. (Einsiedeln: Johannes Verlag, 1986).

59. Balthasar, *Our Task*, 109–10.

> Mission is presented here as a central concept of Christology and the following of Christ. It is in harmony with the whole Ignatian and Johannine theology of Adrienne. The confrontation, which in its most extreme form is between divine freedom and anti-divine demonic freedom, became as dramatic and concrete in Adrienne's life as it was for St. Anthony the Great and the Curé of Ars.[60]

The role of Mary in the Church corresponds to the concept of mission. These are Balthasar's words: "At the foot of the Cross, Mary shared the suffering of her Son and was handed over by him to John, thus becoming the 'Church' (in the Church's innermost being a Bride of Christ). This is Adrienne's constant teaching."[61] Balthasar's book on the ministry of the pope and the nature of the Church (1974) presents Mary as embodying the Church in an all-embracing way.[62]

At the conclusion of part two of his trilogy, Balthasar affirms

> that the grounding of all dogmatics and spirituality leads back in what St. John's Gospel teaches us about Christ's loving obedience to the Father in the Holy Spirit. This is the presupposition of the revelation of the trinitarian mystery of God's love and of Christ's redemption of the world, when he makes atonement for all the disobedience of mankind. . . . It was Adrienne who emphasized in the strongest possible terms, following St. John, the christological foundation of obedience and took it existentially to its farthest limits. . . . As far as I am concerned, the secret center of my work on the Old Testament (*The Glory of the Lord* VI) is the chapter on the frightening obedience of the prophets (down "The Steps of Obedience" to the obedience of

60. *Our Task*, 110.

61. *Our Task*, 111.

62. *The Office of Peter and the Structure of the Church* (San Francisco: Ignatius Press, 1986); German: *Der antirömische Affekt: Wie lässt sich das Papsttum in der Gesamtkirche integrieren?*, 2nd ed. (Einsiedeln: Johannes Verlag, 1989).

> Christ).[63] The question interested me not only in theology and general spirituality, but also in a practical way with regard to obedience in secular institutes.[64]

The theological aesthetics of Balthasar's *The Glory of the Lord* is an eloquent testimony to the input Speyr had on his thinking and writing. He refers to her influence in the final volume of the *Theo-Drama, Last Act*,[65] as well as in the third and final part of his trilogy, the "*Theo-Logic*." Balthasar, in writing about "Hell and Trinity," points to the special charism of Adrienne von Speyr, especially her mystical experiences related to Holy Saturday. He comments, "Luther tore open abysses that no theological or ecumenical soft-pedaling has managed to close. An adequate answer comes only from the doctrine of Adrienne von Speyr, who sounds and expresses these abyssal depths like none before her."[66] She demonstrated in a unique way what it means to do theology on one's knees.

Concrete Collaboration and Adrienne's Themes

How were the dictated works of Speyr composed? Balthasar's theological formation, guided by the insights and work of Adrienne von Speyr, was formed in an objective way. It was a matter of their collaboration and many years of work together. This is what Balthasar wrote about their relationship:

63. *The Glory of the Lord: A Theological Aesthetics*, vol. II, *Theology: The Old Covenant* (San Francisco: Ignatius Press, 1989).

64. *Our Task*, 114–15.

65. Balthasar, *Theo-Drama: Theological Dramatic Theory*, vol. V, *The Last Act* (San Francisco: Ignatius Press, 1998), 13: "Here many passages from the works of Adrienne von Speyr are reproduced and referred to in footnotes. . . . These quotations are not intended to give a full picture of her theology; that would require far more space; I quote her to show the fundamental consonance between her views and mine on many of the eschatological topics discussed here."

66. Balthasar, *Theo-Logic: Theological Logical Theory*, vol. II, *The Truth of God* (San Francisco: Ignatius Press, 2004), 345.

> Initially, we just had a few catechism sessions on the Catholic faith. I was amazed by the way Adrienne immediately grasped everything she was told, as if it were something long expected. The decisive thing at the very beginning was the fact that I "gave her back" the Our Father. This came about as follows. When her husband Emil died, she felt she could no longer say the petition "Thy will be done." "I don't want to lie to the good Lord," she said. A Protestant clergyman advised her to avoid the Our Father and say other prayers. But then she felt a kind of emptiness, "the absence of God, in fact, almost the nonexistence of God." One of the first instructions I gave her was about simple, unselfconscious praying of the Our Father, which at a stroke gave her back all her prayer.[67]

Balthasar affirms: "I never gave A. any proper instructions in theology. She heard my homilies and the instructions I gave to the community."[68]

Adrienne's themes presented her original theological insights and embraced the whole of theology, from the Trinity to Christology, from protology to eschatology. She had a special interest in marriage and virginity, in Christian mission, the Communion of Saints, and in ecclesial mysticism. Balthasar referred to her wide range of interest:

> All the main themes in Adrienne's work which I have here described played no role in my books before 1940, however many Church Fathers and other theologians I may have studied. If these themes emerged in my books and lectures after 1940, it is because they were taken from what I had learned from Adrienne. . . . At the same time, of course, my own ideas and way of thinking were not extinguished but rather enriched by what I received from Adrienne. It is quite

67. Balthasar, *Our Task*, 57–58.
68. *Our Task*, 56–59.

> pointless to try to disentangle what is hers from what is mine in these late works.[69]

Adrienne's special charism were celebrated by Balthasar by the four main concepts in her theology: *indifference, readiness, confessional attitude,* and *virginity and love.*[70] The central theme in her theology revolved around her "confessional attitude" as it related to Trinitarian, Christological, Mariological, and ecclesial issues. Her insights were unique and inspirational to Balthasar.

Adrienne von Speyr's Help with Balthasar's Work

A special help Adrienne gave was during the numerous courses of the Ignatian Spiritual Exercises which Balthasar undertook. He said of her assistance, "She never failed to prepare for these through prayer and special penances. While they were taking place, she would phone and make practical suggestions about how I should deal with certain people."[71] Adrienne also helped him in another practical way: "She checked proofs and read books, about which I wanted her opinion, which always turned out to be very much to the point."[72]

It was difficult for Balthasar to leave the Society of Jesus because of his discernment of God's will for himself. It was also difficult for Adrienne because of her attachment to Ignatian spirituality. But her path led her more deeply into a life of renunciation and suffering. She renounced her many attachments that chained her to this world and her ability to achieve something for herself. In 1954, because of her increasing infirmity and the loss of her sight, she had to give up her medical practice. Balthasar reported:

69. *Our Task*, 72–73.

70. Balthasar, "Adriennes Charisma," in *Adrienne von Speyr und ihre kirchliche Sendung: Akten des römischen Symposions*, ed. Balthasar, Georges Chantraine, and Angelo Scola (Einsiedeln: Johannes Verlag, 1986), 173–78.

71. Balthasar, *Our Task*, 74.

72. *Our Task*, 77.

> On a trip to Mariastein, as we were leaving a church in which we had prayed, she said: "*C'est en ordre*, It is in order." I asked what she meant. "She has now renounced her profession. She really had to tear herself away. This was the last thing chaining her to the world: the feeling of being able to do something, to achieve something earthly. But now this has been given up, or at least it will be given up." In 1954, because of total infirmity and finally loss of sight, she had to give up her medical practice. However, to the very end, by her prayer and suffering, she never ceased to make my journey easier. All this she did increasingly in perceptible contact with heaven.[73]

Hans Urs von Balthasar mentions finally the international catholic review *Communio*:

> In 1945 the demand was repeatedly made that "I should start a magazine" . . . I saw no possibility of it at all. Then came the reply: "Not now. But get on with the planning. Keep in mind the people who can write it with you." And a year later: "Don't forget the magazine!" I gave it no more serious thought, even when one evening, in a café in the Via Aurelia in Rome, a few of us from the International Theological Commission decided to start the international Catholic review *Communio*. . . . The strange blessing that rests on this fragile network linking different countries and continents confirmed me in this supposition, and imperceptibly it became a certainty.[74]

In explaining the complementarity that existed between himself and Adrienne, Balthasar wrote this:

> Complementarity is only possible when the two halves are different. As for my path, Adrienne was told: "It is a different route, but the destination is the same." Adrienne's mission

73. *Our Task*, 80–81.
74. *Our Task*, 81–82.

> was not only one of experience, of the dark night and other Christological states, but also quite expressly one of interpretation. That is why a complementary mission was needed—to introduce and train her practically in the central Christological mystery of the Son's obedience to the Father. This obedience was fundamental to everything. In the end it applied to both of us and was taken to its ultimate consequences. For me, the Society of Jesus was a "homeland," a gift that I loved above all things. . . . In the end I had to leave. The proofs for the correctness of the decision had meanwhile become overwhelmingly clear. Taking responsibility for this was such a crushing burden for A. that she wished she could die, so that I could stay in the Society.[75]

Adrienne von Speyr's Impact on the Church

From September 27 to 29, 1985, an international symposium took place at the Lateran University in Rome titled "Adrienne von Speyr and Her Ecclesial Mission."[76] During the symposium Cardinal Ratzinger offered Mass for the participants in the Lateran Basilica. At the end of the symposium the Pope John Paul II invited them to a private audience with himself.

Adrienne had been given a prophetic gift for the Church. Prophecy, in both the New and Old Testaments, is not just prediction for the future, but a clear understandable message and explanation of what God wants to say to the Church and the world. A characteristically Christian understanding about prophesy and mysticism requires the consent of the receiver (as with Mary) and

75. *Our Task*, 18–19.

76. *Adrienne von Speyr und ihre kirchliche Sendung*. For the 100th anniversary of Adrienne von Speyr in Freiburg im Breisgau,"Hans Urs von Balthasar: Stiftung," organized the symposium "Adrienne von Speyr und ihre spirituelle Theologie" (2002). For the 50th anniversary of von Speyr's death, an international symposium was organized in Rome from November 17–18, 2017, "Adrienne von Speyr (1902–1967): Una donna nel cuore del ventesimo secolo" ["A woman in the heart of the 20th century"].

leaves God the freedom to place that person in a state He deems most suitable for conveying an insight from Him, and for the task He wants accomplished. Balthasar saw in Speyr a gift of "an objective genuine Christian mysticism which is always incarnational."[77]

Contemplation played in important role in Adrienne's theology which originated from her constant prayer and her contemplation of the Holy Trinity. Her theology was ecclesial and thoroughly Marian. Barbara Albrecht said of Adrienne,

> The full openness and readiness for an obedient reception of experiences and insights led Adrienne von Speyr constantly to Mary. . . . It is certainly not unimportant to note that Adrienne's first glance is directed to "Handmaid of the Lord," and with this title from 1948 begins her entire work.[78]

Mary, the mother of Jesus, demonstrated most clearly what prophecy is and what it means for the Church.

> The figure of Mary constitutes the fundamental reference in the Church. One could say metaphorically that Mary is a mirror placed before the Church, in which the Church is invited to recognize her own identity as well as the dispositions of the heart, the attitudes and the actions which God expects from her. The existence of Mary is an invitation to the Church to root her very being in listening and receiving the Word of God. It is from Mary that the Church always learns the intimacy of Christ.[79]

Mary has always been the model for prophecy in the Church, and when we review the history of the Church, we find that most

77. See Adrienne von Speyr, *Das Wort und die Mystik*. Part I, *Subjektive Mystik*; Part II, *Objektive Mystik* (Einsiedeln: Johannes Verlag, 1970).

78. Barbara Albrecht, *Eine Theologie des Katholischen: Einführung in das Werk Adrienne von Speyrs*. Durchblick in Texten 1 (Einsiedeln: Johannes Verlag, 1972), 17.

79. Congregation for the Doctrine of the Faith, *Letter on the Collaboration of Men and Women* (2004), 15.

prophets were women. Cardinal Joseph Ratzinger reflected on this reality when he wrote:

> There is an ancient patristic tradition that calls Mary, not priestess but prophetess. The title of prophetess in the patristic tradition is Mary's supreme title. It is in Mary that there is a precise definition of what prophecy really is, that is, this intimate capacity to listen to, perceive, feel, that allows one to sense the consolation of the Holy Spirit, accepting him within oneself, making him fruitful, bringing him fruitful into the world. It might be said, in a sense, without wishing to be categorical, that it is none other than the Marian line that represents in the Church the prophetic dimension. Mary has always been seen by the Fathers of the Church as the archetype of the Christian prophet and it is from her that the prophetic line comes then to enter into the history of the Church. The sisters of the great saints also all belong to this line. Saint Ambrose owes much to his holy sister for the spiritual pathway he embarked upon. The same holds for Basil and Gregory of Nyssa and for Saint Benedict. Further on, in the late Middle Ages, we meet some great female figures and of them we must mention Francesca Romana. In the 16th century, Teresa of Ávila was very determinant for John of the Cross and, more generally, for the entire development of faith and devotion. The prophetic female line was of great importance in the history of the Church: Catherine of Siena and Brigid of Sweden could be an illustration. Both addressed a Church which had an apostolic college and where sacraments were administered. So the essential things were still there, however threatened with decadence because of internal conflicts. They re-awakened the Church and in it they restored value to evangelical unity, humility and courage and to evangelization.[80]

80. Ratzinger, "Das Problem der christlichen Prophetie: Niels Christian Hvidt im Gespräch mit Joseph Kardinal Ratzinger," *Communio: Internationale Katholische Zeitschrift* 28, no. 2 (1999): 177–188, at 182.

The important role of prophecy in the Church is manifested in a special way in the unity of two people, Hans Urs von Balthasar and Adrienne von Speyr, and their two missions. Before becoming Pope, Cardinal Joseph Ratzinger had this to say about Christian prophecy:

> Hans Urs von Balthasar is unthinkable without Adrienne von Speyr. I believe that it can be proven that for all the great theologians any new theological elaboration is only possible if the prophetic element has first paved the way. While one proceeds with the mind only, nothing new will ever happen. Increasingly more definite systems may well be construed, increasingly subtle questions raised but the true and proper way from which great theology may again flow is not generated by the rational side of theological work but by a charismatic and prophetic thrust. And it is in this sense, I believe, that prophecy and theology go hand in glove. Theology, as theological science in the strict sense, is not prophetic but may only truly become living theology under the thrust and illumination of a prophetic impulse.[81]

81. Ratzinger, "Das Problem der christlichen Prophetie," 183.

6

A Continuing Legacy: Adrienne von Speyr

In 1997, when devotees of Adrienne of Adrienne von Speyr gathered in Mariastein near Basel to celebrate the 30th anniversary of her death, they recalled the special mission of this doctor and mystic. Pope John Paul II, during the Roman Symposium (September 27–29, 1985), said of her, "Let this spirituality, which Adrienne von Speyr lived with such an extraordinary dedication to God and neighbor, help us to reflect better the evangelical and Church's life in the present-day world."[1]

In a 1985 book written about the Roman symposium concerning the work of Adrienne von Speyr, there is this excerpt:

> Marie-Antoniette de Geuser (1889–1918), known as the Consummata, once said: "I would like to leave a long, igneous carpet on the earth." Adrienne's response to this was: "No, no! Not like that. I would not want to leave anything of myself. I would like to completely disappear, no longer be any more than just in Mary's 'Let it happen,' and that completely nameless. I would like one thing only: that people through me could see a bit more the traces of God." This declaration of holiness must be put back into the whole of Adrienne's work. The issue is how she perceived the meaning of her life: how to let the traces of God become more distinct in her life. She did not want to leave any traces of herself behind her.[2]

1. John Paul II, "The Address of the Holy Father John Paul II to the Participants of the Symposium in Rome," in *Adrienne von Speyr und ihre kirchliche Sendung: Akten des ŕomischen Symposiums 27–29 September 1985*, ed. Hans Urs von Balthasar, Georges Chantraine, and Angelo Scola (Einsiedeln: Johannes Verlag, 1986), 182.

2. Patrick Carty, "Spuren Gottes," in *Adrienne von Speyr und ihre kirchliche Sendung*, 19.

Adrienne von Speyr's Special Charism

What follows are some of Hans Urs von Balthasar's reflections on the Roman symposium concerning the work of Adrienne von Speyr. He was closely associated with her, cofounder with her of St. John's community, and her confessor for many years. In a lecture that emphasized the cohesiveness of Speyr's life and work, Balthasar wrote: "We have to look at Adrienne's charism in a certain whole. Its various aspects are like the bright lights on all sides, all of which emanate from a single center, and so they always testify to it."[3]

The depth and extent of Adrienne von Speyr's insights are so multifaceted and rich in content that it is difficult to provide a worthy synthesis. Balthasar developed several basic phrases which attempt to explain Adrienne's insights: the first involves *indifference*, which in Ignatian terminology means taking a stance in which a person is willing to accept anything God wants of him. Then there is an emphasis on *readiness*, adapting Mary's role of complete openness and availability to God which is basic to genuine Christian spirituality. Next, there is a need to take a *confessing attitud*e which for Adrienne von Speyr meant having an unveiled, totally open mind and heart before God and the Church. Hans Urs von Balthasar considered this confessional attitude of Speyr to be a favorite term in her spiritual vocabulary. A "confessional attitude," says Balthasar, however, carries the fourth theme, the simple name of *obedience*, which in turn is the most radical form of evangelical poverty. Balthasar also referred to Speyr's commitment to *virginity* which she considered the essence of Christ's love and relationship with his Church.

This co-work and co-vision of Balthasar and Speyr caused a new theological perspective to open up for the world, based on Scripture and the Incarnation of Christ. Balthasar summed up these insights in these words:

3. Hans Urs von Balthasar, "Adriennes Charisma," in *Adrienne von Speyr und ihre kirchliche Sendung*, 174.

> How else could we conclude these kinds of variations of the same topic—indifference, availability, confessional stance, obedience, poverty, virginity—as with the reality that is in the center of all these glows: with love? Love has mastered the whole of Adrienne's stay all the way from her youth, through the hard experience of her life to her dreadful death. It was a love that was prepared for any sacrifice that did not scare away from any request and was endowed with the ultimate courage; love resonating with everything that is in on the way, even if hidden, being in service for redemption of the world. We have deliberately put this most important word towards the end, as did Ignatius in his Spiritual Exercises. Love had to be propagated through all the variations shown, in order to fully observe Christianity, even though it was, hidden and insignificant, at the beginning of the initiative for all these variations. Here again, the motto of the family von Speyr appears: "faire sans dire," which Adrienne has very consciously repossessed. With all that she said, we find that there was a much larger, tacit activity here.[4]

Adrienne von Speyr's Death

In the previous quote, Balthasar writes about Speyr's "dreadful death." It is significant to note that Adrienne herself, as reported by Balthasar, "requested to die a most dreadful death, and such a request was heard. After several months of dying, she bid farewell on September 17, 1967."[5] Adrienne wanted to return all to God without having anything left. She offered her suffering and difficult death as a ransom for sinners.

These words were written about Adrienne's suffering:

> From the mid-fifties on, her weakness was so great that it was always necessary to consider the possibility of death;

4. "Adriennes Charisma," 177.

5. Balthasar, "Einleitung" [Introduction], in *Adrienne von Speyr und ihre kirchliche Sendung*, 14.

> no physician could understand how she could still be alive at all. From one year to the next, the conviction grew—the absolute rock-bottom of human endurance had been achieved. But always this point was lowered once again to new depth.[6]

Hans Urs von Balthasar, Adrienne's confessor, reported that her slow dying process was the slowest of all slow motion; it was an inconceivable diminuendo.[7] These are his words:

> The last months in bed were a continuous, merciless torture, which she bore with the great equanimity, always concerned about others. . . . One of the last things she said was "*Que c'est beau de mourir!*"—"How beautiful it is to die!" Three days prior to her death, before losing consciousness, she once more gave thanks for everything, promised she would help from heaven, and gave directions and assurances about our work on earth. She died on September 17, 1967, the feast of Saint Hildegard, whom she had always greatly revered and who, like her, had been a physician. She was buried on her sixty-fifth birthday. Albert Schilling carved, as her tombstone, a symbol of the Trinity—the innermost center of her theology.[8]

The Secular Institutes

Adrienne von Speyr had a prophetic gift that was manifest in the Community Saint John, she founded together with Hans Urs von Balthasar. She had wanted to establish something like the Saint John's Community soon after her entrance into the Church. She was convinced that, because of the creative work of the Holy Spirit, a new flourishing within the Church could

6. Balthasar, *First Glance at Adrienne von Speyr*, 2nd ed. (San Francisco: Ignatius Press, 1981), 44.

7. *First Glance*, 44.

8. *First Glance*, 45–46.

take place. She herself continued to be unconditionally open to God for whatever He wanted of her. It was this emphasis that gave rise to the whole concept of founding the secular institutes. These are some of her comments regarding the promoting of the Holy Spirit in her life:

> If someone wants to hinder the action of the Holy Spirit at some institution, then it must set rules right at the very beginning. . . . God needs people who do not get scared at a decisive moment . . . they shouldn't think of themselves while praying, but of God and his needs, to serving others and offering self for the service of substitution.[9]

Adrienne helped the first members of the new community understand that "The community must have strong walls." She also emphasized a spirit of penance for the members that is

> a firm structure rooted in prayer and a sound grounding in the spiritual life. She warned her members against show-off activism. She did not want their spirituality to be considered some kind of special form, set apart from other groups, but rather with a simple but thoroughly Catholic spirituality embracing everything the Church believes.[10]

All the novelty, and at the same time, the grounding in Catholic teaching and spirituality in the new secular institutes were the result of Speyr's charism combined with the theology of Balthasar. They provided the bridge in this new life-form for the Church. The "secular institutes are beyond doubt the unifying midpoint of the Church; they constitute the link between the lay state and the life of the vows and show not only the existential unity of the Church but also her perennial and most 'up-to-date'

9. Balthasar, "Ein Mitglied," in *Adrienne von Speyr und ihre kirchliche Sendung*, 50.

10. "Ein Mitglied," 51–52.

mission in the world," writes Hans Urs von Balthasar in his own retrospective in 1990.[11]

Adrienne von Speyr's Continuing Presence

It is said that Adrienne von Speyr did not want to leave any trace behind her. But the fact is, her work and her influence cannot be overlooked or forgotten. She also did not want to be referred to as a saint, and as she once said, "The worst thing that could happen to me would be if, after my death, I would turn into a plaster post." And as Balthasar said of her, "She wanted to be alive in the Church" and not a dead relic.[12]

Thankfully, Adrienne von Speyr is very much alive in the Church today, according to the promise *Tu vivras au ciel et sur la terre* ("You will live in heaven and on earth"). And even if much of her life remains hidden, the testimony of her friends gives witness that Adrienne's spirit and teaching is very much alive today. Adrienne von Speyr continues to have an amazing impact on many people in many places now and will for many years to come.

11. Balthasar, *My Work*, 58.
12. Balthasar, "Einleitung," 16.

7

Man and Woman under God

THE DIGNITY OF THE HUMAN BEING ACCORDING TO HANS URS VON BALTHASAR

The following words of Hans Urs von Balthasar do not merely apply to the ecclesiastical mission of Adrienne von Speyr, but also summarize his own theology:

> Charisms are not distributed by God to supply what is needful and lacking in his Church at each historical moment. If they are from God, they usually do not flow with the latest fashionable trend but much more likely contain an antidote and remedy for the perils of the time.[1]

There are certain areas regarding human life that lack clarity. One of these areas is the relationship between man and woman. As Balthasar remarks, "The world-wide offensive of 'feminism,' which is battling for the equality of women with men, takes effect within the Church as the women's claim to the ministerial priesthood. As a whole, the battlefront presents a confusing picture."[2] The core of the problem revolves around the dignity of men and women which is central to Christian anthropology. In the drama of God's self-revelation, and the focus of His attention, is the creation of man and woman. Until humans become aware of this revelation, it is not possible to discover the true relationship and proper roles men and women should have with each other in the world and in the Church.

1. Hans Urs von Balthasar, *First Glance at Adrienne von Speyr*, 2nd ed. (San Francisco: Ignatius Press, 1981), 89.

2. Balthasar, *New Elucidations* (San Francisco: Ignatius Press, 1986), 187.

"Male and Female He Created Them" (Gn 1:27)

The relationship between and man and woman, as determined by their creation, involves mystery because it flows from the mystery of God's creative purpose and power. Balthasar addressed this mystery:

> the human being is spirit and body, man and woman, individual and community. These constants are part of his nature, his essence, which does not mean that they solve his riddle; in fact, they render it more profound and more pressing. In all three dimensions, man seems to be built according to a polarity, obliged to engage in reciprocity, always seeking complementarity and peace in the other pole. And for that very reason he is pointed beyond his whole polar structure.[3]

In analyzing the sexual difference between men and women, it is evident that "a human being can only be either male or female. . . . Male and female are the elements of natural dialectics. . . . As a natural being man exists as either male or female.'"[4]

> From the peak of his spirit to his bodily basis, the human being is man and woman, and the personal equality in value of the sexes is interlocked through their oppositeness to produce the spiritual-bodily fruitfulness of love. The Song of Songs is indispensably part of the Old Testament, both as a song of praise of the love of the two sexes before God and as something transparent to the relationship between God and his people, which has an oppositeness that clothes itself in the concepts and images of sexual love. This is pos-

3. Balthasar, *Theo-Drama: Theological Dramatic Theory*, vol. II, *Dramatis personae: Man in God* (San Francisco: Ignatius Press, 1990), 355.

4. Balthasar, *Das Ganze im Fragment* (Einsiedeln: Johannes Verlag, 1963), 327–28. Balthasar, *A Theological Anthropology* (New York: Sheed & Ward, 1968); Balthasar, *Man in God*, 365–82.

> sible because, despite all the personal equality in value, the man has a primacy and is the image of God as the one who begets, shapes and leads, while the woman, as the one who receives and gives birth, is essentially an answer to the man, a 'helper', but also 'fullness' and 'glory' and therein the image of the creaturely world. The teaching in the Old and New Testaments about the difference between the sexes is not conditioned by its time and cannot be superseded (e.g., 1 Cor 11:7–12) but is rather the presupposition for the full unfolding of God's making himself known in his Incarnation. Reductions of the difference between the sexes to a lower level abandon the radicality of the interlocking both in the human sphere and in the sphere of revelation and lead to an ever more indifferent juxtaposition.[5]

The sexual difference between men and women is not only external, but it involves the basic dignity regarding what it means to be a male and female. These are Balthasar's words: "The male body is male throughout, right down to each cell of which it consists, and the female body is utterly female; and this is also true of their whole empirical experiences and ego-consciousness."[6]

However, human sexuality does not solely reside within the physical sphere of man. Indeed, sexual distinction also permeates the most profound depths and highest peaks of the human spirit, so much so that physical differences appear as mere partial aspects when compared to the difference that prevails within the totality of the human personality. Therein lies the nature of man as the image of God: As both body and soul, as males and females, human beings embody the image of God.

5. Balthasar, "Summa Summarum," in *Explorations in Theology*, vol. III, *Creator Spirit* (San Francisco: Ignatius Press, 1993), 378–79. Cf. *Das Ganze im Fragment*, 327–35; *Elucidations*, 101–13; Balthasar, *The Glory of the Lord: A Theological Aesthetics*, vol. VII, *Theology: The New Covenant* (San Francisco: Ignatius Press, 1989), 470–84.

6. *Man in God*, 365.

Man and Woman as Images of God

The fundamental polarity between men and women cannot be resolved and then celebrated until it is viewed in light of Christ and his teaching. As Balthasar puts it, "The Word of God appears in the world as a man, as the 'Last Adam.' This cannot be a matter of indifference."[7]

Balthasar portrays the male as the "word" (*Wort*) and the female as the "response to the word" (*Ant-wort*), or the "counter-image" (*Ant-litz*). Therein lies the mystery of man as the "image of God."

> The first Adam calls nature's animals by name, and as he names them, so they are called. But no adequate response comes to him from them. Only when God forms woman from his side does nature reply ("at last!") with an appropriate word. "This at last is the bone of my bones and the flesh of my flesh; she shall be called Woman, because she was taken out of Man" (Gen 2:23). Thus, woman is essentially an answer (*Ant-Wort*), in the most fundamental sense of "*ant*," which is common to all Indo-European languages. . . . If man is the word that calls out, woman is the answer that comes to him at last (in the end). The two are related and ordered to each other. Furthermore, the second account of creation shows that the word that calls out only attains fulfillment when it is understood, accepted, and given back as a word. This clearly shows us the way in which man can be primary and woman secondary, where the primary remains unfulfilled without the secondary. The primary needs a partner of equal rank and dignity for its own fulfillment. Moreover, the man is incapable of providing this answering dimension; it is latent within him—for there can be no word without an answering word—but it has to be given to him as grace. It can

7. Balthasar, *Theo-Drama: Theological Dramatic Theory*, vol. III, *Dramatis personae: Persons in Christ* (San Francisco: Ignatius Press, 1992), 283.

> only come about in freedom, and only God, fundamentally, can give such freedom.[8]
>
> What *Antwort* (answer) denotes in the realm of speech, *Antlitz* (face) signifies in the visual realm. . . . Thus the "face" is what "faces" us, "looks toward" us. Man and woman are face to face. Here their equal rank is given even more emphasis: man looks around him and meets with an answering gaze that turns the one-who-sees into the one-who-is-seen.[9]

Eve is potentially in Adam, but he cannot produce her from within himself. "It is not good for man to be alone" (Gn 2: 18). This state of affairs cannot be remedied by man on his own; the action of Adam's Creator is required if man is to be complete: "Male and female he created them" (Gn 1:27).

> Thus, the woman, who is both "answer" and "face," is not only man's delight: she is the help, the security, the home man needs; she is the vessel of fulfillment specially designed for him. Nor is she simply the vessel of *his* fruitfulness: she is equipped with her own explicit fruitfulness. Yet her fruitfulness is not a primary fruitfulness: it is an answering fruitfulness, designed to receive man's fruitfulness (which, in itself, is helpless) and bring it to its "fullness." In this way she is the "glory" of the man (1 Cor 1,1:7). So, we can speak of a kind of natural *vocation* on woman's part much more explicitly than in man's case; for the call to "be fruitful" and "subdue the earth" is addressed to both of them (Gen 1:28). To that extent, the woman's *missio* vis-a-vis Adam can be described as the extrapolation and continuation of her *processio* from Adam. Of course, this aspect must not obscure the other truth, namely, that both man and woman *individually* (and not only *together*) constitute an "image of God"; thus each has a guaranteed direct access to God.[10]

8. *Persons in Christ*, 284–85.
9. *Persons in Christ*, 285.
10. *Persons in Christ*, 285–86.

The woman's response is enthusiastic: she not only returns to the man what she has received from him, but also presents him with the common fruit of their encounter.

> Since it is woman's essential vocation to receive man's fruitfulness into her own fruitfulness, thus uniting in herself the fruitfulness of both, it follows that she is actually the fruit-bearing principle in the creaturely realm. (But as we have said elsewhere, we must not be misled into equating man with the principle of 'spirit' or 'heaven' and woman with the principle of 'nature' or 'earth.') In the most general terms, this means that the woman does not merely give back to man what she has received from him: she gives him something new, something that integrates the gift he gave her but that 'faces' him in a totally new and unexpected form. In this way the woman gives him a twofold answer: a 'personal' answer and one that goes beyond the I—thou relationship (and which, in the absence of a more precise word, one may call 'generic' or 'of the species'). She responds through reproduction.[11]

In his book, *The Christian State of Life*, Hans Urs von Balthasar writes:

> The physical union of man and woman is not something accidental to man: It is so essential and central to his nature that almost the whole account of the ideal man as God created him in paradise is concerned with the distinction between male and female. And although man shares this difference of sex with the animals, there is no reason to doubt that the first division between man and woman—based as it was on the spirituality by which man had dominion over all creation—belonged, no less than his dominion over all creation, to the "likeness to God" that was bestowed on him

11. *Persons in Christ*, 286.

alone of all creatures: "'Let us make mankind in our image and likeness; and let him have dominion over the fish of the sea, and the birds of the air, the cattle, over all the wild animals and every creature that crawls on the earth.' God created man in his image. In the image of God he created him. Male and female he created them. Then God blessed them and said to them, 'Be fruitful and multiply; fill the earth and subdue it. Have dominion over the fish of the sea, the birds of the air, the cattle and all the animals that crawl on the earth'" (Gen 1:26–28). Indeed, the fruitfulness of this multiplying that has its source in the union of male and female is the image of that mysterious nature of God that speaks here in an unfathomable plural: "Let us"! God's being in the Trinity is an infinite fecundity that reveals itself externally in creation; whatever is made in his image must, of its very nature, have a share in this fecundity. Since mankind was made male and female and since the first word God spoke to them was 'Be fruitful and multiply,' it cannot be doubted that human beings were created for fecundity. This likeness to God is a likeness of both nature and grace, just as creatureliness and engracement were inseparable in man's original state. Man's natural sexuality is bestowed on him in view of the union of natural and supernatural fecundity in him. In no way does the sexual dominate only the physical sphere while the spiritual sphere, which is deemed to be the true seat of his "likeness to God," remains untouched by it. For the division of the sexes touches man's spirit so totally, from its deepest roots to its highest pinnacle, that the physical difference appears insignificant in comparison with this distinction that affects the whole person.

The mystery of the fecundity for which God created man and by which man becomes an image of the eternally fruitful Trinity is even more closely linked to the divine nature than a reading of the first account of creation might lead us to suspect. God did not simply create mankind male and female as he had created the animals male and female. He not only created them to be one in the duality of sex; he also created their duality out of their own oneness. He created Eve out of the side of Adam, not by a process of natural generation, but in a preternatural manner through the instrumentality of the sleeping Adam, although he accomplished the rest of the work without him and placed the completed result before him: "And the rib which the Lord God took from man, he made into a woman, and brought her to him" (Gen 2:22). The communal oneness of Adam and Eve was thus the oneness of Adam's flesh, which became by grace the source of the duality of male and female. Adam recognized the gift presented him by God as being, at the same time, himself, his own flesh: "Then the man said, 'She now is bone of my bone, and flesh of my flesh; she shall be called Woman, for from man she has been taken'" (Gen 2:23). Hence God's command to Adam and Eve to be fruitful and multiply was not just a moral command subject to their freedom and through the fulfillment of which they were to reflect something of the archetype according to which they had been created, something of the fruitfulness of the Trinity; it was, at the same time, the result of the physical fecundity that God effected in Adam while he slept and that became, by the formation of Eve from the one living body of Adam, a direct physical image of the origin from the Father's substance of the eternal Son who shares his nature. It would be false to say that Adam and Eve were one only in some abstract "human nature" and achieved concrete state of the counsels, even of contemplatives and anchorites. But only God knows what graces he bestows on the souls consecrated to him. For there exists an inner kingdom that eye has not seen, that ear has not heard, and that yet belongs so wholly to the Church that without it the Church would be robbed of its most precious life, of its most vital strength. This kingdom "remains" and must remain until the Lord comes again; but only the Lord has dominion over it.[12]

12. Balthasar, *The Christian State of Life* (San Francisco: Ignatius Press, 1983), 285–86.

The minor and restricted physical fertility of human beings is augmented by the greater catholic and eucharistic fruitfulness of the redeeming love of Christ and the redeemed love of his bride, the Church, which simultaneously incorporates his body. The original unity centers on the Church's birth in Christ the way Eve was taken from the side of Adam. However, the new fruitfulness is completely virginal because it originates from the Cross.

The Primacy of the Feminine

In order to understand Balthasar's teaching regarding feminine and masculine characteristics and their importance in his theology, he emphasized the idea that all creatures are "feminine" in the sight of their Creator. This perspective means that the entire Church is fundamentally bridal, both a wife and bride that lovingly obeys the husband and bridegroom who is Christ. The Church personifies both the bride of Christ and his "assistant." In Balthasar's view, the Church is the second Eve who was created from the pierced side of Christ, the second Adam (*Ecclesia ex latere Christi*).[13]

The creature's relationship with God is secondarily responsive; it is fundamentally receptive and thus feminine. Together, men and women are images of Christ and his bride the Church. As human beings made in God's image, they are necessarily connected with Him. And since everything is created in and through Christ, this means that both men and women are created by him and in his image, especially when they have an open and receiving (feminine) attitude.

As the Creator, God carries within him the primordial image of man and woman. As the one who has been begotten, the Son represents the primordial image of both sexes—the receiving and

13. Balthasar, *Mysterium paschale: The Mystery of Easter* (San Francisco: Ignatius Press, 1995), 129–40; Balthasar, *The Christian State of Life*, 224–49; Balthasar, "Who Is the Church?" in *Explorations in Theology*, vol. II, *Spouse of the Word*, 143–91, esp. 146–47; *Persons in Christ*, 383–92.

responding feminine side and the actively giving masculine. "The One who comes forth from the Father is designated, as a human being he must be a man if his mission is to represent the Origin, the Father, in the world."[14] However, in a certain way, as "wisdom," the attitude of the eternal Son toward the Father is "feminine." This may come as a surprise, but his complete obedience to the Father reveals these characteristics. The eternal Word owes his existence to his paternal origin. Moreover, the Son is and also remains the Child that proceeds every time and again from the womb of the Father.[15] Nevertheless, as "Logos," the Child has to represent the Father in the world by becoming incarnate, a deed that is possible only if he is a man. Christ must be a man to be able to represent the Father in the world.

The primordial image of the Church is that of a woman—Mary. Within the context of this all-encompassing femininity, or motherliness of the Church, all are united: both men and women. "Even the men, even the priest, is in this respect feminine, Marian."[16] Regular, faithful contemplation should result in one's readiness to accept the love of God. This constitutes a typically "feminine" attitude in contradistinction to the "masculine" attitude of the actively mediating human being. The natural difference between the sexes, whose personal dignity must never be taken for granted, becomes a metaphor for man's relationship to God in the course of revelation and throughout the history of salvation. As human beings, we ought to understand our existence as a bridal state. In Balthasar's words,

> The Church and the soul, as they receive the seed of the Word and its meaning, can do nothing but await it in feminine openness and readiness, not struggling or stiffening

14. *Persons in Christ*, 284.

15. Balthasar, *Unless You Become Like This Child* (San Francisco: Ignatius Press, 1991); Cf. Balthasar, *Das Ganze im Fragment*, 274–83.

16. Balthasar, *A Short Primer for Unsettled Laymen* (San Francisco: Ignatius Press, 1987), 94.

> or hardening, not trying to make any answering masculine contribution, but simply surrendering in the dark, conceiving and bearing in the dark, not knowing what, or how much, has been conceived and brought to birth.[17]
>
> Woman is formed out of man, and in the last analysis the wife is, in marriage, formed and molded by the husband. Through what he gives her she becomes mother: her body and spirit ripen from within to which they are meant to be. She is the protecting body and womb to man physically, but he is the womb that contains her spiritually, where dwells and grows the image of her true essence. The Christian and the Church attain to their true essence, their *eidos*, which exists already in Christ the Bridegroom, insofar as they receive and keep within themselves the will of the Father, and the seed of his Incarnate Word.[18]

Elsewhere Balthasar explains that:

> The bride is essentially woman, that is, receptive: one who, through acceptance of the seed but also through all her own female organs and powers is made competent to bring forth and bear fruit. In bringing forth at birth (which, in a broad sense, includes her care of the child and his feeding and upbringing to full independence), woman gives to man the complete, superabundant response. It is to such a Christian womanly role that the creature is educated by the structural, sacramental Church: the office and the Sacrament are forms of communicating the seed; they belong to the male aspect, but their end is to lead the bride to her womanly function and fortify her in it.[19]

A human person (both male and female) cannot conduct oneself in a purely masculine way. Both St. Paul and St. Augus-

17. Balthasar, *A Theology of History* (San Francisco: Ignatius Press, 1994), 122.

18. *A Theology of History*, 122–23.

19. Balthasar, "Who is the Church?" 158.

tine stressed the feminine attachment to God. This led Balthasar to write:

> With God there can be no union of the same sex but only a feminine dependence on God, as taught by Paul and Augustine: no taking but only a being taken. As the individual believer lets himself be taken by God, becoming a handmaid of the Lord, so the Church awakens in him and, in feminine fashion, reflects the Spirit of the Lord. It is both the lowliness and glory of woman to be obliged and to be able to receive in this way. But since we are sinners, this humility must be instilled into us by humiliation: "But we have this treasure in earthen vessels, to show that the transcendent power belongs to God and not to us" (2 Cor 4:7).[20]

In this sense the woman takes precedence. She rear seats that which is personal; he, that which is functional.

Mary as Exemplar of Man and Woman

The feminine nature of the Church takes specific precedence over its masculine counterpart. As (*ecclesia*) *immaculata*, Mary existed prior to the appointment of the Apostles. Mary is privileged by the complete union of the Petrine and the Marian dimensions. That is why: "The Church's Marian dimension embraces the Petrine dimension, without claiming it as its own. Mary is the 'Queen of the Apostles' without claiming apostolic powers for herself. She possesses something else and something more."[21]

What constitutes this "greater" power of Mary?

> By experiencing and accomplishing a living and personal liturgy with the faithful women at the foot of the Cross, Mary earned for herself and for all women a place at the heart of the Church's life. If women are excluded from the functional

20. "Who is the Church?" 188.
21. Balthasar, *New Elucidations*, 196.

> priesthood and thereby reflect in the Church something of the natural order of creation according to which "man . . . is the image and glory of God, but woman is the glory of man . . . [and] man was not created for woman, but woman for man" (1 Cor 11:7, 9); according to which, as a general rule, what is functional is the prerogative of man, but it is unbecoming for a woman to leave "uncovered" what "is a glory to her" (1 Cor 11: 13–15), this exclusion in no way indicates that woman is inferior to man or that any "degree of perfection" is thereby closed to her. Any theory that attempts to evaluate the states of election in terms of their respective "perfection" is an insult to women in general and to the Lord's mother in particular. The super- and subordination of the sexes that has its roots in creation serves rather for paratactic alignment: "Yet neither is man independent of woman, nor woman independent of man in the Lord. For as the woman is from the man, so also is the man through the woman, but all things are from God" (1 Cor 11:11–12).[22]

Mary, the mother of the Lord, the paragon of creation, represents the ultimate measure of the unmistakably feminine. The difference between man and woman is not primarily determined by competition or equal treatment.

God "needs" women to achieve salvation, women who—realistically (as Zion-Mary-Church), and symbolically as man's desired response to God's love—present and surrender themselves. He who follows this precept can truly be called a mature Christian: "Someone who has become entirely 'material' for shaping in the form of Christ—*materia* that is raised from such seeming 'passivity' to the highest degree of activity of the 'Matrix' and 'Mater' of Jesus. For he 'is my brother and sister and *mother*' (Mt 12:50)."[23]

22. Balthasar, *Christian States of Life*, 288–89.

23. Balthasar, *Who Is a Christian?* (San Francisco: Ignatius Press, 2014), 91–92; cf. Balthasar, *Engagement with God* (San Francisco: Ignatius Press, 2008), 39;

> Mary's surrender, indicated here simply as being the supreme instance of the true Christian and human attitude before God, is without a trace of passivity or resignation. On the contrary, it calls for the active participation of man's united powers, a wholehearted effort to banish anything that could spoil the purity of first receiving the divine message and substance, and then living it. The real victors are those who persevere in this to the end.[24]

Mary's is the most perfect example of a Christian life. Anyone who was to follow her example would become a true witness and would embody the essence of being Christian. Balthasar insists that "Mary's life must be regarded as the prototype of what the *ars Dei* can fashion from a human material which puts up no resistance to him. It is a feminine life which, in any case more than masculine, awaits being shaped by the man, the bridegroom, Christ, and God."[25] At the same time, such a life is totally virginal, maternal, and bride-like. It is the kind of life that simply surrenders. Mary's entire life is one of unlimited readiness to do the will of God: "I am the handmaid of the Lord, let what you have said be done to me" (Lk 1:38). This is why Balthasar speaks about the "Marian mold of the Church."[26]

Balthasar, *Der antirömische Affekt*, 2nd ed. (Einsiedeln: Johannes Verlag, 1989), 172; Balthasar, "Die marianische Prägung der Kirche," in *Maria heute ehren*, ed. Wolfgang Beinert (Freiburg: Herder, 1977), 263–79, esp. 276.

24. Balthasar, *A Theology of History*, 123–24.

25. Balthasar, *The Glory of the Lord: A Theological Aesthetics*, vol. I, *Seeing the Form*, 2nd ed. (San Francisco: Ignatius Press, 2009), 548.

26. Balthasar, "Marian Mold of the Church," in *Mary: The Church at the Source*, ed. Joseph Ratzinger and Balthasar (San Francisco: Ignatius Press, 2005), 125–44. Greiner on "Die Würde der Frau. Ihre Bedeutung in der Theo-Logic Hans Urs von Balthasar," in *Hans Urs von Balthasar: Gestalt und Werk*, ed. K. Lehman and W. Kasper (Cologne: Communio, 1989), 283–97. Also Balthasar, *The Threefold Garland: The World's Salvation in Mary's Prayer* (San Francisco: Ignatius Press, 1982).

Equal Dignity of Man and Woman

For Balthasar, this reciprocal relationship between male and female, which eliminates any hint of inferiority of woman toward man, is achieved through the voluntary surrender of Christ.[27] When St. Paul interpreted and systematized the relationship between man and woman, he had the relationship between Christ and the Church in mind (Eph 5). The Church will always retain her clearly feminine character. She is the virgin, the bride, and finally in the Apocalypse, the wife. Any obscurity or, what would be worse, any collapse of the distinction between the sexes into the modern kind of unisexuality would make the understanding of the relationship between Christ and his Church impossible.

> Positively speaking, the special nature of man is one of a donor—sexually speaking—thus remotely reminding us of a reproduction of the divine and eternally uninterrupted fatherhood of God. While negatively speaking, man passes on in almost ludicrously ephemeral fashion the creative forces (by giving life to another immortal human being!) that only God possesses. The special nature of a woman is borne out by the fact that she is truly the one who receives, thus reminding us symbolically—and not only remotely, but very realistically—of created nature with its immense creative potential. Therein lies a woman's special superiority that remains unattainable for a man: Compared to the father in his relationship with the child, she can actively receive, bear, and raise a child in ways that make the child distinctly actively from her flesh. Conversely, a priest is a "servant of Christ," one who transmits something more sublime than that which he possesses, while the receiving community of the Church amounts to more:

27. Balthasar, "The Dignity of Women," in *Explorations in Theology*, vol. V, *Man Is Created* (San Francisco: Ignatius Press, 2014), 166–83, esp. 168–69.

> She represents the genuine recipient and *curatrix* [female guardian] of this sublimity.[28]

Balthasar insists that woman, "as the active power of receiving all that heaven gives, she is the *epitome of creaturely power and dignity;* she is what God presupposes as Creator in order to give the seed of his Word to the world."[29]

This led Balthasar to declare that "the greater the difference between man and woman, the greater also are the possibilities for love and fecundity."[30]

The greater the difference between man and woman who are characterized by the same human nature, the more perfect and fruitful will be their union in love. The actual recipient of this revelation is the Church, the immaculate bride of Christ.[31]

On Being Nuptial

The scope of Balthasar's theology regarding human sexuality is broad because it originates from the triune God and returns and is completed in this same source. In connection with Ephesians 5:21, Balthasar postulates the dialectical oneness of man and woman in the mystery of marriage as the sacrament of the spiritual oneness between Christ and the Church. That is why marriage lies at the center of Balthasar's ecclesiology. The Cross rep-

28. Balthasar, "Kurze Erwägungen zum Frauenpriestertum," *Vaterland* (Luzern) 48 (February 1977), Supplement to *Christ und Kultur* 26; cf. also epilogue of the translator, in Louis Bouyer, *Frau und Kirche* (Einsiedeln: Johannes Verlag, 1977), 87–95.

29. Balthasar, *A Short Primer for Unsettled Laymen*, 90.

30. Balthasar, "Gedanken zum Frauenpriestertum" (manuscript), quoted by Johann G. Roten, "The Two Halves of the Moon: Marian Anthropological Dimension in the Common Mission of Adrienne von Speyr and Hans Urs von Balthasar," in *Hans Urs von Balthasar: His Life and Work*, ed. David L. Schindler (San Francisco: Ignatius Press, 1991), 65–86, at 86.

31. See Balthasar, *The Glory of the Lord: A Theological Aesthetics*, vol. VII, *Theology: The New Covenant* (San Francisco: Ignatius Press, 1989), 89–103.

resents the culmination of Christ's love for the Church, and the love of a husband and wife. "This *nuptial spirit* remains the innermost mystery of the Church, a blissful and at the same time a painful mystery since it originates perpetually in the actuality of the Cross."[32] Balthasar adds: "Nothing could be more contemporary than the deepening of this mystery of marriage between Christ and the Church; an effective reform of the Church can arise solely from this mystery, and not from any changes in traditional structures."[33]

Women Priests?

The issues surrounding ordained priesthood for women, mentioned in the beginning of this book, are now able to be answered. The essentially feminine nature of creation, of revelation, and of the Church as bride already suggest an answer:

> A woman who would strive for the male role in the Church thus strives for something "less" and denies the "more" which she is. This can be overlooked by a feminism that has lost sense for the mystery of sexual difference, which has functionalized sexuality and attempts to increase the dignity of women by bringing about her identification with men.[34]
>
> The priesthood of women would amount to an "exchange of a more for a less."[35]

Balthasar sees clearly that:

32. Balthasar, *A Short Primer for Unsettled Laymen*, 92.

33. Balthasar, Preface to Adrienne von Speyr, *Das Hohelied* (Einsiedeln: Johannes Verlag, 1972), 5–6. Concerning the theme of "nuptiality" see Balthasar, *Theology: The New Covenant* (San Francisco: Ignatius Press, 1989), 470–84.

34. Balthasar, *A Short Primer for Unsettled Laymen*, 94.

35. Balthasar, "Mary in the Church's Doctrine and Devotion," in Ratzinger and Balthasar, *Mary: The Church at the Source*, 99–124.

> women's struggle today for "equality" amounts tragically and largely to a battle for their masculinization in a technological and mechanical pseudo-culture invented and directed by men, a culture where human beings are reduced to sexless ants.[36]

Thus, the Church has become the bearer of the truth that guarantees equal dignity to men and women. Pope John Paul II, who frequently speaks of the "nuptial meaning of the human body," published an apostolic letter on the subject: "*Mulieris Dignitatem*" (1988). So it was that Balthasar began his essay on "*The Dignity of Women*" with this statement: "The promotion of women is intimately connected with the maleness of Jesus Christ."[37] This same understanding led St. Paul to declare that "woman is the reflection of man's glory" (1 Cor 11:7).

36. Balthasar, *Kurze Erwägungen*, 26.

37. Balthasar, "The Dignity of Women," 166. See also Marc Ouellet, "L'existence comme mission: L'anthropologie théologique de Hans Urs von Balthasar," STD diss. (Rome: Pontificia Universitas Gregoriana, 1983).

8

The Theo-Logic *of Hans Urs von Balthasar*

The published works of the Swiss Theologian Hans Urs von Balthasar have no equal in 20th century theology. Indeed, when Pope John Paul II bestowed the International Paul VI Prize on him on June 23, 1984, the accompanying laudation enumerated the reasons for awarding the Prize:

> The vastness and depth of his culture, the multi-lateral nature and breadth of his work, the originality and daring of his concepts have objectively earned the Swiss theologian Hans Urs von Balthasar a role of outstanding importance in the sphere of the dominant figures in the theology in 20th century. Already unquestionably appreciated for its intrinsic value, the thought of von Balthasar is certainly destined to become a "classic" in theological tradition and in the new Catholic systematic in particular. In fact, he is the only contemporary Catholic theologian of importance who has alone dared the formidable undertaking of a theological "summa" which, for its unity of conception and grandeur of system, can be justifiably placed in the line of the great syntheses which have marked the path of Western theology. The undertaking, which opened under the original sign of the search for a theological "aesthetic," is followed with singular coherence in the line of a "theodrama" in it, precisely, the theology of revelation and theology of history explain the principles and themes of their intrinsic correlation.[1]

The following pages introduce the reader to the *Theo-Logic* of Balthasar. These are his words:

1. John Paul II, "Address for the Awarding of the International Paul VI Prize to Hans Urs von Balthasar," *L'Osservatore Romano*, English Weekly Edition, July 23, 1984, 7.

> The third part of our trilogy focuses on theological "logic." It asks, then, just one question: What role does "truth" play in the event of God's self-revelation through the Incarnation of the Logos and the outpouring of the Holy Spirit? . . . From first to last, the trilogy is keyed to the transcendental qualities of being, in particular to the analogy between their status and form in creaturely being, on the one hand, and in Divine Being, on the other. Thus, there is a correspondence between worldly "beauty" and divine "glory" in the *Aesthetics,* and between worldly, finite freedom and divine, infinite freedom in the *Drama.* By the same token, our task in the present theological *Logic* will be to reflect upon the relationship between the structure of creaturely truth and the structure of divine truth.[2]

A brief survey of the three volumes of *Theo-Logic* will follow, covering only a limited number of issues.[3]

The Truth of the World

The first volume of the *Theo-Logic*, entitled *Wahrheit der Welt* [Truth of the world], was first published in 1947, along with an introduction to the three volumes. This first edition of the trilogy resulted in a positive response by scholars:

> A mature book by a master of thought and words which holds the reader's attention with increasing suspense and which delights him with the genuine pleasure of clear and deep insights. Balthasar draws from a rich tradition, yet his work is devoid of rigidity, encrustation, or expiration, rather

2. Hans Urs von Balthasar, *Theo-Logic*, vol. I, *The Truth of the World* (San Francisco: Ignatius Press, 2000), 7.

3. In his "first biography of the theologian of the beautiful," Elio Guerriero treated a lot of factual information regarding the *Theo-Logic*. My modest attempt at Balthasar is also greatly indebted to him. See Elio Guerriero, *Hans Urs von Balthasar: Eine Monographie* (Milan: Edizioni Paoline, 1991); published in German (Freiburg: Johannes Verlag Einsiedeln, 1993).

> it contains surprising vivacity and fertility. . . . There is no question that the book exceeds by far the average in its desire to appeal and to be fruitful.[4]

Balthasar published a second (unchanged) edition in 1985, along with an introduction to the three works. In contrast to the two subsequent volumes of *Theo-Logic* he would publish, the *Truth of the World* presents a clear philosophical investigation which subtly embraces the theme of truth without referring directly to the source of all truth. Balthasar emphasizes the need to absent oneself from a purely inner-worldly truth because "the world as it concretely exists is one that is always already related either positively or negatively to the God of grace and supernatural revelation."[5]

Truth, then, can be defined as the revelation, open, with full disclosure, and the non-concealment (*a-letheia*) of being.[6] As non-concealment, *aletheia* also corresponds to the Hebrew *emeth*, i.e., trustworthiness, constancy, reliability. Non-concealment relates to trustworthiness, constancy, consistency, reliability. These characteristics have in common an openness which extends beyond themselves. Revelation of truth makes possible reliable knowledge and understanding, which includes the mysterious nature of being. Only that which is characterized by mystery is worth loving forever. Something which lacks mystery cannot really be loved. Love possesses infinite depth, without any darkness in that depth.

The ultimate reason for truth is God himself: "All things, therefore, stand completely unveiled before the divine knowledge, and by that same knowledge they are measured. Their truth lies with God, and whoever wants to know them must know them

4. Review in: *Philosophisches Jahrbuch der Görres-Gesellschaft* 58, no. 1 (1948): 74–75.

5. Balthasar, *Truth of the World*, 11.

6. *Truth of the World*, 206–7.

in their adequation to the mind of God."[7] Things are both revealed and concealed. Love itself demands unveiling and concealment and reserve in order to be able to reach the depth and intimacy of the beloved being: "For depths and the means and motive for reverence come only with mystery."[8] Genuine love exists, filled with the constant readiness to disclose itself, to confess. The mystery of being is ultimately revealed with a view to the mystery of God. Through his creation and revelation, he bestows his own truth on the world so that it can be proclaimed.

The absolutely ultimate reason for all things is love. Balthasar writes in the conclusion of this volume:

> God is love. . . . But the very existence of truth, of eternal truth, is grounded in love. If the truth were ultimate in God, we could look into its abysses with open eyes. Our eyes might be blinded by so much light, but our yearning for the truth would have free rein. But because love is ultimate, the seraphim cover their faces with their wings, for the mystery of eternal love is one whose superluminous night may be glorified only through adoration.[9]

This means that we are able to move from the truth about the world to the truth about God. Balthasar, in the next two volumes about truth, emphasizes that the two divisions are in reality superficial because both parts need to be viewed as a whole. Therefore, the line that separates the work of the *Logos* (Word) and the work of the *Pneuma* (Spirit) is also artificial.

The Truth of God

The decisive element in the knowledge and understanding of the truth of God is the self-revelation of the triune God through the

7. *Truth of the World*, 56.
8. *Truth of the World*, 209.
9. *Truth of the World*, 272.

Incarnation of the divine Logos. Jesus clearly says of himself: "I am the truth" (Jn 14:6). He represents and bears witness to truth: "I came into the world for this: to bear witness to the truth" (Jn 18:37). The Johannine witness of God's entry into human history is central to his Gospel. To Balthasar, the truth of God constitutes the self-revelation of God through the Incarnation of the Son, which was ultimately made possible, explained, interpreted, and extended by the Holy Spirit. The works of the Son and of the Holy Spirit cannot be separated from one another. The indivisibly triune God performs all salvific deeds in unison.

"Thus, the one truth—the expression of the Father by the Son (which in turn is expository by the Spirit)—is ultimately a trinitarian truth. But *a-letheia* (unveiling)—this truth is one that is unveiled in and for the world."[10] Truth in a Christological and trinitarian sense states the intrinsic, indissoluble bond between the Father and the Son and the Holy Spirit. The Christological and trinitarian truth is incomparably superior to anything that can be termed true in a human or worldly sense.

What, then, is the relationship between human logic and divine logic? The final word between God and man constitutes simultaneously the most decisive word in the relationship between human beings: *agapan*—to love. Only the logic of love is able to pave the way. At the same time, the principle of fruitfulness plays a decisive role. Fruitfulness denotes not only the law of organic existence, but also that of spiritual life. In the trinitarian mystery, the love relationship which existed before all love relationships constitutes the seminal ground for all trinitarian expressions. The Father surrenders eternally to his Son. The Son owes his being to the Father, and from the eternal love between the Father and the Son originates the Holy Spirit.

The logic of love is perfected in the logic of descent. The Logos descends to where no one expected him to go: human

10. Balthasar, *Theo-Logic*, vol. II, *The Truth of God* (San Francisco: Ignatius Press, 2004), 16.

flesh. The flesh signifies weakness and danger. This flesh is appropriated by the Son of God in order to bear victorious witness to the powerful weakness of God. The Incarnate One also took upon himself the flesh as *caro peccati*, as both lies and negativity. By descending into hell, the Logos ultimately exposes himself to every facet of reality: he samples the diabolic side of existence and the negativity of sin to their very end. Yet, it is exactly his total isolation which permits him to found the Communion of Saints in heaven, on earth, and under the earth. It cannot come into existence until the restitution of the communion of love between the Father and the Son takes place. Both in its beginning and in its perfection, the truth of God is trinitarian.[11]

The Spirit of Truth

Pneumatological logic can constitute only a continuation of Christological logic: "All he tells you will be taken from what is mine" (Jn 16:14). The Holy Spirit is the interpreter of the Son. Christ's redemptive work is constantly accompanied and rendered possible by the Holy Spirit. The Spirit is at work in the Incarnation, during Christ's baptism, in his mission, on the Cross, and throughout his glorification. After the completion of his salvific act, the Spirit becomes fully active. Both Son and Spirit are "the two hands of the Father" (Irenaeus). Balthasar talks about a pairing in joint cooperation. For the two hands of the Father do not act independently—each one for itself, parallel with one another or in successive steps—but act in a joint and intimate effort. The accents are placed differently in the East from those in the West. According to the Greek view, their joint action is seen primarily in deification, while the Latin tradition prefers to speak of the incorporation into Christ.

This all-encompassing activity always takes place within the Church, or, more precisely, through the Church throughout the

11. Cf. Guerriero, *Hans Urs von Balthasar*, 363.

cosmos. For nowhere does Scripture state that the Son came into the world in order to redeem the Church, rather that he came to redeem the world. From this Balthasar concludes that the Church has a missionary function which gravitates toward the world in order to lead the world to Christ.

Balthasar distinguishes between the pre-Easter and post-Easter founding of the Church. "For our sake, since we dwell here in the flesh, all that is spiritual and charismatic must be put into visible structures, but these structures are inwardly filled with the goods dispensed by the risen and now pneumatic Christ."[12] Parallel to this view, we can also distinguish an objectively institutional element from a subjectively existential element. Of course, both aspects must be viewed together, since on the one side there are objective gifts such as tradition, Scripture, Magisterium, proclamation and liturgy, canon law, and theology—while on the other, the subjective side, are found the Spirit and the witness of one's life. Yet it is always one and the same Spirit who "will lead you to the complete truth" (Jn 16:13).

In the conclusion of this third volume of the *Theo-Logic*, Balthasar once again leads us to the original source of all being: "Upward and onward to the Father!" The trinitarian vision of truth is the seal of the love of God which existed before all love. "Through the Son's glory we glimpse the abyss of the invisible Father's love—glory in the Holy Spirit's twofold love. Born of the Spirit as we are, we exist in the fire of love in which Father and Son encounter each other: thus, together with the Spirit, we simultaneously bear witness and give glory to his love."[13]

12. Balthasar, *Theo-Logic*, vol. III, *The Spirit of Truth* (San Francisco: Ignatius Press, 2005), 304.

13. *The Spirit of Truth*, 448.

Symphonic Truth

"Whoever sees more of the truth is more profoundly right."[14] This pronouncement of Hans Urs von Balthasar circumscribes very aptly his complete oeuvre. It applies in a special way to his *Theo-Logic*, which explores the theme of truth. The sun never sets in the kingdom of truth. It is amazing to realize that it is a fact that there is such a reality as existence, nature, and objective truth—and this amazement, instead of diminishing in time continues to increase in the life and research of a genuine thinker. Balthasar's works are a "cathedral which towers over the theological landscape and which both assists the searcher in orienting himself and also causes him to encounter amazing bewilderment."[15] Balthasar himself writes in his epilogue:

> Our trilogy, presenting aesthetics, dramatics, and logic, is built from within this mutual illuminating light. What one calls the properties of Being that transcend every individual being (the "transcendentals") seem to give the most fitting access to the mysteries of Christian theology. From these common properties three were drawn out for separate emphasis: the beautiful, the good, and the true. . . . In fact, they were chosen precisely because together they permeate all Being.[16]

These three are inseparable because jointly they permeate all existence. They lie inside one another.

In a certain sense, the *Theo-Logic* is fundamental to the entire trilogy and theology of Hans Urs von Balthasar. For "love alone is credible,"[17] i.e., the gratuitous love (Father) which constitutes both the most wise (Son) and the most right (Spirit).

14. Balthasar, *Epilogue* (San Francisco: Ignatius Press, 2004), 15, 43.

15. Eugen Biser, "Dombau oder Triptychon? Zum Abschluß der Trilogie Hans Urs von Balthasars," *Theologische Revue* 84, no. 3 (1988): 177–84.

16. Balthasar, *Epilogue*, 46.

17. Balthasar, *Love Alone Is Credible* (San Francisco: Ignatius Press, 2004), 10.

9

Life in Christ

THE CHRISTIAN STATES OF LIFE ACCORDING TO HANS URS VON BALTHASAR

The Second Vatican Council, in the view of Hans Urs von Balthasar (1905–1988) "has been a Council of the Holy Spirit like no other Council."[1] Its purpose was the renovation of the Church. Only Mary is "*Ecclesia immaculata*" and the eschatological form of the Church. But in all her other members, the Church must always be reformed (*Ecclesia semper reformanda*). A new mentality and also a new activity is required: "Everyone in the Church, whether monk or nun, bishop or priest, layman or missionary, is obliged to portray the whole spectrum of the Christ-mystery in his existence."[2] The theology of Balthasar helped lay the foundation of Vatican II and then helped put its aims into practice. Henri de Lubac expressed this acknowledgement of Balthasar's contribution: "He himself is one of those men of whom he has spoken, men who devoted the work of their lives 'to the splendor of theology—theology, that devouring fire between two nights, two abysses: requiring both adoration and obedience.'"[3] And again, Lubac about Balthasar: "He is theologian only to be apostle."[4]

1. Hans Urs von Balthasar, "The Council of the Holy Spirit," in *Explorations in Theology*, vol. III, *Creator Spirit* (San Francisco: Ignatius Press, 1993), 245–67, at 263.

2. "The Council of the Holy Spirit," 266.

3. Henri de Lubac, "The Witness of Christ in the Church: Hans Urs von Balthasar," in *The Church: Paradox and Mystery* (Shannon, Ireland: Ecclesia Press, 1969), 110.

4. De Lubac, "The Witness of Christ in the Church," 115.

The Reality of Christian States of Life

In September 1977, Dr. Hans Urs von Balthasar recommended to this author his new book *Christlicher Stand* [The Christian State of Life] which, with many other of his books, provided the inspiration for much of my own research and study.[5] The theme of Balthasar's book indicates the basic reasons for ministry in the Church. It highlights the "moment of Christian witness" and the determination to be part of the Church's mission. God's irrevocable design for us requires our appropriate response.[6] "Whatever particular Christian state the believer may live in, he lives as one who has died and been resurrected, because his whole existence is an attempt to make a loving and thankful response to God 'by faith in the Son of God, who loved me and gave himself for me' (Gal 2:20)."[7]

Hans Urs von Balthasar, in his *Introduction* written in 1945 stated that:

> One of the great blessings of God is that no one sees himself as he really is; even when he looks at himself in a mirror, he sees himself in a reversed mirror image. But others, who discover much in him that he does not know, in turn know little of what he himself knows about himself. And thus ultimately—if we prescind from the omniscience of God—the least unreliable measure of a man remains his work. 'You will know them by their fruits', and yet, since these fruits can be deceptive, you will not 'judge them' by these. Thus, all that a writer can do is to send his books to the front, if he is to give information about himself—even if he can only laugh at these advocates, who correspond so little to what he fundamentally would have wanted to say.[8]

5. Balthasar, *The Christian State of Life* (San Francisco: Ignatius Press, 1983).
6. Balthasar, *The Moment of Christian Witness* (San Francisco: Ignatius Press, 1994).
7. *The Moment of Christian Witness*, 141.
8. Balthasar, *My Work: In Retrospect* (San Francisco: Ignatius Press, 1993), 9.

Ten years later (1955), the author stressed his intention to bring the Church into dialogue with the world. The title of his book *Razing the Bastions* was considered provocative by some since it contained the assertion that the Church should not erect barriers to protect herself against the world.[9] As he wrote: "My programmatic little book *Razing the Bastions* was the final and already impatient blast of the trumpet calling for a Church no longer barricaded against the world."[10]

During the time he was studying in Lyon, the idea of the universal mission of the Church was already in his mind. He wrote:

> We were a fine group, resolute and exposed, and it was clear to us from the beginning that the bastions of anxiety that the Church had contrived to protect herself from the world have to be demolished; the Church had to be freed to become herself and open to the whole and undivided world for its mission. For the meaning of Christ's coming is to save the *world* and to open for the whole of it the way to the Father; the Church is only a means, a radiance that through preaching, example and discipleship spreads out from the God-man into every sphere. This passion rallied us young theologians (Fessard, Bouillard, Daniélou and many others) in Lyon around our older friend and master Henri de Lubac, from whom we gained an understanding of the Greek Fathers, the philosophical mysticism of Asia and the phenomenon of the modern atheism; to him my patristic studies owe their initial spark. For patristic meant to us a Christendom that still carried its thoughts into the limitless space of the nations and still trusted in the world's salvation.[11]

From this perspective, von Balthasar writes, "All this would remain mere literary chatter were it not at the service of, and obe-

9. Balthasar, *Razing the Bastions* (San Francisco: Ignatius Press, 1993); Balthasar, *My Work*, 43.

10. *My Work*, 51.

11. *My Work*, 48.

dient to, an ecclesial action that has been assigned to me, which I myself have not chosen. This is the center; everything else, even if developed earlier, has been placed around it."[12]

This same fundamental purpose was affirmed by Balthasar in 1975 when he wrote:

> The activity of being a writer remains and will always remain, in the working-out of my life, a secondary function, something *faute de mieux*. At its center there is a completely different interest: the task of renewing the Church through the formation of new communities that unite the radical Christian life of conformity to the evangelical counsels of Jesus with existence in the midst of the world, whether by practicing secular profession or through the ministerial priesthood to give new life to living communities. All my activity as a writer is subordinated to this task.[13]

In an interview titled "Spirit and Fire" given a few months after his 70th birthday, Balthasar emphasized what he considered his apostolic mission:

> My books are not a kind of the theology that belongs to academic guild. . . . I consider my own theology to be like the finger of John pointing to the fullness of revelation in Jesus Christ, which is unfolded in the immense fullness in the reception of the history of the Church, above all in the meditation of the saints. I have to say that for me the only truly interesting theologians are the saints.[14]

In his book *A Theology of History*, Balthasar described the mission of the saints:

12. *My Work*, 43.
13. *My Work*, 95.
14. Balthasar and Michael Albus, "Spirit and Fire: An Interview with Hans Urs von Balthasar," *Communio* 32, no. 3 (2005): 573–93, at 574.

Whenever the Spirit takes the Church by surprise with these gifts, it is going to be, in the main, by the proclamation of some truth which has a far-reaching meaning for the particular age to which it is given, in both Church history and world history. The Spirit meets the burning questions of the age with an utterance that is the key-word, the answer to the riddle. Never in the form of an abstract statement (that being something that it is man's business to draw up); almost always in the form of a new, concrete supernatural mission: the creation of a new saint whose life is a presentation to his own age of the message that heaven is sending to it, a man who is, here and now, the right and relevant interpretation of the Gospel, who is given to this particular age as its way of approach to the perennial truth of Christ. How else can life be expounded except by living? The saints are tradition at its most living, tradition as the word is meant whenever Scripture speaks of the unfolding of the riches of Christ, and the application to history of the norm which is Christ. Their missions are so exactly the answer from above to the questions from below that their immediate effect is often one of unintelligibility; they are signs to be contradicted in the name of every kind of right-thinking—until the proof of their power is brought forth. Saint Bernard and Saint Francis, Saint Ignatius and Saint Teresa were all of them proofs of that order: they were like volcanoes pouring forth molten fire from the inmost depths of Revelation; they were irrefutable proof, all horizontal tradition notwithstanding, of the vertical presence of the living Kyrios here, now and today.

All these concrete norms in which the Holy Spirit expounds the Word of God to the Church are subject to many kinds of perils and contingencies: resistances in those who are thus chosen: resistances in their environment which hinder their work; resistances, finally, in the Church, who may not listen to their message, or only listen sceptically Hence it is never possible to apply these "pneumatic" norms independently of the more "formal" norms of Scripture, tradition, and the teaching and pastoral office. The saints have to allow

> themselves to be measured by these norms, and if the Spirit of God is in them, they will not try to avoid such judgment; for he is the Spirit of the Church. But it is nonetheless true that in the final analysis, these formal norms exist for the sake of the living norm of holiness. And anything that is instituted to test and pass judgment on the holiness in the Church needs to realize that such judgment is possible only in the Holy Spirit. And he, as the Spirit of Christ, is the Spirit of humility. The same humility that is binding upon the individual obliged to submit to the judgment of the official Church is equally binding upon that office itself, which must submit to the judgment of the Spirit of Christ shining forth in the holiness within the Church. Ecclesiastical offices will not sit in judgment with Christ on the last day: the saints will. But because it is the same Holy Spirit who creates both subjective and objective holiness, the two belong most intimately together, and only the spirit of dissension would try to sow suspicion between them or to affirm that they cannot be united.[15]

It is no wonder that Hans Urs von Balthasar gave two of his articles the same title: "Theology and Holiness."[16]

Election, Vocation, Mission

The theme of the Christian states of life is inseparably connected with the life and work of Hans Urs von Balthasar. Several of his assertions help us understand this unity,

15. Balthasar, *A Theology of History* (San Francisco: Ignatius Press, 1994), 109–11.

16. Balthasar, "Theology and Sanctity," in *Explorations in Theology*, vol. I, *The Word Made Flesh* (San Francisco: Ignatius Press, 1989), 181–209. Forty years afterward: Balthasar, "Theology and Holiness," *Communio: International Catholic Review* 14, no. 4 (1987): 341–50. See to this theme: Anton Štrukelj, *Kniende Theologie*, 2nd expanded ed. (St. Ottilien: EOS Verlag, 2004); Russian: *O slave božjej* (Moscow: Izdatelstvo franciskancev, 1999); Slovenian: *Klečeča teologija* (Ljubljana: Družina, 2000); Italian: *Teologia e santità* (Milan-Cinisello Balsamo: Edizioni San Paolo, 2010); Polish: *Teologia i świętość* (Lublin: Polihymnia, 2010).

> Well, just as I was once constrained as a boy to plough my way through the entire undergrowth of Romantic music from Mendelssohn via Strauss to Mahler and Schönberg, before finally I was allowed to see rising behind these the eternal stars of Bach and Mozart—and, for a long time, these two have taken the place of all others a hundred times over—so, too, I had to clear my path through the jungle of modern literature, in Vienna, Berlin, Zürich and other places, until at last the kindly hand of God took hold of me (as once he took hold of Habakkuk along with his bowl /see Dan 14:33–39/ and chose me for a true life.[17]

This assertion indicated a special event that took place in 1959 during the Ignatian Exercises. Hans Urs von Balthasar writes:

> Even today (1959), after thirty years, I could still find again the tree on the lost path in the Black Forest, not far from Basel, under which I was struck as if by lightning. At that time, I was a student in German literature and was making a round of Exercises for lay students. In this university environment, it was seen as tough luck if one withdrew to study theology. However, it was neither theology nor the priesthood that, at that moment, appeared in a flash before my mind; it was this alone: You have nothing to choose; you are called. You will not serve; another will use you. You have no plans to make; you are only a small little tile in a mosaic that has long been ready. I needed only "to leave everything and follow," without making plans, without wishes or ideas: I needed only to stand there and wait and see what I would be used for—and so it happened; and if the thought came to me that the Good God had assigned me to a safe place and given me a clearly outlined mission, I still recognized that—despite the opinions and habits of this instrument that I was—He was free to scrap it all in an instant. Of all this, the only thing worth noting is that this life-law,

17. *My Work*, 10.

> which breaks us and in this breaking heals us (as with St. Ignatius's leg, *Au 1–5*), already appeared to me from the very beginning as a kind of invisible life-motif. To be sure, for the impatient rabbi Saul, it must have been no different.[18]

The maturing Christian who seeks direction for his life is led by Ignatius to a personal encounter with Christ through a contemplation of the concrete Gospel scene which is determined by the "call" which is the same basic reality in the life of Jesus; and the "choice" which comes from the encounter with Christ. He chooses us and calls us; our choice of him is the only answer our obedience can make to him. Consequently, Balthasar states:

> So that we may attain to perfection in whatever state or life that God our Lord places before us for our choice". Consequently, perfection is not an impersonal ethical-religious canon of rules but is the obedience of the person to the Lord in the focus of the Gospel that continues to take place. . . . Love is ablaze with enthusiasm, love makes a choice, demands exclusiveness—this is the source of the "counsels of Christ."[19]

A Christian as "man in God" and "person in Christ" can play his role only in being chosen, called and sent. The notions *Election, Vocation, Mission* have the central significance in Balthasar's *Theo-Drama*,[20] but also in his entire theology of Christian states:

> It is when God addresses a conscious subject, tells him who he is and what he means to the eternal God of truth and shows him the purpose of his existence—that is, imparts a distinctive

18. Balthasar as interviewed in *Por qué me hice sacerdote?* by Jorge Sans Vala and Ramón María Sans Vala (Salamanca: Ediciones Sigueme, 1959); German in: Elio Guerriero, *Hans Urs von Balthasar: Eine Monographie* (Einsiedeln: Johannes Verlag, 1993), 401.

19. Balthasar, *My Work*, 20–21.

20. Balthasar, *Theo-Drama: Theological Dramatic Theory*, vol. III, *Dramatis personae: Persons in Christ* (San Francisco: Ignatius Press, 1992), 263–82.

> and divinely authorized mission—that we can say of a conscious subject that he is a "person." This is what happened, archetypically, in the case of Jesus Christ, when he was given his eternal "definition"—"You are my beloved Son."[21]

In Jesus Christ there is the absolute unique identity between person and mission.[22] A man attains his personal dignity only as a person in Christ. "Being in Christ" is the shortest definition of a Christian.

As early as 1947, Hans Urs von Balthasar had published an essay entitled "The Layman and the Life of the Counsels."[23] In it he outlined the complexity of questions regarding the Church's teaching concerning the states of life for believers. These are his words: "There is assuredly no part of dogmatic theology that is more neglected today than this one."[24]

In his essay, Balthasar examines the relationship between the state of lay persons in the world and the state of those in sacred orders and vowed religious. He maintained that it was possible for lay people to live the evangelical counsels in their lives. He welcomed the new apostolic constitution, *Provida Mater,* issued the same year, 1947, in which the Church recognized a lay movement that had been developing for many years in numerous different countries. He wrote, "'the law of praying is the law of believing' (*lex orandi lex credenda*) and 'the law of action is the law of contemplation' (*lex actionis lex contemplationis*)."[25]

The new papal constitution signified more than just a formal incorporation of lay communities into the canon law of the Church in a manner similar to that of religious orders. It included

21. *Persons in Christ*, 207.

22. *Persons in Christ*, 149–259.

23. Balthasar, "The Layman and the Life of the Counsels," in *The Laity and the Life of the Counsels: The Church's Mission in the World* (San Francisco: Ignatius Press, 2003), 39–126.

24. "The Layman and the Life of the Counsels," 39.

25. "The Layman and the Life of the Counsels," 39.

a formal endorsement of these lay communities as representing (belonging to) the very mind and heart of the Church. It gathered all of the varieties of lay movements into one constitution so that they together had a place within the states of life formally recognized by the Church.[26] "Secular Institutes" means a new form of consecrated life which "becomes here the as yet unnameable ideal of the Christian: to follow the counsels of Jesus in the midst of the world, without abandoning one's post. This is not the religious state in the old sense; it is the radicalism of the Gospel in the particularity of our time."[27]

Balthasar summarized (in 1955) his position with these words:

> At the service of the same idea stands the meditation, which is especially urgent today, on the states in the Church, in which the objective life forms of existence in the Church—as we know—are investigated in terms of their original existence in the Gospel and in their historical development, so that they may appear in their first purity to today's Christian, who is looking for paths to imitate.[28]

Balthasar established: "There are three distinct areas: . . . the revelation of the fullness of God in Jesus Christ—the Church as the fullness of Christ—the radiation of the Church into the world."[29] In few words: "All this strengthened my determination to display the Christian message in its unsurpassable greatness (*id quo maius cogitari nequit*), because it is God's human word for the world, God's most humble service eminently fulfilling every human striving, God's deepest love in the splendor of his dying so that all might live beyond themselves for him."[30]

26. "The Layman and the Life of the Counsels," 41.

27. Balthasar, *My Work*, 43.

28. *My Work*, 31. See Balthasar, *The Christian State of Life* (San Francisco: Ignatius Press, 1983).

29. *My Work*, 20.

30. *My Work*, 50.

The Foundation of Secular Institutes

Together with Adrienne von Speyr, Hans Urs von Balthsar led the foundation for the Community of Saint John in 1945. These are Balthasar's words:

> What Ignatius had intended in his time meant henceforth for me "secular institute"; the hard sacrifice demanded by this transition was accompanied by the certainty of serving the same idea more exactly. It was Adrienne von Speyr who showed the way in which Ignatius is fulfilled by John and therefore laid the basis for most of what I have published since 1940. Her works and mine are neither psychologically nor philologically to be separated: two halves of a single whole, which has as its center unique foundation.[31]

Secular institutes are the new possibility of following Christ in the midst of the world. In the view of Balthasar, this is the most up-to-date form of the Christian mission in the world:

> The true, undiminished program for the Church today must read: the greatest possible radiance in the world by virtue of the closest possible following Christ. At the point where the tension between being a Christian and being a man like other men is at its strongest, indeed so strong that it must appear to the natural man as lacerating and "psychologically" unbearable by every standard of closed and harmonious humanity, there is raised up not only the outer "eschatological" (that is, world-vanquishing) sign—a kind of stimulating irritant—but also the reality itself, either in its visibility or (as with everything weighty in Christianity) in its invisibility. Today this form of existence takes a new ecclesial shape in the"'secular institutes." For these as a structure are beyond doubt the unifying midpoint of the Church; they constitute the link between the lay state and the life of the vows and

31. *My Work*, 89.

> show not only the existential unity of the Church but also her perennial and most "up-to-date" mission in the world.[32]

To support his position regarding secular institutes, Balthasar wrote many essays which were published in a collection *The Laity and the Life of Counsels: The Church's Mission in the World*.[33]

What is the role of various orders in the Church today? Balthasar does not refer only to religious orders, but to a "life according to the counsels of Jesus," as they have been named by the Church: poverty, chastity, and obedience. As Balthasar notes,

> I would include here all that makes up the life of a diocesan priest, who also promises obedience, who should know the spiritual meaning of celibacy, and who certainly should have the spirit of poverty. And moving outward are all those who somehow participate in the spirit of counsels as laymen. All of these from Carmel to the secular institutes should be pillars of the Church. . . . They would be pillars if their total self-giving, which is required by their form of life, really flowed from a love of the poor love of God.[34]

Different Christian States of Life

Balthasar wrote his book *The Christian State of Life* in 1945, but it was not published until 1977. It has the same title as a book by Adrienne von Speyr. In his preface regarding the scope of his work, he wrote, "The sole purpose of this book is to provide a comprehensive meditation on the foundations and background of St. Ignatius's contemplation on the 'Call of Christ,' on the answer we must give if we want 'to give greater proof of love' (*Sp Ex*, 97)."[35] And he continues: "The goal of our meditation is to understand why this

32. *My Work*, 58.
33. *The Laity and the Life of Counsels*.
34. Balthasar, "Spirit and Fire: An Interview," 589.
35. Balthasar, *The Christian State of Life*, 9–10, citing the Spiritual Exercises of St. Ignatius of Loyola.

act of choosing a 'state or way of life' 'within our Holy Mother, the hierarchical Church' (*Sp Ex*, 170) is possible and necessary."[36]

Balthasar, according to Christian tradition, describes two main states of life for Christians.

> The priestly and vowed religious state on the one hand, and the state of lay persons in the world (including marriage) on the other hand. *Jesus Christ is not only the Lord of these different states of life, but he is also the cause of their divisions.* The divine plan of Christ coming from the Father, through his life in the world, and returning to the Father, makes it possible for Jesus to be the *source of both possible* states in life without creating a double standard for his disciples.[37]

> Mary's state in life is a model for both states of life (religious and lay). As mother of Jesus, she can be called cofoundress of both states of life for people. Because she is both virgin and mother, both states of life can claim her as their model and patroness. Yet she belongs to neither; even though she passes successively through both states, she stands, like her Son, above both and, by her transcendence, participates with him in the actual founding of both.[38]

The Priestly State and the State of the Counsels

Balthasar writes:

> The call to the priesthood as an objective ministry in the Church and that to the state of the counsels as a subjective way of life in imitation of Christ are both expression of the ecclesial state of election. . . . *The priesthood is primarily an ecclesial function, an objective ministry, and, on the basis of this ministry, subsequently a way of life. The way of the counsels is primarily a personal way of life and consequently*

36. *The Christian State of Life*, 9–10.
37. *The Christian State of Life*, 194.
38. *The Christian State of Life*, 201.

> *becomes an ecclesial way of life*—similar, therefore, to the official ministry, but lacking the distinguishing mark of such a ministry. Common to both is the fact that they are forms of special election, rooted in the same disposition of Christ and challenging the elect to total and irrevocable commitment to a more excellent law of life: the priest, through sacramental consecration; one in the state of counsels, through the taking of vows and the acceptance of a rule that will henceforth govern his whole life.[39]

The State of Lay Persons in the World

Balthasar writes:

> Members of the Church who are neither in the state of election nor in priestly state belong to the state of lay persons in the world. . . . The consecration of the lay person is that of the Christian in general, namely Baptism, which gives access to all the other sacraments and to the whole perfection of love but is common to all Christians, including priests and those in the state of the counsels. It is true that matrimony is reserved in a special way for those in the lay state and confers on them a new supernatural character that is not accessible to other states. But while matrimony is the basis of the "married state" as a special potential within the lay state, it is the basis of the lay state itself.[40]

The Married State

Balthasar writes:

> Marriage is a possible (but not a necessary) form of "lay" life, contrary to the life of the counsels and closed to priests

39. *The Christian State of Life*, 266–67. See also Balthasar, *Priestly Spirituality* (San Francisco: Ignatius Press, 2013).

40. *The Christian State of Life*, 329–30. See Marc Ouellet, *Charismen: Eine Herausforderung* (Einsiedeln: Johannes Verlag, 2011).

of the Western Church (because of the convergence we noted between office and special election) . . . marriage does not cross the threshold of the eschatological realm (Mt 22:30), and a person who wishes to live eschatologically should therefore renounce marriage if he can (Mt 19:12; 1 Cor 7:8f.). Yet marriage, which was originally instituted by God (Mk 10:6; Eph 5:31), may not be represented as un-Christian and simply obsolete (1 Tm 5:3); in many situations it is urgently recommended (1 Tim 5:14; 1 Cor 7:9). But in the New Testament the ideality of marriage is not to be found in marriage itself but in the suprasexual relationship between Christ and the Church: as a sacrament, it participates in this relationship by orienting itself toward the "great mystery" (Eph 5:32), striving toward and molding itself on it. . . . By the power of Christ's grace, and sacramental grace in particular, this effort can achieve its goal, but not without many renunciations, which lead, again, from the sphere of the proclamation of the Gospel to that of the Cross.[41]

Following Christ Today

The Gospel is not inherently monastic, and its directives have a validity that goes further than this. Mary is not a nun, but she is Mother *because* a virgin. Christ is not a monk, but he is King *because* he is poor and obedient unto death. . . . And it would be in keeping with our advanced age if Catholics were to learn better to understand that responsibility, for the world goes well with obedience, disposition over the world goes well with poverty, experience of the world goes well with virginity—indeed, that the ultimate fruitfulness, even in the realm that is most truly that of the laity, that can be expected precisely from this source. Let the one who can grasp this, grasp it. But the one can

41. Balthasar, *New Elucidations* (San Francisco: Ignatius Press, 1986), 184–85.

> grasp it is not the one who psychologizes but the one who thinks Christologically in obedience to God's word. . . . The fullness of the subjective imitation of Christ lies in the counsel.[42]

and "for every Christian is obliged to the spirit of the counsels."[43]

As a conclusion to this section on states of life in the Church, I want to express my deepest gratitude to Cardinal Hans Urs von Balthasar who wrote the following foreword to my dissertation on Christian states of life, published on 1981. Hans Urs von Balthasar affirms:

> We could quite easily get the wrong impression that the last Council's emphasis on the unity of "God's people" was in favor of putting all states of life in the Church on one level. That this is not true becomes very clear if we take a brief look at the dogmatic constitution of the Church—in fact the very opposite is true. However, something has nevertheless changed: due to the strong emphasis on the truth that all states of life in the Church are called to one and the same holiness in following Christ, there has arisen something like competition between these different states—the married, the priest, and the one who has chosen to live the evangelical counsels. Individuals living in these different states want to and indeed must show with the help of God's grace that they can live Christian love in such a way that it radiates out into the world.
>
> The Middle Ages saw an undoubtedly over-simplified gradation of the objective 'perfection' of ecclesial states of life. This led to an indiscriminate over-rating of the state of the evangelical counsels (observed literally) over the secular and married state. Change was brought about by the "Friends of God," "*Devotio moderna*," and even more

42. Balthasar, *Explorations in Theology*, vol. II, *Spouse of the Word* (San Francisco: Ignatius Press, 1991), 331.

43. Balthasar, *The Christian State of Life*, 360.

radically by the Ignatian Spiritual Exercises: God's sovereign act chooses for each individual a Church "state" in which he or she should strive for perfect love according to Christ's example. Thus, on the basis of subjective choice, arises within the Church a competition, which should never lead to one state considering itself superior to another. Each state should, on the basis of its particular charisma, complement the others. This meant that for the first time, the great importance of an individual's choice of state emerged, emphasizing the timeless relevance of the Spiritual Exercises whose central purpose is to lead to a correct life decision.

Nowadays, in a time in which there is a broad tendency to reduce to the same level all social and anthropological differences, there is a danger in the Church that the distinctions between the different states that have always existed are blurred. Let us consider for example how the equality of women is being defended: instead of their equality being acknowledged, they are being treated as the same! Another example is the clearly defined profile of a bishop-priest which is being reduced to a shapeless mass of ecclesial "services" (*ministeria*) while marriage is being reduced to alternative, disordered sexual relations. Meanwhile, the life-long decision of the states of the counsels for God lived according to the evangelical counsels is being rejected as psychologically unworkable and even unwise in these changing times. However, the clearly defined states of life in the Church help create its fertility in the way the obvious physical and psychological differences between a man and a woman make them fecund even as far as the most elevated domains of the spirit.

Anton Štrukelj must be credited with having tactfully and carefully developed this very complicated subject that must by no means be over-simplified. His work represents the continued study of a rather neglected point of theoretic but also practical teaching of the Church. As he has based his work on my attempts to shed light on this subject, I owe him a warm word of thanks. May this subject have further echoes and stimulate new studies and especially new and fertile practice.[44]

44. Anton Štrukelj, *Življenje iz polnosti vere: Teologija krščanskih stanov pri Hansu Ursu von Balthasarju* (Ljubljana: Družina, 1981, 1986, 1995), 5–8. German: *Leben aus der Fülle des Glaubens: Theologie der christlichen Stände bei Hans Urs von Balthasar* (Graz-Wien-Köln: Verlag Styria, 2002), 7–8. (Second Edition: Ljubljana, 2015). Russian: *Жизнь В Полноте Веры: Богословне чинов христианской Церкви у Ханса Урса фон Бальтазара* (Moscow: Izdatelstvo franciskancev, 2016), 3–4. Croatian: *Život iz punine vjere: Teologija kršćanskih staleža u Hansa Ursa von Balthasara* (Zagreb: Kršćanska sadašnjost, 2017), 9–13 (foreword in Croatian and German).

10

Hope Does Not Disappoint

"We rejoice in the hope of . . . the glory of God" (Rom 5:2). "Christ in you, the hope of glory" (Col 1:27). "Our blessed hope, the appearing of the glory of our great God and Savior Jesus Christ" (Ti 2:13). This blessed hope is the ultimate goal of our lives, but the beginning of this fulfillment is joy. Christian history begins with the word "rejoice." The Gospel is the "glad tidings" that give us true hope.

The hope we have as believers for salvation and glory "does not disappoint us, because God's love has been poured into our hearts through the Holy Spirit who has been given to us" (Rom 5:5). Hope does not disappoint because it is trinitarian in origin (not human) and because of this we can speak of faith, hope and charity as "theological" virtues.

The Form of Christian Hope

Pope Benedict XVI begins his encyclical letter *Spe salvi* (*On Christian Hope*) as follows:

> "*Spe salvi facti sumus*"—in hope we were saved, Saint Paul says to the Romans, and likewise to us (Rom 8:24). According to the Christian faith, "redemption"—salvation—is not simply given. Redemption is offered to us in the sense that we have been given hope, trustworthy hope, by virtue of which we can face our present: the present, even if it is arduous, can be lived and accepted if it leads towards a goal, if we can be sure of this goal, and if this goal is great enough to justify the effort of the journey.[1]

1. Benedict XVI, Encyclical Letter *Spe salvi* (November 30, 2007), 1.

> Paul reminds the Christians of Ephesus of the time when they were not yet Christians. Their situation was characterized by a lack of promise. They lived in this world without hope and without God (Ephesians 2:12). A similar observation is found in 1 Thes 4:13, where Paul speaks to the Christians of this Greek port city about a hope that looks beyond death, so that they will not have to live "like those who do not have any hope." Therefore, it can be concluded from these two passages that, for Paul, hope defines the Christian, and inversely that the absence of hope defines the atheist. To be a Christian is to be one who hopes; it is to situate oneself on the foundation of a sure hope. According to these texts, hope is not just one virtue among others; it is the very definition of Christian existence.[2]

Christian hope is primarily vertical (generated from above). And just as the anchor which has been the traditional Christian symbol of hope extends down vertically and hooks into the sea floor, so does hope, the anchor of the soul, and also reaches up vertically hooking into the Holy of Holies, into the life of God. We "have strong encouragement to seize the hope set before us. We have this as a sure and steadfast anchor of the soul, a hope that enters into the inner shrine behind the curtain, where Jesus has gone as a forerunner on our behalf" (Heb 6:18–19). The text from Hebrews brings out clearly the essential difference between the hope of Christians on the one hand and that of Jews and pagans on the other. Pagan hope is limited to things the human mind can grasp. Jewish hope, on the other hand, is always oriented to future promise—it is always messianic even when the Messiah is not present.[3]

Christian hope can justly claim to be a "better hope," because it is founded in the reality of the Resurrection of Jesus Christ. The

2. Joseph Ratzinger, "On Hope," *Communio: International Catholic Review* 12, no. 1 (1985): 71–84, at 71.

3. Regarding the entire issue, see Anton Strle, *Živo upanje: Velikonočna skrivnost* [Living Hope: Paschal Mystery] (Ljubljana: Družina, 1990), 331–78.

Resurrection, in fact, realizes the Jewish eschaton, while bringing about what no pagan eschatology ever dared hope for: the salvation of the whole man, body and soul. Christ's Resurrection is not merely the object, but also the effective source of this "better hope." This is solemnly proclaimed in 1 Peter 1:3–5: "Blessed be the God and Father of our Lord Jesus Christ! By his great mercy we have been born anew to a living hope through the resurrection of the dead, to an inheritance which is imperishable, undefiled and unfading, kept in heaven for you, who by God's power are guarded through faith for a salvation ready to be revealed in the last time."

"An unfading inheritance," St. Peter proclaimed. This glorious inheritance will be our fulfillment, but "as long as we are on earth we participate in this fulfillment only in a veiled form."[4] This veil is necessary because we must be purified "by various trials" before we are ready to be open to the full glory of God. Man can only hope "that it is something glorious." It is by hope that we are saved: *Spe salvi!* (See Romans 8:24).

The Spirit himself intercedes before the Father "with sighs too deep for words" in those filled with this hope. He intercedes so that the Son's saving work may be completed in the world. Hope, then is essentially divine, trinitarian, and essentially "theological" because it is rooted in the life of the Trinity: "Hope is a theological virtue, a virtue springing from the life of the Trinity."[5]

The Little Hope Which is Pleasing to God

It is in this context that Hans Urs von Balthasar undertook a new translation of Charles Péguy's "mystery" poem, *The Portal of the Mystery of Hope*. In Péguy's poem, God says that he is not "surprised" by faith or charity. "What surprises me, says God, is hope.

4. Adrienne von Speyr, *Die katholischen Briefe I* (Einsiedeln: Johannes Verlag, 1961), 254.

5. Hans Urs von Balthasar, *Theo-Drama*, vol. V, *The Last Act* (San Francisco: Ignatius Press, 1998), 146.

And I can't get over it. . . . This little hope which seems like nothing at all."[6] Péguy attributes to hope a pivotal, mediating position between two "big sisters," faith and love.

The reality is that hope always presupposes faith, since faith has first to present the object to be hoped for. However, the salvation which faith promotes is realized only "in hope." Indeed, faith itself is "the assurance of things hoped for, the conviction of things not seen" (Heb 11:1). In self-entrustment [to God], faith gains its objective certainty, which is so solid that Paul can refer to it simply as "knowledge": "We, too, believe . . . knowing that he who raised the Lord Jesus will raise us also with Jesus" (2 Cor 4:13–14).

At the same time, hope is also a mediator on the way to love. The love revealed in Christ is the only reason to live by faith (Gal 2:20). Christian love is itself the response to God, who loved us first in the sacrifice of his Son (1 Jn 4:10). Christian love is primarily, then, love of God. In this way it is also love for Christ and, because of God's incarnation, love for one's neighbor, indeed, "for all" without exception.

"'Faith, hope and love: these three' (1 Cor 13:13) shape the content of Christian existence."[7] But love sums up the three theological virtues. It would thus be erroneous to confine faith and hope to temporal existence while associating love only with eternity. "*Love bears* all things, *believes* all things, *hopes* all things" (1 Cor 13:7). Faith and hope are an expression of the love that "does not insist on its own way" (1 Cor 13:5). Accordingly, hope is

6. Charles Péguy, *The Portal of the Mystery of Hope*, trans. David L. Schindler (Grand Rapids: Eerdmans, 1996), 7.

7. Heinrich Schlier, *Nun aber bleiben diese Drei: Grundriß des christlichen Lebensvollzuges* (Einsiedeln: Johannes Verlag, 1972); Adrienne von Speyr, *Korinther I* (Einsiedeln: Johannes Verlag, 1956), 422–29; Balthasar, "Fides Christi: An Essay on the Consciousness of Christ," in *Explorations in Theology*, vol. II, *Spouse of the Word* (San Francisco: Ignatius Press, 1991), 43–80; Balthasar, "Movement toward God," in *Explorations in Theology*, vol. III, *Creator Spirit* (San Francisco: Ignatius Press, 1993), 15–55.

the readiness [*Bereitschaft*] that says "yes" to everything with a disposition of total availability. In this way it expresses a love that remains infinitely open because it knows that God is ever-better. Likewise, faith is the attitude of the creature by which it surrenders everything and prefers God's ever-greater, ever-truer truth to its own. If hope and faith contain such infinite openness, then at their core they are genuine modes of the love that "never ends." Christian hope, distinct from merely human hope, can be understood only as a modality of love. This is why Hans Urs von Balthasar holds that the "common root of the three theological virtues is the selflessness, that is particularly visible in love but which also grounds faith and hope."[8]

Péguy brings out the connection between hope and self-surrender in love in his meditation on sleep, night, and the cross in *The Portal of the Mystery of Hope*. Péguy praises the self-entrustment that sleep embodies:

> It has come to my ears
> That there are men who do not sleep.
> I cannot abide people who do not sleep, says God.
> Sleep is, perhaps, the most glorious thing in my creation.
> And I myself rested on the seventh day.[9]

Commenting on this passage, Hans Urs von Balthasar writes:

> The poet does not insist, does not theologize. He simply takes the best God has designed for children, namely, the renewal of hope in sleep, and combines it with the darkest reality of trinitarian forsakenness (the Father having witnessed the execution of his Son) and the night that has seen the burial of this horror. There is no mention of the Resurrection; it is latent but unsaid in God's address to his 'most

8. Balthasar, *Explorations in Theology*, vol. V, *Man Is Created* (San Francisco: Ignatius Press, 2014), 352.

9. Péguy, *The Portal of the Mystery of Hope*, 125.

> beloved daughter of all', night. For night does for him what every man has the right to do for himself—to bury his son. God, however, cannot, for 'this adventure means that his hands are tied'. Night does it, here at the end, having taken the place of a hope that can no longer be named. This is because self-surrender is ultimate; it is ultimate in God the Father, in the Son and in the Spirit, it is the ultimate in man, too, when he has reached the end of his crazy path.[10]

Hope for All

This text from Balthasar's *Theo-Drama* brings us to the question of universal hope. Balthasar himself emphasizes our "duty to have hope for all men."[11] At the same time, he decidedly rejects apocatastasis and the assertion of an "empty hell." In an effort to clarify his position against vehement criticism, Balthasar published two pamphlets, *Dare We Hope "That All Men Be Saved"?* and *Short Discourse on Hell*, the contents of which are briefly examined in the following paragraphs.[12]

Without exception, we all stand under Christ's judgment. As the Apostle Paul says, "It is the Lord who judges me" (1 Cor 4:4). But we also have confidence and hope for salvation, because our judge is also our savior. Christ died for all, carrying the sins of each and every human being on his shoulders. Jesus' expiatory death [*Sühnetod*], his descent into hell, and his Resurrection are the foundation of Christian hope for the salvation of all. In his abandonment, the Son experienced rejection more than any other human person has or will experience it. For this reason, we

10. *The Last Act*, 188.

11. Balthasar, *Dare We Hope "That All Men Be Saved"? With a Short Discourse on Hell* (San Francisco: Ignatius Press, 1988), 129, 169–77.

12. *Dare We Hope*. See also Elio Guerriero, *Hans Urs von Balthasar: Eine Monographie* (Freiburg: Johannes Verlag Einsiedeln, 1993), 382–88. For an informative look at the controversy, see Jan Ambaum's "An Empty Hell? The Restoration of All Things? Balthasar's Concept of Hope for Salvation," *Communio: International Catholic Review* 18, no. 1 (1991): 35–52.

are permitted to hope that all men are lovingly embraced in God's arms. "Mercy triumphs over judgment" (Jas 2:13). Balthasar comments: "I think that the most serious thing that exists is not God's punitive justice but rather his love. . . . The seriousness that we are confronted with is the seriousness of a love that goes beyond all justice."[13]

Hope is thus grounded in the mercy of God. Moreover, it is a duty to hope for all men. Balthasar cites Cardinal Jean Daniélou in this connection:

> Too often we think of hope in too individualistic a manner as merely our personal salvation. But hope essentially bears on the great actions of God concerning the whole of creation. It bears on the destiny of all mankind. It is the salvation of the world that we await. In reality, hope bears on the salvation of all men—and it is only in the measure that I am immersed in them that it bears on me.[14]

The hope for the salvation of all human beings is grounded in the Christian faith, although this does not mean that every individual person has this knowledge in mind. "How can anyone equate hoping with knowing? I hope that my friend will recover from his serious illness—do I therefore know this? But: if I hope for you, for others, for everyone, then in the end I am also allowed to include myself."[15]

Nevertheless, although

> the Church has sanctified so many men, she has never said anything about the damnation of any individual. Not even about that of Judas, who became in a way the representative example for something of which all sinners are also guilty.

13. Balthasar, *Dare We Hope*, 130 and 140.

14. Jean Daniélou, *Essai sur le mystère de l'histoire* (Paris: Éditions du Seuil, 1953), 340, cited in Balthasar, *Dare We Hope*, 132.

15. *Dare We Hope*, 131.

> Who can know the nature of the remorse that seized Judas when he saw that Jesus had been condemned (Mt 27:3)?[16]

Cardinal Joseph Ratzinger concurs in this judgment: "Christ condemns nobody to perdition. . . . He does not mete out damnation. Rather, damnation occurs wherever a human being has remained distant from him."[17]

Hope in Patience

It is the Church's task to bring this "hope that does not disappoint" into the world. This means, as we have seen, that Christian hope is not primarily individual, but universal. But is this an invitation to idleness? The response of Joseph Ratzinger is clear:

> On the contrary: because the Christian knows that meaning exists, he can and must perform the work of history cheerfully and without hesitation. . . . The new world described in the Apocalypse as the final Jerusalem is no utopia; rather, it is a certainty towards which we are journeying in faith. There is a redemption of the world: it is this confidence that sustains the Christian and still makes it worthwhile to be Christian even today.[18]

What does it mean to live out this confidence born of hope in the midst of time? In his book *To Look on Christ*,[19] Joseph Ratzinger offers three biblical examples in illustration of Christian hope. First, there is the prophet Jeremiah, who strongly opposes

16. *Dare We Hope*, 149.

17. Ratzinger, *Eschatologie* (Regensburg: Pustet Verlag, 1977), 169; also in Ratzinger, *Auferstehung und ewiges Leben*, JRGS 10 (Freiburg: Herder, 2012).

18. Ratzinger, *Einführung in das Christentum* (München: Kösel Verlag, 1968), 299–300. New Edition: JRGS 4 (Freiburg: Herder, 2014). English: *Introduction to Christianity* (San Francisco: Ignatius Press, 1990).

19. Ratzinger, *To Look on Christ: Exercises in Faith, Hope and Love* (New York: Crossroad, 1991). German: *Auf Christus schauen: Einübung in Glaube, Hoffnung, Liebe* (Freiburg: Herder, 1989).

the prevailing optimism of public opinion. "From the point of view of the official optimism, the prophet's realism appears as a crass and inadmissible form of pessimism."[20] But:

> In the light of Israel's catastrophic downfall and the collapse of all previous optimism, the pessimistic Jeremiah proves to be the genuine bearer of hope. Everything appeared to have come to an end with this downfall, yet to Jeremiah this moment is a new beginning. God is never defeated, and his promises are never brought down by man's defeats. Indeed, they grow greater, just as love grows in the measure that it is needed by the beloved.[21]

The second example is taken from the Apocalypse of Saint John. The magnificent, frequently terrifying visions of the disciple of love reveal how God sees world history. "Despite all its horrors, human history will not drown in the night of self-destruction; God will not permit it to be wrested from his hands."[22] God remains God; he remains the savior whose mercy is indestructible. Man is not the only player, and death does not have the last word.

Cardinal Ratzinger cites the Beatitudes as the third example. "The paradoxical message of the Beatitudes mirrors precisely the paradoxical figure of the prophet Jeremiah as well as the view of history of Revelation. . . . The Beatitudes tell us that if we lead Christian lives we will always be accompanied by this paradoxical tension."[23]

This means that in living as a follower of Christ, man may bear much suffering, but he also enjoys the privilege of God's consoling nearness. St. Augustine reaffirms the hope of the Church with these famous words: "The Church has gone forward on pil-

20. Ratzinger, *Auf Christus schauen*, 53.
21. *Auf Christus schauen*, 54.
22. *Auf Christus schauen*, 58.
23. *Auf Christus schauen*, 59.

grimage amid the persecutions of the world and the consolations of God.[24]

The significance of these three examples regarding life beyond the grave is highlighted when we recall the Letter to the Hebrews (Heb 11:1) which defines faith as the substance (*hypostasis*) of what is hoped for, the certitude of what one does not see. In this basic biblical text both an ontology and a spirituality of hope are affirmed. The word "hypostasis" is crucial.

> Believing is leaving the shadowy play of corruptible things to reach the firm ground of true reality, 'hypostasis'—quite literally therefore, what stands and that on which one can stand. In other words, to believe is to have touched ground, to approach the substance of everything. With faith, hope has gotten a footing. The cry of waiting wrung from our being is not lost in the void. It finds a point of solid support to which we must for our part hold fast.[25]

The Dimensions of Hope: Its Franciscan Element

Hope and Possession

Even in the loss of our "substance," our possessions, we Christians have solid ground that no one can take from us. Our true "substance," our life, is "hidden with Christ in God." A luminous example of the free man who has found imperishable joy beyond earthly goods is Francis of Assisi. In the midst of the almost unbearable pains of his illness and of the most inhospitable lodging, Francis becomes aware of the treasure which has already been given him. Because he had found freedom from the many hopes, he became the great witness of the fact that man has "hope," is a creature of hope. "Francis is the witness and guardian of hope because he has helped us 'accept with joy' (Heb

24. Augustine, *De Civitate Dei* XVIII, 51:2.

25. Ratzinger, "On Hope," *Communio: International Review* 12, no. 1 (1985): 71–84, at 77.

10:34) the loss of rank, of position, of possessions, and has made visible, behind the false hopes, the true, the genuine hope—the one that no one can confiscate or destroy."[26]

Hope and Recollection of Being

To approach the spirit of Francis from another point of view, a passage taken from St. Bonaventure's sermons for Advent highlights the theology and spirituality of hope in the Franciscan tradition. These are Ratzinger's words regarding the Canticle of Canticles of St. Francis:

> "I sat down in the shadow of the one I had longed for" (2:3). The shadow of Christ, says Bonaventure, is grace, which for us is a cool retreat from the scorching heat of the world. "To be seated" signifies composure of the spirit, recollection, the opposite of a thought going round and round endlessly and without purpose. To enter into the domain of the One toward whom our interior expectation tends, we must stop "being open to the outside and be recollected interiorly. Let nothing prevent the taste of eternal goodness from penetrating one's being."[27]
>
> If these words sound a bit abstract, they are clarified when we consider them in conjunction with what the legends of St. Francis tell us of the origin of the Canticle of the Sun. In the midst of almost unbearable pains of illness, and in an inhospitable lodging, Francis becomes aware of the treasure that he has already received. God's voice says to him: "Live henceforth in serenity, as if you are already in my kingdom." In his last years Francis had lost everything—health, possessions, his own foundation (*ta hyparchonta*). And it is precisely from this man that the most delightfully joyous words issue. With all his hopes taken away, all his disappointments experienced, there shines forth the "fundamental

26. "On Hope," 79.
27. "On Hope," 79.

hope" in its invincible grandeur. Francis had truly left the "accidental" to enter into "substance." Free of the multiplicity of hopes, he has become the great witness that man has hope, that he is a being of hope.

Still more concretely, do we not all run the risk of losing the grace of hope amid the everyday vexations? The more our life is turned toward the exterior, the less the great and true hope can counterbalance the havoc caused by daily worries. Gradually these become the only reality, existence is depressing, hopes wear thin, initial optimism is exhausted, and ill humor becomes an insidious form of despair. We can remain people of hope only if our life is not contentedly grounded in the everyday but is solidly rooted in "substance." The more we recollect ourselves the more hope becomes real and the more it illumines our daily work. Only then can we perceive the brightness of the world which otherwise withdraws farther and farther from view.[28]

The Social and Cosmic Dimension of Hope

What has been written above concerning hope does not mean that we should tend toward escaping into interiority (one's interior life) because the exterior world tends to create hopelessness in us. Rather, Christians should strive to create positive living conditions which help prevent flight into one's inner self as a sole alternative. Human suffering, which is part of life, becomes tolerable when one has reason to hope for future relief and peace. This kind of hope that St. Francis proclaimed and lived did not come from any kind of retreat into an interior life or isolated individualism. Rather, his hope allowed him to live a life of poverty so that he could be detached from things, and at the same time helped him form a community of men who shared his values and insights. He was able to develop new rules for a common life for his brothers, and through the Third Order he founded, he helped

28. "On Hope," 79–80.

his followers live a life of simplicity with their eyes focused on a fullness of life in the Lord.

St. Bonaventure was able to focus the spirit of Francis, in one of his Advent sermons, on the hope that could sustain their faith. He wrote that the experience of hope resembled the flight of birds, when they opened their wings and concentrated their strength, totally involved in soaring to new heights: "The one who hopes must lift up his head."[29] So it is, Bonaventure said, that one who hopes uses his energy to rise towards the object of his hope. He presented in detail the Franciscan formula for intertwining the interior life of the soul with an external life lived in common with others. These are Joseph Ratzinger's words:

> "To the dynamism of hope, to the comprehensive movement of man that hope wants to realize, belongs the physical and practical work without which one cannot raise oneself." Let us restate it, this time without the imagery. In the Franciscan pattern of hope, which takes up exactly the model traced by the epistle to the Hebrews, it is a question of surmounting the wish to possess. Possession as a foundation of being is surpassed by a new foundation so that man is freed of the former. It is precisely this greed for possession that shuts man out of paradise. Here is the key to the economic as well as the ecological questions which are both without hope unless a new "fundamental hope" comes to free man. This is why the way to the interior traced by the New Testament is the only way to the exterior, to free air.[30]

The reason we can live with hope, and even with joy, is rooted in the message of Jesus recorded in the Gospel, the Good News, because he is resurrected from the dead as he promised, and he

29. "On Hope," 79, citing Bonaventure, "Dominica prima Adventus, sermo XVI," in *Opera Omnia*, vol. 9 (Quaracchi: Collegium S. Bonaventurae, 1901), 40a.

30. Ratzinger, "On Hope," 80–82. See also Ratzinger, *The Yes of Jesus Christ: Exercises in Faith, Hope, and Love* (New York: Crossroad, 2005).

wants to share his resurrected life with us. For those who are troubled and carry heavy burdens, the possibility of experiencing joy in their lives comes with their faith in the risen One. As Cardinal Ratzinger wrote, "One who is cheerful from the bottom of his heart, one who has suffered but not lost joy, cannot be far from the God of the *evangelium*, whose first word on the threshold of the New Testament is 'Rejoice!'"[31] Christian hope, which "does not disappoint," empowers us to rejoice. For God's might bestows on us the "blessed" hope that gives us life and a future.

31. Ratzinger, "Faith as Trust and Joy—Evangelium," in *Principles of Catholic Theology: Building Stones for a Fundamental Theology* (San Francisco: Ignatius Press, 1987), 75–84, at 84.

11

Lord Jesus Christ as Judge and Savior

In his Encyclical letter *Spe salvi*, Pope Benedict XVI presents the Last Judgment as a setting for learning and practicing hope. "Christ himself, the Judge and Savior. The encounter with him is the decisive act of judgment. Before his gaze all falsehood melts away. This encounter with him, as it burns us, transforms and frees us, allowing us to become truly ourselves."[1] Earlier, Cardinal Joseph Ratzinger had presented similar ideas in his *Eschatology*:

> Christ inflicts pure perdition on no one. In himself he is sheer salvation. Anyone who is with him has entered the space of deliverance and salvation. Perdition is not imposed by him, but comes to be wherever a person distances himself from Christ. It comes about whenever someone remains enclosed within himself. Christ's word, the bearer of the offer of salvation, then lays bare the fact that the person who is lost has himself drawn the dividing line and separated himself from salvation.[2]

Man Is Judged by Truth

Jesus Christ is our Judge and Redeemer. A glance at the Pierced One on the cross testifies to this truth. And the Lord's judgment is the ultimate truth for each person.[3] As Ratzinger points out:

> In death, a human being emerges into the light of full reality and truth. He takes up that place which is truly his by right.

1. Benedict XVI, Encyclical Letter *Spe salvi* (November 30, 2007), 47.
2. Joseph Ratzinger, *Eschatology: Death and Eternal Life*, 2nd ed. (Washington, D.C.: The Catholic University of America Press, 2007), 205–6.
3. Ratzinger, *Behold the Pierced One: An Approach to a Spiritual Christology* (San Francisco: Ignatius Press, 1986).

> The masquerade of living with its constant retreat behind posturings and fictions, is now over. Man is what he is in truth. Judgment consists in this removal of the mask in death. The judgment is simply the manifestation of the truth. Not that this truth is something impersonal. God is truth; the truth is God; it is personal. There can be a truth which is judging, definitive, only if there is a truth with a divine character. God is judge inasmuch as he is truth itself. Yet God is the truth for us as the One who became man, becoming in that moment the measure for man. And so, God is the criterion of truth for us in and through Christ. Herein lies that redemptive transformation of the idea of judgment which Christian faith brought about. The truth which judges man has itself set out to save him.[4]

Eternal Judgment Means Separation and Division

Within the concepts of judgment and salvation, and Christ as judge and savior, it is important to consider the various aspects of the judgment itself. Christ himself, as the One through whom all creation exists, has a decisive role in judgment: "He shall come to judge the Living and the Dead." Hans Urs von Balthasar comments on this article of the Apostles' Creed with the following words:

> "*To judge*," according to the German word *urteilen*, judging means dividing things fundamentally into distinct parts; without a division between yes and no, there is no judgment. According to the German word *entscheiden*, judging means separating things out from each other; without a separation into right and left, there is no judgment. This process of dividing and separating is vividly represented for us in the great judgment scene in Matthew 25. And right now, in the world and its history, there is undoubtedly much that needs to be divided and separated if the truth about the whole and the particular is to come to light. Further, this judgment does not merely aim at establishing what really

4. Ratzinger, *Eschatology*, 205–6.

> existed in secrecy, but beyond that, at opening up, through its verdict, the way into coming, the eternal. We all stand under this judgment, except the Mother of the Lord, in whom there is nothing to be separated out; thus the icons depict her as the intercessor next to her judging Son ("Pray for us sinners, now and at the hour of our death").[5]

Before the Tribunal of Christ

Again, Balthasar expands on the concept of judgment:

> How the Lord will judge, no one knows in advance; he tells us just one thing, namely, what he will judge about: "I was hungry, and you gave me food (or you gave me no food)." Me, in the least of my brethren. Have we shown mercy, or only loved ourselves? Once the documents have been presented, there is no longer any need at all to pronounce the verdict: "I will condemn you out of your own mouth, you wicked servant!" (Lk 19:22). "Should not you have had mercy on your fellow servant, as I had mercy on you?" (Mt 18:33). "Judgment is without mercy to one who has shown no mercy; yet mercy triumphs over judgment" (James 12:13).
>
> Where will we stand, left or right? From what we know of ourselves, we can assume: most probably, on both sides. Much in us will appear to us ourselves, and especially to the Judge, as worthy of damnation; it belongs in the fire. That not everything in us was reprehensible, that we have not, our whole life long, from childhood on, said only no to love, is something that we might hope for from the grace of the Judge. Should it be fully in vain that he "died for us"?[6]

Ending Self-Delusion

The individual human being will be confronted, after his death, with unveiled truth and the demands of God on the creatures

5. Hans Urs von Balthasar, *Credo: Meditations on the Apostles' Creed* (San Francisco: Ignatius Press, 2000), 65–66.

6. Balthasar, *Credo*, 66–67.

made in his image. This is the frightening dimension of judgment—the greater the love God has offered and demonstrated for man, the more that is expected of him in return, in his response to such love. Adrienne von Speyr addressed this issue: "The greater a man's intimacy with the Lord, the greater the danger that he will become estranged." If a person withdraws from the Son's judgment of love, "the Father has no other course but to replace love with judgment and sentence."[7] Hans Urs von Balthasar wrote:

> As long as man lives in the carapace of his senses, he can lull himself to sleep with ever-new illusions as to the extent of his guilt; indeed, sin's mendacious nature absolutely requires this kind of self-concealment and constant self-justification. Once he is released, however, from this outer shell, it is no longer possible to deceive himself; man "sees himself: he sees who he was and what he has become. . . . The scales fall from his eyes." Of course "the light that enables us to see all this does not come from ourselves" but from "the decisive encounter with the living God," with the light of truth that streams from him. Origen was the first to describe the Judgment as the radiance of the light of Christ, so that "not only no righteous man but no sinner either will be able to mistake the nature of Christ"; even sinners "will recognize their evil deeds in the light of his countenance." For the light of his divinity will illuminate everything with far more clarity than faith—even the most lively faith—can now perceive it.[8]

Man Judges Himself

Balthasar goes on:

7. Adrienne von Speyr, *Korinther I* (Einsiedeln: Johannes Verlag, 1956), 348 and 351.

8. Balthasar, *Theo-Drama*, vol. V, *The Last Act* (San Francisco: Ignatius Press, 1998), 291–92.

> Basil takes up the theme: The face of the Judge radiates a divine light that illuminates the very depths of hearts, and we shall have no other accuser but our own sins, thus made present to us. Similarly Gregory Nazianzen: Judgment is "the internal burden that weighs upon each man's conscience." Ambrose, as so often, follows Origen: The "opened books" and "judgment seats" are simply images of our own conscience, which, in the presence of Christ, "can no longer hide itself"; according to Ambrose, the sentence is nothing other than the confirmation of each person's just deserts. "Thus", says Augustine, "there is a certain divine power whereby everyone is reminded of all that he has done, good or evil. This knowledge, which either accuses or excuses the conscience, is presented to him with such inconceivable rapidity that everyone, every individual, is judged simultaneously. This divine power is called a "book" in which we read, as it were, what is set forth in it.[9]
>
> To that extent . . . judgment can be regarded as a kind of *judgment upon oneself*, albeit in the light of the divine truth, which is, as such, the truth of what God has done for mankind in Jesus Christ. It is hard to imagine that any man, faced with this standard of action that God puts before him, could so much as mention his supposedly "good works." It is precisely those who have acquired a deeper insight into the absolute nature of the divine act of love on the Cross who are forced to admit that they fall utterly short of the model presented for their imitation.[10]

The One Judgment and the Process of Purification: A New Perspective

This is true since the Scriptures make it clear that there can be only one single judgment, which includes all individual judg-

9. Balthasar, *The Last Act*, 292.
10. *The Last Act*, 292–93.

ments at the time of death. The following reflections and references are taken from the *Theo-Drama* of Hans Urs von Balthasar:

> The famous passage of St. Paul concerning God's fire, which tests every "building" raised by man, sparing every well-built building (with Christ as the foundation), but consuming all poorly-built ones, allowing man to escape (be spared) but only through fire (1 Cor 3:10–11). The image of God coming to judge by fire (Is 66:15–16) is a metaphor for the majesty of God as he reveals himself in Scripture. This image of Christ as judge is reflected in the writings of Joseph Ratzinger, saying that Christ the Judge is the eschatos, which means that it is impossible to distinguish between the Judge of the Last Day and him who judges us after our death. Stepping into the realm of his manifest reality, a man steps into his ultimate destiny and so is drawn into the eschatological fire. The transforming "moment" of this encounter is beyond the earthly calculation of time.[11]

According to Origen, it is God who makes himself a purifying fire; in Jesus Christ he stands in the stream of fire with his flaming sword, "to baptize in this stream all those who are destined for paradise after death yet still need purification." Ambrose follows Origen: "The resurrected who wish to return to paradise must face an ordeal by fire;" they must undergo the baptism of fire announced by John; they must pass the angel's fiery sword at the entrance of paradise. Only sinners, however, will be touched by it. Augustine, in a commentary on this passage in St. Paul, says that the sinner will be "saved as by fire," but "what he has possessed through the seductions of love will now be lost through burning pain."

The doctrine of purgatory has a complicated history, from its Jewish roots, in the era immediately following Christ ("Gehenna" is sometimes given a purifying dimension), early Christian intercessions for the dead, numerous

11. *The Last Act*, 360.

later patristic writings (Gregory the Great), and medieval versions (Bede, St. Patrick) that associate purgatory with the pains of hell—and the definitive teaching that comes from the twelfth century. These are some of the characteristics assigned to the doctrine of purgatory. First, there is a temporal prolongation of the Last Judgment, allowing the Pauline fire of testing (purifying) to be completed. Then there is the concept of two fires; one that purifies individuals prior to the general judgment, and the fire of judgment that will destroy the world and the dross that still remains in the righteous. With this theological development regarding judgment, then comes an increasing emphasis on the doctrine of the communion of saints, the relationship between those in heaven and those on earth, and with those currently in purgatory. And finally, there is the speculation about those in purgatory who are no longer capable of free decision, whether they can surrender themselves to purification with a certain freedom of will since they understand there is no other way for them to be prepared to be in the presence of an all-holy God.

Fire is "an essential trait of the triune God, who cannot endure anything impure, but must devour it" (cf. Heb 12:29). Right from the beginning, however, the Son has exposed himself, in love, to this fire: "In his cry of forsakenness on the Cross, he allows himself to be consumed by his Father's fire because he has gathered together in himself everything that hinders him from actively sharing in the burning of this fire." So, in passivity, he becomes fuel for the fire. In purgatory he makes us to be fuel for the fire that consumes him. . . . Unleashing this fire upon us, he is the first to plunge into it," so that "I am drawn into his fire, which is a fire of love." Properly speaking, therefore, purgatory comes into existence on Holy Saturday, when the Son walks through hell, introducing the element of mercy into the condition of those who are justly lost. Purgatory "has its origin in the Cross. The Father makes use of the fruit of the Cross in order to temper divine justice, which held the sinners captive, with

> new mercifulness. From the Cross, hope is brought down to the netherworld; from the Cross, a fire is unleashed in which justice and mercifulness are intermixed. Through the Lord's arrival there, the powers of the netherworld, of death and of evil are driven, as it were, into the back most recesses of hell, and the devil's chain is made shorter. Purgatory arises as if under the Lord's striding feet; he brings comfort to this place of hopelessness, fire to this place of iciness." It is this fire, according to Paul, that tests a man's life's work to see if it is built on the foundation of Christ; thus, the fire of testing is one with this foundation. The proven righteousness of this testing, then, is a work of love, even though, in its objectivity, the process of transformation may begin with fear and some resistance.[12]

More commentary by Hans Urs von Balthasar:

> "The Day of the Lord will disclose it" (1 Cor 3:13), not the day when, in death, we go to the Lord, but the day on which the Lord will come. It is his day because he has died for us, because his fire is the fruit of his Holy Saturday, because he planned to begin with us once we had come to the end of ourselves. Hence the testing is something that takes place between himself alone and the individual; all human works are now concentrated on the Lord: "Whatever you did—or did not do—to one of these, you did it—or did not do it—to me" (Mt 25:40,45). Purgatory is "experienced in total isolation," the soul is "essentially isolated in a kind of 'solitary confinement,' entirely taken up with God's relationship with it"; "one's fellow men play no part whatsoever in this whole process; they do not exist, and so there is no need of communication, no desire to know how they are faring in this condition." The soul is "totally preoccupied, not susceptible to any distraction." "For a moment, the communion of saints is suspended. When the time of testing has

12. *The Last Act*, 363.

come, it is impossible to have recourse to what others have done, to be carried by them. Everyone stands there in isolation. . . . Though this does not mean that prayers for the dead in purgatory are ineffectual." "The soul sees itself only in [the Lord's] mirror. . . . The one being purified does not see his neighbor and his faults at all. He is wholly occupied with God and with himself. He sees his brother only after he is so cleansed by the Lord's love that he can regard him with the Lord's eyes." "For the moment my neighbor is exclusively the Lord, I have no other. Only at the very end, before entering heaven, is one given back one's fellow man by the Lord himself, for now I can encounter him as the Lord does and as God loves him." For the present "the only necessity is to be face to face with the Lord and respond to him." It is clear that this descent from the impersonal "one" into personal being is the genuine point of departure for a new, authentic and definitive community.

Man stands before God objectified in his life's work. This is the "test material"; "in the work that is exposed to view, naked, one's confession is already made; it speaks for itself. Any light the person himself might want to shed on it, any commentary he might want to give, is too late. His confession is already objectified in his deeds." "Man's love for the Lord has now taken the form of his work, and the Lord's love for man has taken the form of fire." A man's work embodies "the thoughts and intentions of the heart" (Heb 4:12), "not only those at the hour of his death, but those of his whole life." "All sins" of this life "are intimately connected with one another." Thus, it is possible "to evaluate the difference between what was and what might have been." In this experience man is helpless and stripped: he stands "for the first time naked before the Lord" and realizes that the Lord "has always seen him naked." This gaze is now the only thing that matters. What is important is not how I love the Lord but "how he wishes to be loved."[13]

13. *The Last Act*, 365.

Justice and Grace

We all stand under the Judgment of Christ: "The Lord is my Judge" (1 Cor 4:4). The Lord died for all mankind. He shall come to judge the living and the dead. The Judge is our Savior. In his Encyclical letter *Spe salvi*, Pope Benedict XVI writes:

> Both these things—justice and grace—must be seen in their correct inner relationship. Grace does not cancel out justice. It does not make wrong into right. It is not a sponge which wipes everything away, so that whatever someone has done on earth ends up being of equal value. Dostoevsky, for example, was right to protest against this kind of Heaven and this kind of grace in his novel *The Brothers Karamazov.* Evildoers, in the end, do not sit at table at the eternal banquet beside their victims without distinction, as though nothing had happened.[14]

The ultimate judgment belongs only to God, who is love: *Deus caritas est* (1 Jn 4:16).

> The judgment of God is hope, both because it is justice and because it is grace. If it were merely grace, making all earthly things cease to matter, God would still owe us an answer to the question about justice—the crucial question that we ask of history and of God. If it were merely justice, in the end it could bring only fear to us all. The incarnation of God in Christ has so closely linked the two together—judgment and grace—that justice is firmly established: we all work out our salvation "with fear and trembling" (Phil 2:12). Nevertheless, grace allows us all to hope, and to go trustfully to meet the Judge whom we know as our "advocate," or *parakletos* (cf. 1 Jn 2:1).[15]

14. Benedict XVI, *Spe salvi*, 44.
15. *Spe salvi*, 47.

12

From Mutable to Immutable Life

Life into Death

Hans Urs von Balthasar addressed the mystery surrounding death:

> Dying is the most ordinary thing—newspapers list pages and pages of obituary and funeral notices to which no unaffected person pays any attention—and yet in an individual case it is the most incomprehensible thing because it crushes the little bit of meaning that has been arduously gathered in a lifetime and disperses it to the four winds. Where the death of a valued and beloved person makes its presence felt, all meaning of his life is put in brackets by it; the validity of this meaning is not definitive but is fragmentary at best. We see islands of meaning in an infinite sea of meaninglessness. And, the view beyond is barred to us, all peeking behind the curtain, all guesswork—spiritism, the teaching of reincarnation, and whatever else men might contrive—will not reveal the mystery. Even less so materialism; extending the chain of these fragments of meaning to the future in hope that it may someday become something whole is more than utopian. We have to content ourselves with the fragmentary, but does this not contain a contradiction: that we know of something like meaning but are unable to trace the line of it?[1]

This paradox surrounding death is, from a human perspective, unsolvable. The Second Vatican Council speaks specifically about the mystery of death:

1. Hans Urs von Balthasar, *Life Out of Death: Meditations on the Paschal Mystery* (San Francisco: Ignatius Press, 2012), 9–10.

> It is in the face of death that the riddle a human existence grows most acute. Not only is man tormented by pain and by the advancing deterioration of his body, but even more so by a dread of perpetual extinction. He rightly follows the intuition of his heart when he abhors and repudiates the utter ruin and total disappearance of his own person. He rebels against death because he bears in himself an eternal seed which cannot be reduced to sheer matter. All the endeavors of technology, though useful in the extreme, cannot calm his anxiety; for prolongation of biological life is unable to satisfy that desire for higher life which is inescapably lodged in his breast.[2]

On the Theology of Death

Cardinal Joseph Ratzinger, in his essay "On the Theology of Death" writes

> The physician and the pastor both care for the life of men. Each one, on his own level and in his own way, tries to ensure that the life of man becomes richer, fuller, more secure, that it becomes freer and happier, in a word: that it becomes to a greater extent "living." The saying in which the Lord clothed the meaning of his mission is also the expression of their commission, whose authority they acknowledge: "I came that they may have life, and have it abundantly" (Jn 10:10). But this very care for life necessarily includes an encounter with the phenomenon of death. Working for human life automatically means also coming into conflict with the reality of death. For human life is centrally marked by death. At every moment it already bears its contradiction within itself. That is why in every age man's consciousness of life has been at the

2. Vatican Council II, Pastoral Constitution *Gaudium et spes* (December 7, 1965), 18.

same time a consciousness of death also, or at least of mortality. This can be substantiated by the words of that early Father of the Church Gregory the Great: "In comparison to eternal life, temporal life should be called death rather than life. For what else is this daily exhaustion and decline than a long, drawn-out dying?" just as it can be substantiated by the medieval saying "In the midst of life we are surrounded by death" or by Heidegger's observation about man, who is cast into nothingness and must attempt to travel upon the roaring sea of nothingness armed with joy. Most impressive perhaps is the wonderfully terse formula by Claude Bernard: "La vie, c'est la mort" (Life is death). This also expresses the fundamental insight that death does not simply punctuate the conclusion of a life, which for its part would then be only life while death would remain, as it were, outside of that life and touch upon it only from outside; rather, "living" itself is "dying": dying is inherent to life, the *processus* of living is per se also the *processus* of dying into that life, so that that whole life is imbued, as it were, by death and in its movement is both a movement of living and: a movement of dying. Hence understanding human life means understanding a process of dying.

The question about death is therefore raised peremptorily by life itself. It is posed inescapably to anyone who really cares about life. And if he does not just want to care for and preserve this life externally but also tries to fill it with meaning and thus give it its true greatness and potential, then he will not be able to avoid the question about the meaning and senselessness of death. In this meditation, I would like to try to show briefly how this question about the meaning of death is answered from a Christian faith perspective. Of course, in doing so we cannot forget that questions like those about life and death can in the final analysis never be answered simply with a formula but, rather, find their true answer only in the lived appropriation of the formula. In this regard,

> everything that is merely *said* here is evidently provisional in character.[3]

Christian Meaning of Death

The Christian announcement about a death should not be a flowery eulogy. The Church recognizes the shock that every death is to loved ones. But at the same time, she announces the hope that the death and resurrection of Jesus has a bearing on each person's death—that Baptism associates us with the death and Resurrection of the Savior—and this reality fills Christians with hope. While sadness and mourning are part of our response to the death of a loved one, our faith consoles us and helps us accept this death with hope.

Therefore, a Christian does not beautify nor diminish the deep shadows that cover human existence in this world. And yet even these shadows are a sign of hope; these shadows would not exist without the light he is generating. If shadows prevail in the present, light will prevail in the future.

The Second Vatican Council addressed the mystery of death with these words:

> Although the mystery of death utterly beggars the imagination, the Church has been taught by divine revelation and firmly teaches that man has been created by God for a blissful purpose beyond the reach of earthly misery. In addition, that bodily death from which man would have been immune had he not sinned (Cf. 2 Thes 3:6–13; Eph 4:28) will be vanquished, according to the Christian faith, when man who was ruined by his own doing is restored to wholeness by an almighty and merciful Savior. For God has called man and still calls him so that with his entire being he might be

3. Ratzinger, "On the Theology of Death," in *Dogma and Preaching: Applying Christian Doctrine to Daily Life* (San Francisco: Ignatius Press, 2011), 243–54, at 243–44.

> joined to Him in an endless sharing of a divine life beyond all corruption. Christ won this victory when He rose to life, for by His death He freed man from death. Hence to every thoughtful man a solidly established faith provides the answer to his anxiety about what the future holds for him. At the same time faith gives him the power to be united in Christ with his loved ones who have already been snatched away by death; faith arouses the hope that they have found true life with God.[4]

The *Catechism of the Catholic Church* (nos. 1005–1014) states that human death is transformed into new life by Christ. We know that Jesus, the Son of God made man, suffered the death that is part of the human condition. Yet, despite his anguish as he faced death, he accepted it in an act of complete and free submission to his Father's will (Cf. Mk 14:33–34; Heb 5:7–8). The obedience of Jesus has transformed the curse of death into a blessing (cf. Rom 5:19–21).

Because of Christ, Christian death has a positive meaning: "For to me to live is Christ, and to die is gain" (Phil 1:21). "The saying is sure: if we have died with him, we will also live with him" (2 Tm 2:11). What is essentially new about Christian death is this: through Baptism, the Christian has already "died with Christ" sacramentally in order to live a new life; and if we die in Christ's grace, physical death completes this "dying with Christ," and so completes our incorporation into him in his redeeming act. Saint Ignatius of Antioch says: "It is better for me to die in Christ Jesus than to reign over the ends of the earth. Him it is I seek—who died for us. Him it is I desire—who rose for us. I am on the point of giving birth. . . . Let me receive pure light; when I shall have arrived there, then shall I be a man."[5]

In death, God calls man to himself. Therefore, the Christian can experience a desire for death like St. Paul's: "My desire is to

4. *Gaudium et spes*, 18.

5. Ignatius of Antioch, *Ad Romanos*, 6, 1–2.

depart and be with Christ" (Phil 1:23). The Christian vision of death receives privileged expression in the liturgy of the Church (Cf. 1 Thes 4:13–14): "Lord, for your faithful people life is changed, not ended. When the body of our earthly dwelling lies in death we gain an everlasting dwelling place in heaven."[6]

The Church encourages us to prepare ourselves for the hour of our death. In the Litany of the Saints, for instance, she has us pray: "From a sudden and unforeseen death, deliver us, O Lord" (*Roman Missal*, Litany of the Saints), in the Hail Mary to ask the Mother of God to intercede for us "at the hour of our death"; and to entrust ourselves to St. Joseph, the Patron of a Happy Death. In the Canticle of the Creatures, Saint Francis of Assisi says: "Praised are you, my Lord, for our sister bodily Death, from whom no living man can escape. Woe on those who will die in mortal sin! Blessed are they who will be found in your most holy will, for the second death will not harm them."

Practical Consequences

Cardinal Joseph Ratzinger summarized the response of the Church to death with these words:

> Christian preaching about death, accordingly, does not need to launch into misleading trivializations. It acknowledges the upsetting seriousness of death. Yet at the same time it can proclaim the new event that has taken place in Christ: that this same seriousness, in all its earnestness, is divine worship (seen from man's perspective) and blessing (from God's perspective), as Althaus says. Death as a whole, that is, that *processus mortis in vitam* which permeates our whole life, is as such our baptism, the gradual success of the new Adam. It is divine worship if we acknowledge therein our finitude and our unworthiness before God, our true insignificance, just as human worship of God ultimately must

6. *Roman Missal, Preface of Christian Death I.*

always be this acknowledgment of one's own lowliness and of the divine majesty. It is a grace-filled event, inasmuch as God snatches away from us our natural, self-willed, rebellious life at the tribunal of death so as to recreate us for the life of holiness and love. Basically, everything is said with the observation that death (taken in each case as a whole) is the realization of our baptism. At the same time, it becomes evident how this theology of death is connected with the innermost intentions of Christian doctrine about morality and salvation. If its core precept is to love God and neighbor as oneself, then that means precisely the radical dethroning of self, becoming free from the ego, and, thus, the spiritual movement of death: the movement of death is identical to the movement into radical love. Thus, it becomes clear that I can just as well say "All that matters in Christianity is death and Resurrection" as "All that matters in Christianity is love" or "All that matters in Christianity is the humility of faith." Viewed from within, Christianity is completely simple; it receives its wealth of content from the external multiplicity of human realities in which this one truth is proclaimed anew in each instance.

Another consequence of this Christian understanding of death, then, is the Christian attitude of the survivor. When Augustine at his mother's grave believed that he was not supposed to weep, that was not Christian but idealist thinking. From the idealist standpoint, mourning at the graveside (at least in the case of a "good" person) is in fact meaningless. Idealism means the negation of sadness. Not so Christianity: the attitude of the Christian is not the denial of sadness, and certainly not being disconsolate either (although the materialist has grounds for that), but rather consoled sadness. This means that sadness remains and has its rightful place, but it is actually at the same time consoled sadness, sadness that notwithstanding its seriousness can and should nevertheless be profoundly comforted and surpassed by consolation.

At the end of the day, this attempt at a theology of death produces a picture of the basic spiritual attitude that one

> might call the Christian man's realism. The Christian does not gloss over and deny the deep shadows that fall upon man's existence in this world. And yet these very shadows are also signs of hope for him, because he believes and, in believing, knows that they are shadows, which would not be there without the great light that casts them. And if the present belongs to the shadows, then the future is that much more in the possession of the light.[7]

Purgatory as a Possibility for the Final Purification

The Church's doctrine regarding purgatory is presented in the *Catechism of the Catholic Church* (nos. 1030–1031 and 1471). The Church gives the name purgatory to this final purification of the elect, which is entirely different from the punishment of the damned. The Church formulated her doctrine of faith on purgatory especially at the Councils of Florence and Trent. The tradition of the Church, by reference to certain texts of Scripture, speaks of a cleansing fire: "As for certain lesser faults, we must believe that, before the Final Judgment, there is a purifying fire. He who is truth says that whoever utters blasphemy against the Holy Spirit will be pardoned neither in this age nor in the age to come. From this sentence we understand that certain offenses can be forgiven in this age, but certain others in the age to come."[8]

The formula adopted by *Ecumenical Council of Trent* (1563) is the most succinct of all:

> The Catholic Church, instructed by the Holy Spirit, has, following the sacred writings and ancient tradition of the Fathers, taught in sacred Councils and very recently in this ecumenical Council, that there is a purgatory, *purgatorium*, and that the souls detained therein are aided by

7. Ratzinger, "On the Theology of Death," 253–54.
8. Gregory the Great, *Dialogues*, in PL 77:4, 39. Cf. Mt 12:31.

> the suffrages of the faithful and chiefly by the acceptance of the altar.[9]

Cardinal Joseph Ratzinger referred to this purgatorial process in his book *Eschatology: Death and Eternal Life*.[10] In it, he presented the basis for the doctrine on purgatory and its development in the Church's teaching. These are his words:

> What is the authentic heart of the doctrine of Purgatory? What is its rationale? In listening in to the patristic discussion, we had occasion to mention First Corinthians 3, 10–15. For this text, there is a foundation, Jesus Christ, on which some build with gold, silver and precious stones, and others with wood, hay and straw. What each one has in fact built will be brought to light by the Day of the Lord. It will be revealed with fire, and the fire will test what sort of work each one has done. If the work which any man has built on the foundation survives, he will receive a reward. If any man's work is burned up, he will suffer loss, though he himself will be saved, but only as through fire. . . . If one presupposes a naively objective concept of Purgatory, then of course the text is silent. But if, conversely, we hold that Purgatory is understood in a properly Christian way when it is grasped Christologically, in terms of the Lord himself as a judgment fire which transforms us and conforms us to his own glorified body (Rom 8:29; Phil 3:21), then we shall come to a very different conclusion.[11]

What is contained in the permanent Catholic doctrine on purgatory? Purgatory is an extension of the Lord himself whose burn-

9. Heinrich Denzinger et al., ed., *Compendium of Creeds, Definitions, and Declarations on Matters of Faith and Morals*, 43rd ed. (San Francisco: Ignatius Press, 2012), 1820.

10. Ratzinger, *Auferstehung und ewiges Leben*, JRGS 10 (Freiburg: Herder, 2012), 220–33.

11. Ratzinger, *Eschatology: Death and Eternal Life*, 2nd ed. (Washington, D.C.: The Catholic University of America Press, 2007), 228–29.

ing flame sets free a person's closed off heart, melting it, pouring it into a new mold that makes it worthy of an all-holy God. The transforming "moment" of the soul's encounter with its Judge cannot be quantified by the measurements of earthly time. Consequently, one's personal judgment at the time of death, and the judgment on the Last Day are indistinguishable. These are Ratzinger's words:

> The essential Christian understanding of purgatory has now become clear. Purgatory is not, as Tertullian thought, some kind of supra-worldly concentration camp where man is forced to undergo punishment in a more or less arbitrary fashion. Rather it is the inwardly necessary process of transformation in which a person becomes capable of Christ, capable of God and thus capable of unity with the whole communion of saints. Simply to look at people with any degree of realism at all is to grasp the necessity of such a process.... Man is a recipient of the divine mercy, yet this does not exonerate him from the need to be transformed. Encounter with the Lord *is* this transformation. It is the fire that burns away our dross and reforms us to be vessels of eternal joy.[12]

There is still an important issue regarding the doctrine on purgatory: praying for the departed in its many forms in the Judeo-Christian traditions. The Church Militant on earth praying for the Church Suffering in purgatory, and the Church Triumphant—the saints—praying for the other two which is the doctrine of the Communion of Saints. Joseph Ratzinger quotes Hans Urs von Balthasar here:

> The intercession of the saints with the Judge is not . . . some purely external affair whose success is necessarily doubtful since it depends on the unpredictable benevolence of the Judge. It is above all an inner weight which, placed on the scales, can bring them to sink down. This intercession is the

12. *Eschatology*, 229–30.

> one truly fundamental element in their "judging." Through their exercising of such judgment they belong, as people who both pray and save, to the doctrine of Purgatory and to the Christian practice which goes with it. As Charles Péguy so beautifully put it, "J'espère en toi pour moi"—"I hope in you for me."[13]

This brings us to an important truth in Catholic theology: that self-substitutional love (the sharing of the love in one's heart with another) is central to Christian unity. This means that the possibility of helping others does not cease to exist when one dies. The capacity to love, which is our Christian duty, stretches beyond the grave to embrace to the Communion of Saints on both sides of death's portals. This capacity to love beyond the grave is basic (primordial datum) to the Church's tradition in both East and West, and it was never questioned until the Reformation's rejection of the development of doctrine in the Catholic Church.

Encountering Infinite Love

The Apostle Paul's hymn of love claims that "love never fails" (1 Cor 13:8). Every genuine love somehow requires an eternal dimension. The philosopher Gabriel Marcel wrote, "To love a being means to say to him: 'Yourself, you will not die!'"[14] Joseph Ratzinger added these thoughts: "All love wants eternity, and Gods love not only wants it but effects it and is it."[15]

13. *Eschatology*, 232.

14. Gabriel Marcel, *Trois pieces: Le regard neuf, Le mort de demain et La chapelle ardente* (Paris: Plon, 1931), 161: "Aimer un être, c'est lui dire: Toi, tu ne mourras pas." See also David S. Crawford, "The Gospel of Life and the Integrity of Death," *Communio: International Catholic Review* 39, no. 3 (2012): 364–80; Romano Guardini, *Die letzten Dinge* (Kevelaer: Topos plus Taschenbuch, 2008), 46. Ludwig Gerhard Müller, "Fegefeuer," in *Lexikon für Theologie und Kirche*, vol. 3 (Freiburg: Herder, 2009), 1204–1210.

15. Ratzinger, *Introduction to Christianity* (San Francisco: Ignatius Press, 1990), 271.

Servant of God Anton Strle, whose life and work are presented at the end of this book, affirmed: “I believe in Purgatory. I will go to Purgatory for a while.” In his first will, written on January 1, 1947, he wrote: “The funeral should be simple. I rather prefer no fame, less of Purgatory, and more joy at God.” Anton Strle said that he might be scared of God, who is Love, even at the time of his death:

> I came to Jesus of Nazareth and come again and again to the conviction that God is by nature love. But I know that in me there is full of what is not in harmony with God’s love. “There is no fear in love, but perfect love casts out fear” (1 John 4:18). But I have not completed myself in love. So I never feel safe in myself. Thus I am inclined not to condemn people who reject what is absolutely clear to me—that, as the ultimate foundation and goal of all, is the incomprehensible secret of love that goes beyond all knowledge (cf. Eph 3:19). Furthermore I am not inclined to rely on emotions, adventures and experiences, as if this could be the last foundation. Perhaps, even at the time of death, I will feel the fear of God who is Love. But I firmly hope that grace will also then be granted to me, a grace—an undeserved gift—to lean on the Heart of Jesus of Nazareth, who was trembling in the deadly fear on the Mount of Olives, and I will be able to say with him: “It is completed! Alleluia!”[16]

Hans Urs von Balthasar addressed the unspeakable wealth that will be ours, the eternal life that we will have with the triune God:

> We believe in the life everlasting without being able to foresee what it will be. . . . For anyone who is permitted to step

16. Anton Strle, “Kaj mi pomeni Jezus iz Nazareta?” [What does Jesus of Nazareth mean to me?], *Communio: Mednarodna katoliška revija* 30, no. 4 (2020): 299–324, at 301. Originally published in Družina on November 24, 1974; Anton Strle, *Živo upanje: Velikonočna skrivnost* [Living Hope: Paschal Mystery], (Ljubljana: Družina, 1990).

out of his or her own narrow and finalized life, and into this life of God, it seems as if vast spaces are opened up before one, taking one's breath away. Spaces into which one could hurl oneself in uttermost freedom, and these spaces are themselves freedoms that entice our love, accept it, and respond to it. Who, while still here below, could penetrate to the ground of another freedom? Impossible! Thus, in the communion of saints in God, the adventures of creative, imaginative love are intensified beyond all counting. Life in God becomes an absolute miracle. Nothing is given in a concluding way, the act of giving goes on unfolding boundlessly. The heavenly are therefore always ready to help in cases of earthly need—certainly through eternal, perhaps also through temporal, gifts—so as to rekindle our courage to strive, despite everything, toward the life everlasting, and to grant us a foretaste of that which awaits us. And if we are given to suffer, deeper shafts are sunk in us than we thought we could contain, depths destined to become, in the life everlasting, reservoirs of greater happiness, wells still more productive. Wells that flow forth of themselves, gratis; for in the life everlasting, all is gratis. The words "without money," "for no payment," when it is a matter of God's gifts, run through the whole of the Bible (Is 55:1; Sir 51:25; Mt 10:8; Rev 21:6; 22:17). This "gratis" is the innermost essence of divine love, which has no other ground than itself; and by it, everything that exists in eternal life with God is determined. And precisely because this love is without any ground, its depths cannot be plumbed; one never gets to the bottom of it, it remains deeper than anything that can be grounded or "put into concepts." Hence, Paul quite accurately says: "Know the love . . . which surpasses knowledge, in order to be filled with all the fullness of God" (Eph 3:19).[17]

17. Balthasar, *Credo: Meditations on the Apostles' Creed* (San Francisco: Ignatius Press, 2000), 95–97.

13

"In God I Trust"

SERVANT OF GOD ARCHBISHOP ANTON VOVK

The Life of Archbishop Anton Vovk

Anton Vovk was born on May 19, 1900, in Vrba (Gorenjska), in the same room where his famous great-uncle France Prešeren (1800), the most renowned of all Slovenian poets, was born. He attended school in both Breznica and Kranj, where he completed the first six years in grammar school. His parents died early—his father before Anton was four years old, and his mother when he was seventeen. In the autumn of 1917, he entered the minor seminary of Škofovi zavodi (St. Stanislaus Institute) in Šentvid near Ljubljana. He completed his secondary school exams there in 1919 and then entered the seminary in Ljubljana. He was ordained a priest for the diocese on June 29, 1923.

Anton Vovk spent his first three years of priesthood as an assistant pastor in Metlika. He was appointed associate pastor at Tržič in 1926 before becoming the pastor there in 1928. He inherited a large parish financial debt but succeeded in paying it off in a relatively short time. The stress, however, caused him some health problems that would remain with him throughout his life. As pastor of the parish, he was able to respond well to the pastoral, cultural, spiritual, and social needs of his people. He renovated the parish church, other parish buildings and published a monthly "Church Herald," which was recognized throughout the whole diocese. Because of the way he was able to manage the parish of Tržič, he was appointed diocesan spiritual councilor on June 6, 1936.

One year before the outbreak of the Second World War, on April 15, 1940, Anton Vovk was appointed cathedral dean in

Ljubljana. It was rumored that he would eventually become rector of the new Baraga seminary. The outbreak of the war, however, changed these plans and Vovk became president of the diocesan committee assisting refugee priests. A large number of priests were forced into the Ljubljana province, or simply fled there, from territories which had been occupied by Nazi German forces (Štajerska and Gorenjska). The committee tried to provide shelter for these priests and take care of their other needs. This became a difficult task because of war-time conditions. On July 26, 1944, Vovk was also appointed rector of the seminary.

At the beginning of the war, Bishop Gregorij Rožman had appointed a group of vicars general to be charged with managing the diocese in case anything should happen to him. Vovk was the last name on this list of new vicars general. But as it turned out, at the end of the war and with the arrest of Vicar General Ignacij Nadrah, Anton Vovk was given the responsibility of leading the Ljubljana diocese. On June 15, 1945, at a time that was particularly difficult for the Church in Slovenia, Anton Vovk became vicar general of the diocese, or "the poor general" as he called himself. A year later, the papal nuncio to Yugoslavia, Archbishop Joseph Patrick Hurley, asked Father Vovk on behalf of the Holy Father if he was willing to become Ljubljana's auxiliary bishop. This is what Vovk wrote about the request:

> I could not believe it. I had been asked to do something which (God is my witness) I had never before considered in my life and for which I had never prepared myself. I asked for half an hour to think it over. When I emerged from the room, overwhelmed, I headed off to the cathedral and to the altar of Our Lady of Perpetual Help from Brezje to make my decision there. I had never knelt before the picture of Our Lady of Perpetual Help with a greater matter in my heart. How good it had been, when so many times as a schoolboy I made the pilgrimage on foot all the way from Vrba to Brezje. In the summer I went almost every Sunday, strengthening my vocation there in the presence of Our Lady.

> Together with Mary, I prayed that God's will and the will of the Church might be fulfilled.[1]

For his bishop's motto, Vovk chose the words "*In Domino Confido*" (I trust in the Lord), and it was this very trust that helped him to guide the diocese of Ljubljana wisely through times of great tribulation. Due to the new territorial divisions between geographical areas, Vovk became responsible for the apostolic administration of the Slovenian parts of the dioceses of Reka (from 1951 to 1961) and Trieste-Koper (from 1951 to 1955).

As Bishop of Ljubljana, Anton Vovk faced serious opposition by the new government. When communist authorities learned about the appointment of Anton Vovk as auxiliary bishop, they immediately made it clear to him that they would not recognize him either as a bishop or as vicar general, and that he should prepare himself to face considerable opposition. This was the only promise that the Communists faithfully fulfilled all the years that he was bishop. Vovk found himself, first as vicar general, then as auxiliary bishop, as apostolic administrator, bishop, and finally as Archbishop of Ljubljana in difficult times that were unprecedented in the history of the archdiocese. The new "people's government" had, through revolution, created a new social order over which it had complete control. The Communist regime repudiated all political structures that existed prior to 1941. The Catholic Church was the only institution which managed to maintain a degree of autonomy in the new order, so it stood as the sole alternative to the Communist party structure. Communist leaders were aware of the Church's moral authority and would do anything it took to break it apart.

At the end of the war, nearly 300 priests and consecrated men had departed Slovenia—185 of them from the Diocese of Ljubljana

1. Anton Vovk, *V spomin in opomin: Osebni zapisi škofa Antona Vovka od 1945 do 1953* [For remembrance and warning: Personal records of Bishop Anton Vovk from 1945 to 1953], ed. Blaž Otrin (Ljubljana: Družina, 2003), 91, 92.

alone. Some were executed without trial. The government jailed priests on a regular basis, many with lengthy prison sentences. In May of 1945, there were 50 priests in prison. By 1961, 429 priests had been charged in court—339 of them received prison sentences, many of them with multiple sentences. Nine priests were condemned to death; four of these sentences were eventually carried out.[2]

The Political Persecution of the Church

The Communist government continued to find new ways of undermining the Church in Slovenia. It planned a long process of "de-christianizing" the Slovenian people, or as Matija Maček said: "The ideological battle against religious prejudices will be long and hard and will be particularly difficult here because the Slovenians are the most religious nation, so it will take us generations to accomplish this."[3] The agrarian reform and the process of nationalization deprived the Church of all its material resources. Most of her social, cultural, and educational activities were discontinued since the state monopolized all these fields. Religious gatherings were banned, printed materials were confiscated, and religious processions were obstructed. Only the most basic religious practice was tolerated, accompanied by strict control and constant obstruction by government officials. Only one seminary for training priests was allowed to remain open, one small Catholic newspaper, the *Oznanilo* (Announcement), was permitted to continue publication, and everything was done

2. Tamara Griesser-Pečar, *Boj proti veri in Cerkvi (1945–1961): Razstava, September 5–December 2, 2007; Muzej novejše zgodovine Slovenije* [Fighting against religion and the Church (1945–1961): Exhibition, September 5–December 2, 2007; National Museum of Contemporary History], (Ljubljana: Družina, 2007), 19.

3. Matija Maček, *Zapisniki politbiroja CK KPS/ZKS 1945–1954* [The records of Politburo Central Committee of the Communist Party of Slovenia 1945–1954], ed. Darinka Drnovšek, Arhivsko društvo Slovenije, Viri 15 (Ljubljana: Darinka Drnovšek, 2000), 66.

to interrupt any kind of religious education. After World War II, the Communist authorities allowed some religious education in schools where they had control, but in 1952 they banished all religious instruction in all the schools of Slovenia. One of the aftermaths of the Communist regime is that religious education continues to be excluded from Slovenian schools to this day.

Immediately after the war, the so-called "consent" regulation was instituted by the government. It was a measure by which every priest who had not served in his parish during the war could either be permitted to return to the parish or be prohibited from doing so. Later, this rule was extended to cover the annual transferrals of priests and even the assignment of newly ordained priests. This policy, which was used by the government to control the appointment of priests, was enforced until 1952. Even though there was no written law on the books, this policy was simply used by authorities to control priests in Slovenia.

The impoverishment of the Church in Slovenia was made even worse by additional government restrictions. In 1946, the so-called government of the People's Republic of Slovenia prohibited priests from collecting money in churches, which was the only source of income for the Church in some rural parishes. Every year, voluntary donations by people to the Church became more problematic. Between 1949 and 1953, everyone who donated to the Church had to obtain special permission from local authorities, and then they could only give their donations to priests who were members of the Association of Catholic Priests of Sts. Cyril and Methodius which had been set up by the Communist government. Any special collections, for example for the seminary, were completely forbidden. And then the government allowed the taxation of income from religious ceremonies on an arbitrary basis by local authorities, even baptisms, for which no stipend had ever been required. Individual priests were required to pay sales tax on everything that was purchased. By 1955, the taxes imposed on the Diocese of Ljubljana were so great that the bishop was not able to pay them. Consequently, in 1955, the state confiscated the diocesan manor in Goričane and 10 hectares of land (24.7 acres), under the pretext of agrarian reform.[4]

Abuse and Attacks on Archbishop Vovk

Archbishop Vovk, as leader of the Church in Slovenia, was subject to constant harassment and brutality by Communist leaders. There was a variety of continual pressures placed on him, mostly by the Communist Party's secret revolutionary police—the so-called State Security (UDV). Their tactics included frequent interrogation of the archbishop, their presence at all Confirmation conferrals and parish visitations, incessant analysis of his sermons, and the interrogation and abuse of priests and lay people who were supportive of the archbishop. Government agents wrote reports on his activities each day, recording with whom he had spoken and what his opinions were on various matters. They conducted regular searches of the archbishop's office, looking through all his incoming and outgoing mail. And finally, they made several attempts on his life, culminating with the awful assault on January 20, 1952, in which Archbishop Vovk was attacked by a mob and set on fire in Novo Mesto.

During his time as leader of the Ljubljana Diocese, Archbishop Vovk was interrogated by the UDV at least 90 times. He accepted these interrogations patiently, recognizing them as an evil imposed by the Communist government. But at the same time, he retained his personal dignity and maintained his principles and values despite extreme pressure for him to renounce them. In the course of these interrogations, Vovk was brutally bullied, humiliated, and

4. Tamara Griesser-Pečar, *Boj proti veri in cerkvi (1945–1961)*, 45–47. Anton Vovk, *V spomin in opomin*, 180, 246. "Zapisnik o razgovoru med Antonom Vovkom in presednikom KOVS Borisom Kocijančičem" [Protocol of the discussion between Anton Vovk and President Boris Kocijančič], Arhiv Republike Slovenije [Archive of the Republic Slovenia] (SI AS) 1211, Komisija za odnose z verskimi skupnostmi [Commission for Relations with Religious Communities of Slovenia], box nr. 108, June 10, 1955.

insulted. The interrogations were carried out by committed Communists such as Mitja Ribičič and Zdenko Roter. He was interrogated throughout his tenure as bishop, at various locations, at all times of the night and day—even when he was sick in bed.

The contents of these interrogations of the Archbishop have been published. A detailed examination reveals that the most common subjects until 1952, when relations between Yugoslavia and the Holy See were severed, were about the Papal Nuncio or the Vatican. The Archbishop was constantly questioned about his relationship with the Nuncio, his whereabouts, what they had discussed together, what instructions he had been given, what information that he had shared with the Nuncio, and what kind of secret network the Church had set up in Slovenia. The UDV tried to force the Archbishop to allow the Church in Slovenia to become independent of the Vatican, but they soon realized they were not going to convince him to do such a thing. Consequently, they urged him to be as "patriotic" as he could be regarding the Yugoslav state. When they failed to make him a puppet for the government, they began to try to convince him that his attitude of noncompliance would incur the disapproval of the Vatican, which they told him was uneasy with bishops who had strained relationships with civil authorities. Since he refused to cooperate with the UDV and Communist leaders, they considered Vovk to be working "against the people" which would cause harm, of course, to the faith of the people. Because of his "obstinacy" and failure to comply with their wishes, the UDV accused the Archbishop of supporting a US-Vatican policy against Communism, of being a lackey of Dr Anton Korošec and Marko Natlačen, and therefore a reactionary leader against the state. This made him an unpatriotic Slovenian.

At times the pressure on the Archbishop became extremely intense. During an interrogation on August 4, 1949, they tried to persuade him to steal the Nuncio's briefcase, cooperate with them in doing so, or at least allow somebody from the UDV to be secretly present at a meeting between the Archbishop and the Nuncio. In October 1952, the Archbishop was interrogated while seriously ill in bed, and they tried to gain information from him in this condition. Interest in the relationship between the Archbishop and the Holy See quieted in 1952 but resurfaced in 1958 when Archbishop Vovk travelled to Rome to see the pope.

The interrogations of the Archbishop often included malicious forms of extortion, offering him various privileges, and above all promising to release imprisoned priests. Because the Archbishop remained steadfast in his loyalty to Christ and to the Church, officials continued to punish him and put further pressure on him by imprisoning priests that were close to him, as well as seminarians. For example, on December 23, 1948, when he did not consent to their demands, the UDV interrogators replied: "As a consequence you will find out tomorrow the priests who are put into prison because you would not fulfill our demands."[5] That same night, they arrested, jailed, and sentenced the Archbishop's secretary, Božidar Slapšak, to six-and-a half years in prison. He had just recently been released from prison. They imprisoned the dean of St. Nicholas Cathedral, Franc Kimovec, for one year. The Archbishop simply replied to his interrogators: "I do not know why you do not put me in prison if I am really to blame for all these priests being in jail. Here I am, take me." To this, UDV officials gave him a cynical response: "We know that you would like to be put into prison. That would please the Nuncio and the Vatican, who would write all about it and explain the reason another bishop had been locked up in Slovenia. We do not wish to give the Nuncio and the Vatican this pleasure. Just be aware of the consequences of your own deeds."[6]

Psychological Pressure on the Archbishop and Attempts on His Life

Psychological pressures on the Archbishop were unrelenting, but he was also the target of assassination attempts and physical

5. Vovk, *V spomin in opomin*, 417.
6. Vovk, 418.

attacks. At the Confirmation ceremony in Kočevje in May of 1947, the authorities stopped all public transport so that people from the surrounding villages would not be able to attend the ceremony. They also cut off water and electricity, prohibited the sale of food and drinks, and slashed all four tires on the car the bishop was using to travel. In August 1947 he went to the spa Dolenjske Toplice for treatment of rheumatism which he had suffered since taking over leadership of the diocese. The UDV organized protests in front of the parish house where the Archbishop was staying. The demonstrators, who were either hired or forced to participate, smashed the windows of the parish house and broke into the rectory to attack the Archbishop. However, his firm and self-confident manner bewildered them to such an extent that they simply turned around and left. At the Confirmation in Škofja Loka in May 1951, the UDV gave someone a bottle and instructed them to pour it into the soup which the Archbishop was going to eat. The order was not carried out, but it was later discovered that the bottle had contained a harmful mixture of castor oil and old oil. In June 1951, a hired mob smashed the ground floor of the parish house at Bled where the Archbishop was spending the night. At the time of Confirmations and visitations, parish priests were always interrogated and often locked up, their people were intimidated in various ways, and the ceremonies were always obstructed in some way by Communist officials. For example, the tall "maypoles" set up for religious ceremonies were cut down, protests were organized, churches were sometimes smeared with feces and hateful graffiti, and disruptions were arranged on the day of the ceremony.

Archbishop Vovk is Attacked and Set on Fire

The culmination of violence toward Archbishop Vovk took place in Novo Mesto, January 20, 1952, when he was attacked and set on fire by a mob. He had taken the train from Ljubljana to Novo Mesto with several people and was to bless the renovated organ in the parish of Stopiče. While they were passing through a tunnel en route to Novo Mesto, somebody poured a foul-smelling fatty liquid over him.

When the train arrived at Novo Mesto, the Archbishop exited the train together with his escort. A crowd of protesters had gathered at the station; they began to insult the Archbishop and physically attack him. The wild mob forced him back into the railroad car and surrounded him. Accompanied by shouts of "Let's kill the devil!" somebody poured oil on him and set him on fire. The Archbishop's coat began to burn with a strong blue flame that seriously burned his face. While the Archbishop struggled to douse the flames, the crowd shouted: "Burn, devil, burn! Let the devil die!" He threw off his burning coat and extinguished the burning celluloid collar which had caused him serious burns. He was left with an ugly scar on his neck that remained for the rest of his life. It was a visible sign of his persecution.

A policeman then stepped into the car and told the Archbishop to go to the station waiting room, promising to protect him from the mob. But his suffering continued when the crowd forced the exhausted Archbishop to stand on a table while they mocked him. An hour-and-a-half after the train had arrived at the station, the UDV arrived, promised to protect him from the crowd, and told the Archbishop to get back on the train. The demonstrators then blocked the arrival of a doctor and tried to block the automobile in which the Archbishop was to be transported to the local hospital. He received only basic care there so that he could return to Ljubljana by train to receive proper medical care. The Archbishop had spent a total of four-and-a-half hours in Novo Mesto and in all this time, neither the police nor the representatives of the UDV did anything to control the enraged mob. And the persecution did not end there. When the Archbishop was being treated in hospital for his burns, which were so severe that he was at times in a semi-conscious state, the UDV used this opportunity to interrogate him twice.

The authorities tried to portray the incident to the public as an unpleasant event perpetrated by a multitude of patriots, for whom the Archbishop represented all the evil which they had suffered at the hands of occupying armies and local traitors. However, the course of events that day in Novo Mesto, and the preserved archive documents of the Communist Party, indicate very clearly that the incident was carefully organized by the Party in cooperation with the UDV. Those who had directly participated in the attack on the Archbishop were never punished. In fact, later documents indicated that they were rewarded by the authorities for their action against the Archbishop.

Archbishop Vovk's Love for His Priests

Anton Vovk showed great concern and love for his priests. He was always anxious to welcome them, talk with them, visit them, and encourage them. Many times, he interceded with the authorities, the UDV, and the Religious Commission for Priests, even though most of the time it was in vain. In his spiritual testament, he wrote:

> I am sorry that I cannot ordain these new priests today. I pray that they will be good. Keep them, Lord, and bless all our priests! I love them very much because they belong to the Lord and work and suffer for him. I am very sorry if ever I was a little hard on any of them. Truly, it was only a consequence of all the hardship and my exhausted nerves. I was always happy to forgive straight away, to forget everything, and I ask the same of all my dear fellow priests.[7]

Archbishop Vovk also showed great concern for members of religious orders, since many of them were expelled from Slovenia and were also persecuted. His care and concern for religious was manifested by his action on the last day of his life, when he sent a get-well note and some peaches to a religious sister who was ill in the hospital.

7. Anton Vovk, "Duhovna oporoka [Spiritual last will]," Nadškofijski arhiv Ljubljana [Archive of Arcidocese Ljubljana] (NŠAL) 333, box nr. 1, June 29, 1963.

A major source of suffering for Vovk was the Association of Catholic Priests of Sts Cyril and Methodius (CMD) which was founded and run by Communist authorities. Its aim was to set up divisions in the Church at all levels: between the priests and prelates, between the ordinary and the "patriotic" clergy, between other bishops in Yugoslavia and those in Slovenia. It was a tool of the government's divide-and-conquer strategy. Archbishop Vovk, however, was able to foil the government plan thanks to his wise leadership. He refused to accept the existence of any association which was setup by the Communist authorities to be independent of Church leadership. However, he imposed no sanctions against the Slovenian priests who joined the association because he knew the pressure exerted on them, the worst in all of Yugoslavia.

The Archbishop suffered coercion and criticism from both state authorities and from certain church circles. At UDV interrogations, he was repeatedly the target of forceful attempts to make him convince priests that they should join the Communist "liberation front" and later the CMD; that he should recognize their rules, and that the CMD should become the official association of priests for Slovenia. His refusal to fulfill their demands meant that the priests who were close to him were imprisoned for years on end. On the other hand, he was reproached by some Slovenian émigré priests and called the "red bishop," because of his frequent contact (forced) with Communist authorities. He also experienced some conflict with a few Croatian bishops who did not comprehend his situation. At the bishops' conferences for Yugoslavia, he had to defend himself frequently against certain Croatian bishops, who did not understand his refusal to cooperate with government officials. At one time, the matter was referred to the Vatican.

Pope John XXIII and Archbishop Anton Vovk

Following the death of Bishop Gregorij Rožman, Anton Vovk was named the presiding bishop in Ljubljana on November 26, 1959.

Two months later, he finally received from government authorities all the necessary papers to allow him to travel to Rome. For the first time since the conclusion of the Second World War, he went to visit the tombs of the apostles Peter and Paul (the *ad limina* visit), and to meet with the Holy Father, Pope John XXIII, on February 1, 1960. Bishop Vovk apologized to the Pope, saying that his illness prevented him from genuflecting before him, but the Pope replied: "I should kneel before you." Bishop Vovk left a deep impression on many of the people he met every time he visited Rome. Many recognized him as a contemporary martyr. Pope John XXIII reestablished the Diocese of Ljubljana as an Archdiocese on its 500th anniversary, December 22, 1961, and Bishop Anton Vovk became the first Archbishop of Ljubljana.

Trust in the Lord Was His Strength

Despite all his troubles, Vovk remained remarkably happy as a bishop. He was very popular with his people, who responded well to his charismatic nature and his robust physical appearance. They saw in him a true spiritual shepherd and a defender of the faith. His sermons gave people a sense of hope and courage. With his deep voice, Vovk had no trouble in commanding any venue. He liked to attend popular ceremonies, where he gained new strength and encouragement despite suffering serious illness. In 1957 he wrote:

> I have never fallen unconscious and in summer I can survive two Confirmation ceremonies in one day. I must say that I am a unique kind of healthy sick person who is not thwarted in his work by illness and even looks well. For as long as God wishes it to be so![8]

8. "Pismo Antona Vovka Antonu Prešernu" [the letter of Anton Vovk to Anton Prešern], Zapuščina Anton Vovk [Legacy of Anton Vovk], NŠAL 333, box nr. 15, Ljubljana, January 1957.

The Archbishop was concerned about the condition of churches throughout the archdiocese. He worked to improve the aesthetic appearance of churches despite the weak financial condition of parishes; he kept drawing attention of the people to the need for repair and renovation of churches.

He was surely a product of Gorenjska: firm, proud, unwavering, and direct, but also easygoing and humorous at times. There are many anecdotes about his humor, and he was able to remain cheerful even when his adversaries caused him heartaches. For example, when the authorities forbade him to travel to a Confirmation by car, he travelled in a horse-drawn carriage with a broad smile on his face. He was full of inner peace!

Even though mentally and spiritually the Archbishop was able to sustain the many pressures to which he was subjected, his health gradually weakened. Soon after he took charge of the diocese, he began to suffer from rheumatism and diabetes. These became particularly severe after he was set on fire in Novo Mesto. When, in 1948, he was diagnosed with diabetes he said: "There's not really going to be time for illness! But I accept this cross too." His blood-sugar level was so high—between 320 and 345 milligrams (the normal level is around 120), which should have caused him serious damage and even episodes of unconsciousness. He died of the illness on July 7, 1963, following a period of serious illness and was buried, according to his wishes, in the priests' section at the Žale cemetery in Ljubljana.

Anton Vovk suffered almost constantly from the very first day he became responsible for the Diocese of Ljubljana. Until the end of his life, he was a faithful witness to Christ's gospel, in the spirit of his bishop's motto: "In God I trust." He was a martyr in the true sense of the word, even before he was set on fire in Novo Mesto on January 20, 1952. The diocesan procedure for his beatification was completed in Ljubljana on October 12, 2007. All the documentation was handed over to the Congregation for the Causes of Saints in Rome on October 26, 2007.

14

"God in All Things"

SERVANT OF GOD ANTON STRLE

Anton Strle (1915–2003), prelate and professor in Slovenia, was considered by the people who knew him to be an exceptional person and priest. The process for his beatification began in April 2014 supported by Pope Benedict XVI. Strle demonstrated by his life and scholarship what it meant to do theology on one's knees. This short presentation consists of three parts: a brief biography; Strle's accomplishments as an academic and professor of theology; Strle's importance in the development of theology as a recognized discipline in Slovenia.

The Life of Dr. Strle

From the very beginning of his ministry, Anton Strle was considered to be a holy person.[1] For his first Mass, celebrated July 13, 1941, at the beginning of World War II, he chose as his motto "God in all things." He remained faithful to this motto his whole life.

Strle's father died in 1921, his mother in 1932. He completed primary education in the village of Sveti Vid, an hour's walk from his home. Despite the financial situation of his family, his mother took his primary teacher's advice and sent Anton to grammar school in Šentvid near Ljubljana. In the autumn of 1930, he joined the Institute of St. Stanislaus where he passed his final exams in 1936. He then decided to enter the seminary for the diocese. As a fifth-year seminarian, he was appointed prefect of the Marijanisce

1. For some of my writings on Prof. dr. Anton Strle, see the section of the bibliography, "Writings of Anton Štrukelj concerning Anton Strle."

boarding school. He prepared for his priestly ordination during his time at the boarding school and was ordained in 1941 at the Ljubljana cathedral. Strle was appointed curate at the cathedral. In 1942, he was asked to resume the role of prefect at the Marijanisce boarding school. The diocese also asked him to begin writing his doctoral thesis and to prepare for his final examination, which he passed before Christmas 1943. A few days later, he successfully defended his thesis entitled "The Natural Yearning for a Supernatural End according to the Teaching of St. Thomas Aquinas."

At this time, the leadership of the Catholic Action movement offered Anton material with which he could write a biography of the late Alojzij Grozde, who had been a prominent member of the movement, and whose life was an example of a fervent and faithful faith. Strle was persuaded to write a booklet about Grozde in 1944. For this biography, he spent five years in government prison. The martyr Grozde was beatified in 2010 for his heroic life and death.[2]

In the fall of 1944, Strle was appointed teacher of catechism at the grammar school in Novo Mesto. In early May 1945, he made his way to Ljubljana with several lay people, but near Zalog/Črnuče reports of the bombing of Ljubljana forced the group toward Gorenjska and Carinthia. There, Anton Strle was arrested by the Liberation Army and taken to the former Institute of St. Stanislaus. He was released without trial. On July 18 of that year, Strle was named curate of St. Peter parish in Ljubljana.[3] In the spring of 1946, he was also appointed catechist at the Ledina primary school where he taught until the end of the 1946–1947

2. Alojzij Hribšek, *Blessed Aloysius Grozde: A Teenage Witness for Christ the King* (Ljubljana: Družina, 2012).

3. A confirmation from the headquarters of the POW camp at Št. Vid near Ljubljana wrote: "We confirm that comrade Strle Anton! Born _____ is released on 18.7.1945 by OZNA (security agency) of Ljubljana from the Šentvid camp and must report to the relevant headquarters." Two signatures, undated. This confirmation is in Strle's archive.

school year. In December 1946 he was named curate at the cathedral of Ljubljana.

On July 26, 1947, Anton Strle was arrested by the Communist Yugoslav government and spent two months in custody before being sentenced to five years in prison and three additional years without any civil rights. He was accused of giving moral support to a member of the girl's branch of Catholic Action, and because some of his sermons condemned servile work on Sundays. (The government claimed this undermined their five-year plan of development for the country). He was in prison until July 26, 1952.[4] Sixty-one years later, on June 6, 2013, the Slovenian Supreme Court ruled the following:

> The request for protection for legality is granted and the contested verdict concerning the convicted Anton Strle is changed so that Anton Strle, son of Jože and Ivana (née Intihar) born January 21, 1915 in Osredek near Cerknica, priest, who died October 20, 2003 is acquitted for reasons set forth in point 1 of Law 358 of the Criminal Procedure Act.[5]

The Faculty of Theology (cofounder of the University of Ljubljana in 1919) was expelled from the University by the

4. The official confirmation of the KPD in Ljubljana from July 26, 1952, wrote: "The undersigned administration confirms that com. Anton Strle, born 20. [mistake!] 1. 1915 in Osredek Št. Vid nad Cerknico, living at Lj. Dolničarjeva 2 in the prison here from 1. 9. 1947 until 26. 7. 1952 when a warrant issued by . . . III. [illegible word at the dots] allowed him to be set free. Strle was convicted by the Novo Mesto district court on 1. 9. 1947 to a prison sentence of 5 years with limited civil rights. S.F.— S.N.! Warden: Oblak Ivan[?]" Confirmation on the reverse side: "After completing the sentence, Anton Strle reported at this administration, Ljubljana on 29.6.1952. S. f.—s. n.! Referent . . . [illegible]."

5. Supreme Court of the Republic of Slovenia, Verdict in the name of the people (I Ips 188/2013), Ljubljana, June 6, 2013, Minute-taker Ines Hiter, l.r., President of the senate: Branko Masleša, l.r. (page 7).—See Tamara Griesser-Pečar, "*Anton Strle v zaporu in pred sodiščem*" [Anton Strle in prison and before the court], Lecture at the Strle symposium at the Faculty of Theology in Ljubljana, April 22, 2015, *Communio: Mednarodna katoliška revija* 25, no. 2 (2015): 162–73.

Communist government by a documented dated June 31, 1952 (a nonexistent date, but a valid document!). The Faculty continued its mission as a separate ecclesiastical institution. Then, in 1992, the Faculty of Theology was reinstituted as a full member of the University.

After his release from prison in 1952, Strle was sent to the parish in the village of Planina near Rakek. He was never a member of any organization other than those connected with the Church. He and his family were never politically active. At the time of the Axis occupation, the house where Strle was born and its outbuildings were burned down by Italian troops. His older brother Jože, who lived in the family home, was killed as a hostage together with many other villagers. Two of his other brothers were held in prison for over a year. As a family they survived much hardship but remained proud of their Slovenian heritage. Anton Strle was always interested in speculative theology, though he was never able to go abroad to further his education. He suffered from physical weakness, and his superiors were concerned about his weak health caused by physical suffering over the years. But Strle continued his studies in Mariology.

Dr. Strle began teaching part-time on the ecclesiastical Faculty in 1956. However, there were complications for Strle from the beginning of his teaching career. In 1957, he was sentenced to six months in prison for "inciting religious intolerance"; the sentence was reduced to two months in prison in Ljubljana. The reasons for the charges against him seemed arbitrary. He had visited a family in his parish and asked why their son was not attending catechism classes—and the mother had reported him to authorities. His feelings were made clear in a diary entry February 20, 1957:

> If I will have to go to prison again I leave this to God. Perhaps God wants this for me for penance as I voluntarily do too little. And how badly penance is needed! In his work a priest comes in contact with a river of sin. If I have offered

> myself to God as sacrifice—oh, what a poor one—I will not swallow my words. While I am free, my asceticism must be above all in the form of disciplined work. Perhaps I have harmed my health with my self-will so that I cannot muster as much feeling or fasting. Perhaps God wishes to purify me of so many transgressions and subconscious secular intentions that wallow in me. Confido![6]

It was this steadfast trust (confidence) in God that would sustain Anton Strle as it had the Servant of God Anto Vovk in the face of harassment and persecution. Since Dr. Strle was part-time lecturer in dogmatics at the Faculty, the Communist authorities agreed that he could serve his sentence during the summer months.[7]

A few days after being released from prison along with a few fellow inmates, Strle noted, "my resolution: *age quod agis*! I must maintain my composure and rootedness in God."[8] His fellow inmates reported that as far as possible, Strle made careful use of his time in prison for prayer and study. During July and August 1958 while Strle was in Paris at the Institute Catholique, he made entries in fluent French. He was there to perfect his French and to receive a diploma from the Institute. While in Paris, he was able to view the great works of art in churches and museums. He also made pilgrimages to Lisieux and Lourdes which nourished his contemplative spirit.

It was this same year, 1958, that Strle became a senior lecturer at the Faculty of Theology of Ljubljana, approved by the chancellor of the Faculty, Anton Vovk, then bishop and administrator of the

6. Strle's diary from February 20, 1957.

7. Summons to begin the sentence: Document OLO Ljubljana from March 19, 1957, addressed to Dr. Strle Anton, Planina pri Rakeku no. 33: "Verdict III Ks 13/57 from 22. 1. 1957 by the District Court in Ljubljana condemns you to 2 /two months in prison according to article 119 of the Penal Code (Inciting religious intolerance). You must come to the district prison in Ljubljana at Miklošičeva 9 on 27. 3. 1957 to begin your sentence, otherwise you will be brought there by the police."

8. Strle's diary from May 9, 1957: "Do what you're doing!"

diocese. Soon afterward, Strle received the same recognition from the Roman Congregation for seminaries and universities. And at the same time, Bishop Vovk gave Dr. Strle his canonical mission at the Faculty. These were Vovk's words: "As you have been a professor at the Faculty of Theology in Ljubljana for some time now and you will have to devote all your time to this work, I relieve you of your function as parish priest in Planina near Rakek."[9]

In November 1964, the current chancellor and Archbishop Jožef Pogačnik named the senior lecturer Dr. Anton Strle professor extraordinaire of systematic theology, and in 1972 he named Strle a full professor of systematic theology.

It is noteworthy that between the years 1959 and 1966, this eminent theologian continued pastoral ministry in several parishes in the vicinity and after 1966, at Holy Trinity parish in Ljubljana. He retired from teaching at the end of the academic year 1985–1986. In 1977, Pope Paul VI named Anton Strle an honorary prelate. He died in Ljubljana October 20, 2003. His funeral was attended by all the Slovenian bishops and a large number of priests, religious, and lay people.

Dr. Anton Strle's Career as Professor and Academic

Dr. Strle lectured in dogmatic theology, and sometimes in patristics, for thirty years (from 1956 to 1986) at the faculty of theology in Ljubljana. He published numerous treatises and articles in the *Compendium* of the faculty and the "Theological Journal." Many of his works were published in different reviews, in the archdiocesan newspaper (Družina), and in other journals in Slovenia and Croatia.

Despite his humble demeanor and quiet, unassuming lifestyle, Anton Strle produced an amazing body of theological works which included 46 books and major papers, 82 dissertations, 70 studies, 345 articles, 70 reviews, 36 translations, and 49

9. All these documents are kept at the Faculty of Theology in Ljubljana.

forewords. He also served as mentor for 100 undergraduates, 10 candidates for master's degrees, and 13 doctoral candidates.

Professor Strle was known, especially by his priest students, for presenting them every year with a new set of lecture notes in dogmatic theology: the sacraments, Christology, Mariology, matrimony, truths about Jesus and his mother Mary, grace, the role of the Holy Spirit, the mystery of Triune God, theological anthropology, the virtues of faith, hope and love, indulgences, the faith of the Church, eschatology, the decrees of Vatican II, Christian existence, and entering the third millennium with Mary. In any given year, Strle would often have five or six sets of his lecture notes published which he freely provided for his students. His work *The Mystery of God* was published in 1977,[10] and after his retirement, four volumes of his work were published in Slovenian: *I Know Whom I Have Believed: Faith and Revelation*, 1988; *Living Hope: The Easter Mystery* in 1990; *God's Glory, the Living Man: Theological Anthropology* in 1992; *Theologians for the Future* in 1998.[11] The forewords to volumes 1, 2, and 4 were written by the Archbishop of Ljubljana, Dr. Alojzij Šuštar, while the foreword to volume 3 was written by Cardinal Joseph Ratzinger, which indicated the close tie between Strle and the future Pope Benedict XVI.

For anyone who looks through Strle's articles, the breadth of his scholarship and the depth of his personality becomes obvious. Beside the many articles he wrote, there are 50 masterful presentations of the Lord's and Mary's feast days during the liturgical year. These are published in two editions of a monumental work entitled *Leto svetnikov* (*Saints through the Year*).[12] Slovenian

10. *Skrivnost Boga* (Ljubljana: Družina, 1977).

11. Respectively, *Vem, komu sem veroval: Vera in razodetje* (Ljubljana: Družina, 1988); *Živo upanje: Velikonočna skrivnost* (Ljubljana: Družina, 1990); *Božja slava—živi človek: Teološka antropologija* (Ljubljana: Družina, 1992); *Teologi za prihodnost* (Ljubljana: Družina, 1998).

12. Anton Strle, multiple articles in *Leto svetnikov* [The Year of Saints], 5 vols, 2nd ed., ed. Marijan Smolik and Andrej Kropej (Celje: Mohorjeva družba, 1999–2001).

readers consider this work by Strle demonstrative of his genius and holiness. Every year, before celebrating the Feast of All Saints, Fr. Strle would quote the words of Cardinal John Henry Newman: “Be my soul with the saints.”[13]

His reviews and presentations of theological and spiritual works in foreign languages, his numerous translations of Church documents and other important papers—all this demonstrated the special ability and character of Anton Strle. He was and is now considered a special man of the Church (*anima ecclesiastica*). He proofread an amazing number of theological documents with scrupulous accuracy, including a whole series of Church documents, treatises, and spiritual essays. As diocesan censor, he carefully reviewed many books and journals, including the *Catechism of the Catholic Church* and the international Catholic review *Communio*.[14]

An important contribution Strle made to theology in the Slovenian language was his translation of Denzinger-Schönmetzer’s compendium of the sources of Catholic Tradition with his in-depth introduction. He called his work *The Faith of the Church*.[15] He also produced an updated translation of all the documents of the Second Vatican Council, complete with new introductions and table of contents.[16] He strove in every way possible to interpret the Council in a genuine and accurate way and worked for a true renewal of Christian life in Slovenia according to the content and spirit of the Council. This included many intro-

13. John Henry Newman, *Apologia pro Vita Sua* (New York: Longmans, Green, and Co., 1908), 116. Originally published, revised edition 1865.

14. Slovenian Bishops’ Conference, *Katekizem katoliške Cerkve*, Slovenian translation of the *Catechism of the Catholic Church* (Ljubljana: Slovenska škofovska konferenca, 1993).

15. Anton Strle, *Vera Cerkve*, 2nd ed. (Celje: Mohorjeva družba, 1997).

16. Anton Strle, *Konstitucije, odloki, izjave, poslanice 2: Vatikanskega vesoljnega cerkvenega zbora (1962–1965)* [Second Vatican Council: Translation and introductions to all documents (1962–1965)], 2nd ed. (Ljubljana: Nadškofijski ordinariat, 1995).

ductions, forewords, and tables of contents that he assembled meticulously on note pads before the use of computers. His goal was the complete acceptance of the documents of the Second Vatican Council and their practical conclusions and resolutions—namely the new evangelization and a renewed Christianization of Europe (and the rest of the world).

Strle the theologian was completely familiar not only with classical theological literature and tradition, but also with the work of current leading theologians. This is the reason that the scholarship of leading theologians, both past and present, echoed in Strle's work. He was able to integrate the best of Catholic theology from many sources and share this wisdom with the larger Church. The whole Church today is in need of theologians like Anton Strle, who can read the signs of the time while preserving Catholic tradition as intended by the Church.

Strle's Contribution to a "Holy Theology" in Slovenia

As indicated above regarding Strle's academic work, it is clear that the broad scope of his scholarship flowed from a creative mind, and that the center of his energy was a desire to achieve a "holy theology"—a theology that emerged from his prayer life. These are the words he wrote in a letter:

> Toward the end of June 1958, Dr. Franc Jere died. Two or three days before his death I visited him for the last time in his room on the second floor of the seminary in Ljubljana . . . my visit was very brief—and upon leaving, Dr. Jere again uttered the words that became indelibly engraved in my memory: "May God help you contribute much to holy theology!"—how many times I then remembered with great clarity these last words of Jere! "Holy Theology. Holy."—when I came across strange theological treatises and books which tried to force upon me opinions that were dressed in the multicolored and garish plumage of modernity, they could not win my heart and soul, not even for a second. It

> was as though the eyes of the emaciated Professor Jere were looking straight at me, and his withered lips, which were nevertheless so full of life, were calling to me with their last strength, to move me to the core: "May God help you contribute much to holy theology!" "Holy theology!" Not just cerebral but holy theology! Better nothing than the theology that is being proposed in this gaudy book! I would rather go and work in a quarry than accept and pass on such unevangelized sawdust! No, never!—And when I felt utterly exhausted and fed up with everything, how many times did I hear the words about holy theology for which something, at least something must be done! To do something not for ideology but for "holy theology," for the "holy" which alone can be "theology serving man" and his salvation. For man, not for abstraction! For God therefore for man. Precisely therefore for man because for God!

Professor Strle, who made it a point to know each one of his students personally, wanted to prepare them for a holy life, and not just an academic or professional life. This was the basis of Pope John Paul II's 1992 exhortation *Pastores dabo vobis* (*I will give you shepherds*), which emphasized the need for professors to prepare their seminary students for a holy, balanced life, for the sake of the people they would serve. These are the Pope's words: "The professors of theology who introduce future priests to the holy sciences have a special educative responsibility. Experience tells us that their responsibility for developing the priest's personality is often more decisive than the responsibility of other educators."[17]

Professor Strle welcomed each one of his students to his office (his den) to help prepare them for the examination in compulsory reading material for which they would be responsible. The most important legacy he gave them was the witness of his own life. He

17. John Paul II, Post-Synodal Apostolic Exhortation *Pastores dabo vobis* (March 25, 1992), 67.

demanded a great deal of himself, and he was demanding of his students, for their own good. In the 1957–1958 school year, when he was giving his first lecture, he wrote this note:

> *Ego repellam te* . . . if I love God, I will willingly accept the effort necessary to penetrate as deeply as possible into the truths he has revealed to us—many people are doomed through ignorance, but ignorance all too often stems from laziness as well as distractions. A person who has dedicated his life to God should really dedicate himself completely and not be preoccupied with all sorts of other things in the seminary. In the past we mostly survived various student illnesses while still in grammar school, now many of my students suffer them during these academic years—they 'study at the academic level while still living at the grammar school level or even worse'. Lack of theological knowledge is one of the great obstacles to successful pastoral care. Of what help is skill if there is no depth? Depth is achieved by thorough study and prayer.

Even though he could be demanding of his students, he let them know that he was a teacher of theology because he was a shepherd and an apostle. He said that he had actually been a shepherd when he was a young boy and always remained one.

The last book Anton Strle wrote had the title *Theologians for the Future*. It was prophetic about the impact he would have on the future of theology in Slovenia. Archbishop Alojzij Šuštar wrote the following on Strle's 75th birthday,

> The years which passed more or less quickly for Professor Strle were very rich, literally lived for others in offering himself up in so many different ways: in pastoral work, at the pulpit and in the confessional, in teaching catechism and in lecturing at the Faculty of Theology, in countless treatises, article and conversations . . . not only the people, pupils and confreres of Professor Anton Strle and so many others who enjoyed his spiritual wealth, his heartfelt

> goodness and his help that drew from faith, hope and love, but also his books and essays will for a long time speak of this man, priest, academic, and writer.[18]

Anton Strle was and remains one of Slovenia's greatest theologians. Cardinal Joseph Ratzinger said of him:

> I had the privilege of meeting Professor Strle in 1974 when we had a meeting of members of the International Theological Commission. I believe I may say the meeting with him left a strong impression on all the members of this group of thirty scholars from the most varied countries of the world. Professor Strle always kept humbly in the background; he wanted only to learn and speak when he had anything truly original to say that others did not see. But it was this very modesty of stepping into the background of his own accord and giving priority only to a better understanding of the truth that drew attention to him. From his humble and benevolent personality emanated a great interior light; we felt this lean man had been pervaded through and through by contact with God. Although it was possible to see a deep ascetic life in him, this ascesis spoke of what is positive: of inner nearness to the Lord which relegated everything else to second position. This life and thinking in communion with Christ gave professor Strle the strength of judgement and the capacity for discernment which cannot derive from mere learnedness. He had a sharp sense for what is right and what is wrong, for what purifies faith and gives it growth, and what destroys it; he knew—in one word—how to discern spirits and it was for this reason that his judgement was precious and cogent.
>
> This is why I am very pleased that this compilation of his anthropological essays is being published. It will help make his contribution to the search for the true likeness of man become better known and more effective. The path of

18. Alojzij Šuštar, Foreword to *Živo upanje* by Strle, 5–6.

> the Church is man, said our Holy Father (Pope John Paul II), and added that man's path is Christ. Our common question is the confusedness of our time is how man should find his way. This is after all the questions of how man is able to meet Christ again in our time. Professor Strle provided an important contribution to this integral anthropology in this book, which I hope will enjoy a broad readership.
>
> Given from Rome on the Feast of the Apostle Saint James, July 25,1991.
>
> —Joseph Cardinal Ratzinger.[19]

People who knew Strle spoke about his capacity for discerning spirits mentioned by Cardinal Ratzinger which they sometimes experienced in their meetings with him. And it was his patience and continuing self-denial that gave evidence of Strle's increasing abandonment of himself to divine providence. Even when he was a young priest, this unconditional surrender to God was evident when he had to go to prison. And his book, *Lojze Grozde. The disciple of Christ the King*,[20] which was the main reason for his prison sentence, is about dependency on God rather than on oneself. This book by Strle was a decisive contribution to the beatification of Blessed Aloysius Grozde.

What is most likely Strle's autobiographical statement was written on a small piece of paper and revealed after his death:

> Someone reported that there has been much suffering in my life. I was in prison for many years. A number of times I have been seriously ill. Sometimes very ill. But if I look back I can see that in my life there have been incomparably more

19. Joseph Ratzinger, Foreword to *Božja slava—živi človek* by Strle, 5–6 (German), 7–8 (Slovenian).

20. Anton Strle, *Lojze Grozde: Mladec Kristusa Kralja* [Lojze Grozde: The disciple of Christ the King], (Ljubljana: Salezijanci, 1944). Later a French translation was published with a foreword by Bishop Gregorij Rožman that was reprinted many times, including *Un martyr des temps modernes: Alöïs Grozďe* (1923–1943) (Paris: La Colombe, 1957).

> moments of beauty and happiness than of bitterness. Oh, there have been bitter moments, even bitter days and weeks. However, following struggles that lasted some time, God gave me the grace to again find peace in being united with Christ's suffering. So it was that in very difficult circumstances I experienced much inner joy. I understand the following: the path to deep happiness does not lie in one's searching for joy and consolation but in putting all one's effort into fulfilling God's will. And in doing so to always unite with Christ who always fulfilled God's will, and with Mary who only wanted to be God's servant. When faced with the worst moments I always joined in spirit the suffering Lord in the mystery of his suffering on the Mount of Olives and on the cross or in the terrible time he spent chained to the pillar where he was scourged. And after a few days, if not sooner, my spirit was filled with joy, quiet yet bright, and peace that was deeper than I had enjoyed before the onset of the affliction.

Another typed text (undated) about himself had the title "Christ in My Life." These are Strle's words:

> Let me begin with what I once wrote in Družina (11.24.1974). It is with great difficulty and reluctance, because this is something intimate, a mystery that is very personal and that cannot be shared with others, that I try to share with others. I truly and always experience Christ as a liberator. Or to put it better: alongside Christ I always feel most free of the various boundaries I come up against. It was once said in the theological course that one should feel completely at ease. I never feel completely at ease except before God as he reveals himself to me in Jesus Christ. He knows me through and through and accepts me unconditionally. Of course, I must meet some conditions myself: I must give myself to him. However, I know that he himself must make up what is missing in me; he is the one who removes the obstacles. And he can! How nice it would be if one were allowed to do

> whatever one wanted. How nice it would be if there were no God! There was something distinctly Nietzschean in me: as though God was an annoying observer waiting to find something on me about which he could pester me, to destroy me—to this day I can feel how I was plagued by various fears of being doomed and I constantly repeated the act of contrition. Then I gradually realized that the Lord accepts me, that he loves me, that I can give myself to him completely. We were once singing litanies to Our Lady before the Blessed Sacrament, and I felt very strongly that God was calling me to strive to live by the Gospel . . . the only power I saw being victorious over death was Christ. Easter was the high point for me, especially the Easter procession on Easter Saturday evening—he was the only victor over death, the only true liberator. Against the terrible dark background of this drama, man can see the risen Lord shining all the more brightly. "Did not the Christ have to suffer these things and then enter his glory?" Whenever I read this report by Luke about the disciples coming from Emmaus I have to make an effort to contain myself.

This was an entry from Professor Strle's diary dated August 6, 1960:

> I am supposed to have an operation tomorrow. I feel as though I am going on a voyage. There is some nervousness and fearing for the unknown, as well as reluctance to have to separate myself from what surrounds me. However, one day I will indeed have to set out on a very long journey but whose distance will be covered in an instant. I do not know if I want this or not. In 1945 I quietly yearned for life to end and to pass on into true afterlife. I felt purified back then. Now many things bind me to this world. Is everything purified with a supernatural purpose or not? Am I God's through and through or not? My God, you know me. I give myself to you in the sacred hearts of Jesus and Mary. What is certain is that there is at least so much grace active in me that the

> world cannot offer me anything if I am not in a very close relationship with God. I cannot enjoy worldly happiness if there is not consideration for God. How grateful I must be for this in the depths of my worthlessness.[21]

In another note, Strle wrote:

> Heartfelt thanks to all the benefactors I have been meeting throughout my life, great benefactors also in providing an example of Christian and priestly life. "Through Mary's hands I give myself entirely to Jesus Christ, that I may patiently bear any cross all the day of my life"—this is my final and main guiding principle in life.[22]

In order for him to fulfill his desire for holiness, Strle strove to be, as he said, a "hidden man of heart." For example, at the beginning of advent one year he made the following resolutions:

> This Advent better prayer, morning and evening, sanctification of daily duties connected with being a priest, more patience; more good deeds, not just physical and also spiritual works of mercy; to be more fully prepared to receive Christ so that Christmas will be part of my life. Let me not delay—if we put things off again now, we may put them off forever. And then it may be too late. And receiving the Sacraments—this is connected to all sorts of things. This week should be spent in preparing for Our Lady's greatest feast day, in dedicating ourselves to Our Lady. Salvation is approaching: raise your heads in trust, in expectation of God's deliverance. Preparation must be taking place in our very selves—we should look to God himself to help us in our conversion—that we may be so prepared as to be able to welcome Christ with our whole heart.

21. From the diary dated June 8, 1960.
22. From the will dated March 12, 1974.

These are some other resolutions Strle made regarding the Christmas mystery:

> I could hardly stand the mighty force of the great Christmas mystery had on my work. I felt that I must do as much as possible for Mary's honour, which is the same as God's honour: everything that is in my power, supported by God's grace. The introductory Mass celebrated in the chapel of the Faculty of Theology—this sung Mass really appealed to me, especially the sung bidding prayers during the offertory. And the First Saturday Mass—*Missa de Beata*—what a beautiful Gospel reading it had—the instruction to fulfill God's will. Oh, if only I could do this as I yearn for this in the depths of my heart—but I am so weak. I must become only a tool—and a tool can be weak if it gives way to God's grace. I am fully aware of the importance of standing before those to whom the Lord will say in the moment of their priestly ordination: You are my friends! Every morning I recite the *Veni, Sancte Spiritus* ("Come Holy Spirit") in union with Our Lady—this helps me focus the strength I need to fulfill the goal I set for myself. With God's grace I was able to see it clearly, but I have obscured it on so many occasions with small infidelities—which were great offenses against the Lord who has been for infinitely faithful to me even in the darkest hours. That he called me to priesthood so early on and protected me so wonderfully in the most difficult circumstances I am most grateful.

The personal reflections Strle shared with his friends give us an insight into his priestly life given wholly to God and from which his theology blossomed. His theology was entirely a "kneeling theology." He knew, like Hans Urs von Balthasar, "that theology is breached between the chasm of worship and obedience and humble love." He knew with Joseph Ratzinger-Pope Benedict XVI that theology can only spring from contact with the living God and is realized only in prayer.

Anton Strle, in the last week before his death, while reading the book of the Servant of God Anton Vovk, *For Remembrance and Warning*,[23] said to this author: "This is the history of the Church in Slovenia." There are many people who are convinced that the name of Anton Strle will be written in large letters in the history of the Slovenian Church. And it will surely be written in the book of life by the triune God whom he loved with total devotion and served with great wisdom, deep prayer, and a life of suffering. He said often with the apostle Paul, "For our light and momentary troubles that can be so painful at times—they are achieving for us an eternal glory that far outweighs them all" (2 Cor 4:17). This was Anton Strle's priestly motto, "God in all things."

23. Anton Vovk, *V spomin in Opomin: Osebni zapisi škofa Antona Vovka od 1945 do 1953*, ed. Blaž Otrin [For remembrance and warning: Personal records of Bishop Anton Vovk from 1945 to 1953], (Družina, Ljubljana, 2003).

15

The Purification of Memory

The penitential liturgy of the recently canonized Pope John Paul II on the First Sunday of Lent (March 12) in the Holy Year 2000 at St. Peter's in Rome was an important event, one of the high points in the Jubilee Year. The Pope's prophetic gesture was new and nevertheless deeply in continuity with the history of the Church. The public liturgical prayer was well-considered and carefully prepared. More than once Pope John Paul II asked forgiveness for the Church's guilt in the past. In his Apostolic Letter *Tertio millennio adveniente*, he expressed the wish that the Holy Year not only should be a special occasion for individual penance, but also ought to signify for the Church a "purification of memory," in which she should reflect on the guilt of the past that weighs upon Church history.

Pope John Paul II emphasizes: "Acknowledging the weaknesses of the past is an act of honesty and courage."[1] It shows the vitality of the Church, which can offer to individuals and to society an example of repentance and conversion. Pope Benedict XVI puts it bluntly: "This act of the purification of memory, of self-purification, of opening oneself to the Lord's grace, which spurs us on to do good, serves also to make us credible in the eyes of the world."[2]

The Church's Request for Forgiveness

In his Bull of Indiction of the Holy Year 2000, *Incarnationis mysterium* (November 29, 1998), John Paul II highlights among the

1. John Paul II, Apostolic Letter *Tertio millennio adveniente* (November 10, 1994), 33.

2. Joseph Ratzinger, "Nur die Wirklichkeit der Vergebung macht das Bekenntnis der Sünden möglich," in *Kirche: Zeichen unter den Völkern*, JRGS 8/1 (Freiburg: Herder, 2010), 504.

"signs . . . which may help people to live the exceptional grace of the Jubilee with greater fervor" the "purification of memory." The "purification of memory . . . calls everyone to make an act of courage and humility in admitting the wrongs done by those who have borne or bear the name of Christian."[3]

Pope John Paul II said in his homily on March 12, 2000:

> Before Christ who, out of love, took our guilt upon himself, we are all invited to make a profound examination of conscience. One of the characteristic elements of the Great Jubilee is what I described as the "purification of memory" (Bull *Incarnationis mysterium*, n. 11). As the Successor of Peter, I asked that "in this year of mercy the Church, strong in the holiness which she receives from her Lord, should kneel before God and implore forgiveness for the past and present sins of her sons and daughters" (ibid.). Today, the First Sunday of Lent, seemed to me the right occasion for the Church, gathered spiritually round the Successor of Peter, to implore divine forgiveness for the sins of all believers. *Let us forgive and ask forgiveness!*
>
> This appeal has prompted [in the ecclesial community] a thorough and fruitful reflection, which led to the publication several days ago of a document of the International Theological Commission, entitled: *Memory and Reconciliation: The Church and the Faults of the Past*. I thank everyone who helped to prepare this text. It is very useful for correctly understanding and carrying out the authentic request for pardon, based on the objective responsibility which Christians share as members of the Mystical Body, and which spurs today's faithful to recognize, along with their own sins, the sins of yesterday's Christians, in the light of careful historical and theological discernment. Indeed, "because of the bond which unites us to one another in the

3. John Paul II, *Homily on the Day of Pardon in the Holy Year 2000*, March 12, 2000. In-text citation is to John Paul II, Bull of Indiction of the Great Jubilee of the Year 2000 *Incarnationis mysterium* (November 29, 1998), 11.

> Mystical Body, all of us, though not personally responsible and without encroaching on the judgement of God who alone knows every heart, bear the burden of the errors and faults of those who have gone before us" (*Incarnationis mysterium*, n. 11). The recognition of past wrongs serves to reawaken our consciences to the compromises of the present, opening the way to conversion for everyone. *Let us forgive and ask forgiveness!*[4]

At this point we can ask ourselves with Joseph Ratzinger/Benedict XVI

> What is forgiveness, really? What happens when forgiveness takes place? Guilt is a reality, an objective force; it has caused destruction that must be repaired. For this reason, forgiveness must be more than a matter of ignoring, of merely trying to forget. Guilt must be worked through, healed, and thus overcome. Forgiveness exacts a price—first of all from the person who forgives. He must overcome within himself the evil done to him; he must, as it were, burn it interiorly and in so doing renew himself. As a result, he also involves the other, the trespasser, in this process of transformation, of inner justification, and both parties, suffering all the way through and overcoming evil, are made new.[5]

In her request for forgiveness, the Church turns first of all to God. She praises and professes his magnificent grace and mercy.

> This request for pardon must not be understood as an expression of false humility or as a denial of her 2,000-year history, which is certainly richly deserving in the areas of charity, culture and holiness. Instead [the Church] responds to a necessary requirement of the truth, which, in addition

4. John Paul II, *Homily on the Day of Pardon in the Holy Year 2000.*
5. Ratzinger, *Jesus of Nazareth*, vol. 1, *From the Baptism in the Jordan to the Transfiguration* (New York: Doubleday, 2007), 158–59.

to the positive aspects, recognizes the human limitations and weaknesses of the various generations of Christ's disciples.[6]

"Spotted by Sins, Yet Beautiful"

Then Cardinal Joseph Ratzinger, as Prefect of the Congregation for the Doctrine of the Faith, perceived the idea proposed by the pope as an important challenge to theology. The new elements of the Pope's idea and of the penitential liturgy of the Church that he had planned confronted theologians with the task of reflecting on the theological significance of such a process. The International Theological Commission, under its president, Cardinal Joseph Ratzinger, received directions to prepare the way for this act of requesting pardon with a scholarly study and to explain its deeper meaning. The document *Memory and Reconciliation: The Church and the Faults of the Past* was presented by the Cardinal Prefect Joseph Ratzinger on March 7, 2000,[7] in the Press Office of the Holy See.[8] Cardinal Georges Cottier, OP, as Secretary of the Theological Commission, explained the text in greater detail.[9]

"The Church, in Christ, is in the nature of sacrament—a sign and instrument, that is, of communion with God and of unity among all men."[10] Hans Urs von Balthasar says: "All Christians are sinners, and if the Church does not sin as Church, she does sin in all her members, and through the mouths of all her

6. John Paul II, *General Audience*, September 1, 1999, 3.

7. International Theological Commission, *Memory and Reconciliation: The Church and the Faults of the Past* (December 1999).

8. Ratzinger, "The Church's Guilt: Presentation of the Document *Remembrance and Reconciliation* from the International Theological Commission," in *Pilgrim Fellowship of Faith: The Church as Communion* (San Francisco: Ignatius Press, 2005), 274–83.

9. Georges Cottier, *Memoria e pentimento: Il rapporto fra Chiesa santa e cristiani peccatori, la purificazione della memoria, l'importanza della richiesta di perdono per l'ecumenismo* (Cinisello Balsamo: Edizioni San Paolo, 2000).

10. Vatican Council II, Dogmatic Constitution on the Church *Lumen gentium* (November 21, 1964), 1.

members she must confess her guilt."[11] The Church is holy because she is the salvific instrument of the Holy Spirit. For this reason, she is indestructible in professing God's saving deeds, in her faith, in her teaching, and in the sacraments that Christ instituted in her. Neither interior decay nor hostility from the outside will ever overcome her (Mt 16:18).

Cardinal Joseph Ratzinger analyzes the

> *phenomenon of animosity toward the Church.* Protestantism tried to show that "the Catholic Church was not merely stained with sin, as she had always known and said, but that she was, allegedly, completely corrupted and ruined and no longer the Church of Christ; rather, she has, on the contrary, become an instrument of the Antichrist." The position became still worse in the course of the Enlightenment; let us recall Voltaire's "Écrasez l'Infâme!" Ultimately, the accusations were growing in scope right up to those of Nietzsche, in which the Church appears, no longer as merely failing to do the will of Christ, but as the great evil of all evils afflicting mankind, as effecting the alienation of man from himself, something from which he must finally be liberated in order to become once more himself. We see the same theme, differently worked out, in Marxism. . . . Since the Enlightenment, many deplorable historical realities have been exaggerated into real myths—the Crusades, the Inquisition, the burning of witches—and these have grown far beyond the historical facts into mythical bugbears that not merely justify but positively demand the rejection of the Church.[12]

In this often-unfriendly situation the Church admits with great candor her own weakness, asks for forgiveness, and shows the way to reconciliation. This is actually her prophetic charism. The Catholic Church, by her own example, presents to civil soci-

11. Hans Urs von Balthasar, "Casta Meretrix," in *Explorations in Theology*, vol. II, *Spouse of the Word* (San Francisco: Ignatius Press, 1991), 193–288, at 245.

12. Ratzinger, "The Church's Guilt," 280–81.

ety also the way out of many even more profound crises. The request for pardon is an important sign for the New Evangelization, which is always reconciliation with God and among human beings. Pope Benedict XVI explains the liturgical prayer, the *Confiteor*, which introduces the celebration of the liturgy every day.

> The priest, the pope, the laymen all confess with their "*I*"—each one of them and all together before God and in the presence of their brothers and sisters—that they have sinned, with their own sin, their own most grievous sin. Two aspects of this opening of the holy liturgy seem important to me. On one hand, we speak in the first person singular: "I" have sinned; I am not confessing the sins of other people; I am not confessing the anonymous sins of a collective entity; I am myself confessing with my "I." Yet at the same time it is all the people at prayer who with their "I" are saying, "I have sinned." . . . Thus in this fellowship of confession is expressed that image of the Church which was formulated by the Second Vatican Council in Lumen gentium, chapter 1, number 8: "*Ecclesia . . . sancta simul et semper purificanda, poenitentiam et renovationem continuo prosequitur*": the Church is at the same time holy and constantly in need of purification; she is always treading the path of penitence and of renewal. This picture of the Church, formulated by Vatican II and put into practice daily in the liturgy, for its own part reflects the Gospel parables of the darnel [weeds] growing amid the corn [wheat] and of the fishing net that catches all kinds of fish, good and bad. In all generations the Church has recognized these parables as being the Lord's way of expressing in anticipation her own experiences. . . . The Church of Jesus Christ cannot separate herself from sinners; she has to accept that there are all kinds of fish in her net and that in her field the darnel is always growing along with the corn.[13]

13. "The Church's Guilt," 276–77.

Confessio fidei—Confessio peccati—Confessio laudis

Alongside this self-critical attitude of the Church, which again and again admits her own "*Mea culpa*," we must still declare that the Catholic Church—despite the sins which are undeniable and more than obvious—nevertheless remains Holy Church. With the request for pardon and with the document of the Theological Commission, the Church of today is not condemning the Church of the past. Rather she is admitting the roots of her own failings in the past. The Church is very much aware of the fact that there is sin in her; she has always fought against the notion of a Church in which there is room for saints only. "Admitting sin is an act of honesty by which we can make it clear to people that the Lord is stronger than our sins. An anecdote comes to mind that is related by Cardinal Consalvi, the Secretary of State of Pius VII. When someone told him, 'Napoleon wants to destroy the Church,' he replied: 'He will not succeed; that is something that not even we have managed to do.'"[14]

Joseph Ratzinger lists the three criteria for understanding correctly the reality of the request for pardon. First, the Church of the present cannot present itself as a tribunal that passes judgment on past generations. Second, admitting, according to Augustine, means "doing the truth."[15] Third:

> Again in accordance with Augustine, we have to say that a Christian confessio peccati [confession of sin] always has to go hand in hand with a *confessio laudis* [confession of praise]. In any honest examination of conscience we can see that for our part in every generation we have done much that is evil. Yet we can also see that, in spite of our sins, God has always purified and renewed the Church and has always

14. Ratzinger, "Nur die Wirklichkeit der Vergebung," 504.

15. On this topic, cf. Ratzinger, "Originalität und Überlieferung in Augustins Begriff der *confessio*," *Revue d'études augustiniennes et patristiques* 3, no. 4 (1957): 375–92, esp. 385. See also Ratzinger, "The Church's Guilt," 282.

> entrusted great things to fragile vessels. And who could fail to recognize how much good has been done, for example, in the past two centuries by new religious congregations and by lay movements in the sphere of education, in the social sector, in efforts on behalf of the weak, the sick, the poor, and the suffering, even while those centuries were at the same time ravaged by the atrocities of the atheistic systems? It would be failing in honesty to see only our evil and not the good that God has effected through the faithful—in spite of their sins. The Church Fathers saw this paradox of guilt and grace as being summed up in the words of the Bride in the Song of Songs: "*Nigra sum sed formosa*" (Sg 1:5). "I am stained with sins, yet beautiful"—beautiful through your grace and through what you have done. The Church is able to confess the sins of the past and of the present in all openness and confidence, in the knowledge that evil will never completely stain her; in the knowledge that the Lord is stronger than our sins and renews his Church again and again, that she may continue to be the instrument of God's good works in our world.[16]

The memory of the scandals of the past cannot hinder the witness of the Church of today. Conversely, however, acknowledgment of the failings of the Church's sons and daughters in the past can foster renewal and reconciliation in the present. This is why the whole Church, with the confession of the sins of her members, confesses also her faith in God and his infinite goodness and willingness to forgive. This conviction prompted the Church Fathers, Saint Ambrose for example, to make lapidary statements. "Let us, then, be on our guard, lest our fall be the Church's wound (*Caveamus igitur, ne lapsus noster vulnus Ecclesiae fiat*)."[17]

16. "The Church's Guilt," 282–83.

17. Ambrose, *De virginitate*, Patrologia Latina (PL) 16 (Paris: Garnier Fratres, 1844), 10, 48, 278D. See also Balthasar, "Casta Meretrix," 246.

The Church's request for pardon is a healing and prophetic act. Saint Augustine says:

> The saints themselves are not free of daily sins. The Church as a whole says, "Forgive us our trespasses!" She thus possesses spots and wrinkles. But through confession the wrinkles are smoothed out, the spots washed away. The Church stands in prayer in order, through confession, to be purified, and as long as men live on earth, that is how she stands.[18]

18. Augustine, *Sermo 181*, 5, 7 (PL 38, 982). See also Balthasar, "Casta Meretrix," 284.

BIBLIOGRAPHIC NOTES

These chapters previously appeared in other forms and various languages in the following publications, and are re-presented here with grateful permission from the copyright holders.[1]

Chapter 1. "Servants of Your Joy": Joseph Ratzinger as Priest, Professor, Prefect, and Pope

Slovenian: "Duhovnik Joseph Ratzinger." *Communio: Mednarodna katoliška revija* 19 (2009): 285–319. Reprint in Štrukelj. *Zaupanje in pogum*. Ljubljana: Družina, 2015, 35–89.

German: "Diener eurer Freude: Joseph Ratzinger als Priester, Lehrer und Hirte." In Štrukelj. *Vertrauen: Mut zum Christsein*. St. Ottilien: EOS Verlag, 2012, 35–74. Partial reprint: "Die persönliche Bindung des Priesters an Christus." *Kirche heute* 19, no. 7 (2012): 4–7. Reprint: "Diener eurer Freude. Joseph Ratzinger als Priester, Lehrer und Hirte." In *Gott ver(w)orten: Festschrift für Bernhard Körner*, edited by Eduard Prenga and Stefan Ulz, 191–214. Würzburg: Echter Verlag, 2014.

Polish: "Sługa waszej radości: Joseph Ratzinger jako kałan, nauczyciel i pasterz." In Štrukelj. *Zaufanie odwaga bycia chrześcijaninem*. Radom: Wydawnictwo Diecezji Radomskiej, 2019.

Chapter 2. "Coworkers of the Truth": The Ecclesial Vocation of the Theologian in the Light of Pope Benedict XVI

German: "Mitarbeiter der Wahrheit: Die Kirchlichkeit des Theologen im Licht von Papst Benedikt XVI." *Bogoslovni vestnik* (Slovenia) 71 (2011): 511–24. Reprint: "Mitarbeiter der Wahrheit:

1. Also, an earlier draft of this text was printed in English in Ljubljana in 2018 by Publisher CH4 under the same title *Kneeling Theology* and can be found in a handful of libraries worldwide.

Die Kirchlichkeit des Theologen im Licht von Papst Benedikt XVI." *Klerusblatt* 92, no. 4 (2012): 74–78. Reprint in Štrukelj. *Vertrauen: Mut zum Christsein*. St. Ottilien: EOS Verlag, 2012, 11–34.

Slovenian: "Cerkvenost teologa—v luči papeža Benedikta XVI." *Communio: Mednarodna katoliška revija* 21 (2011): 297–310. Reprint in Štrukelj. *Zaupanje in pogum*. Ljubljana: Družina, 2015, 15–34.

Polish: "Współpracownik prawdy: Eklezjalność teologów według papieża Benedykta XVI." In Štrukelj. *Zaufanie odwaga bycia chrześcijaninem*. Radom: Wydawnictwo Diecezji Radomskiej, 2019.

Chapter 3. From a Sitting to a Kneeling Theology: Theology and Holiness in Hans Urs von Balthasar

Slovenian: "Od sedeče h klečeči teologiji: Teolgija in svetost pri Hansu Ursu von Balthasarju." *Communio: Mednarodna katoliška revija* 4 (1994): 333–43. Reprint in Štrukelj. *Klečeča teologija*. Družina: Ljubljana, 2000, 13–26.

Italian: "Dalla teologia 'seduta a tavolino' alla teologia 'prostrata in ginocchio:' Teologia e santità in Hans Urs von Balthasar." *Communio: Rivista Internazionale di Teologia e Cultura* 143 (1995): 58–69.

Hungarian: "Az üldögélő teológiától a térdelő teológiáig: Teológia és szentség Hans Urs von Balthasar megfogalmazásában." *Communio: Nemzetközi katolikus folyóirat* 3, no. 3 (1995): 67–78.

Dutch: "Van een zittende naar een knielende theologie: Theologie en heiligheid bij Hans Urs von Balthasar." *Communio: Internationaal katholiek tijdschrift* 20, no. 5 (1995): 366–76.

German: "Von der sitzenden zur knienden Theologie: Theologie und Heiligkeit bei Hans Urs von Balthasar." *Klerusblatt* 76, no. 5 (1996): 103–5. Reprint: *Folia theologica* (Budapest) 7 (1996): 21–32. Reprint in Štrukelj. *Kniende Theologie*, 2nd ed. EOS Verlag, St. Ottilien, 2004, 11–22.

Polish: "Od teologii 'siedzącej za biurkiem' do teologii 'modlącej się na kolanach': Teologia i świętość u Hansa Ursa von Balthasara." *Communio: Międzynarodowy przegląd teologiczny* 19, no. 3 [111] (1999): 101–11. Reprint: "Teologia i świętość w ujęciu Hansa Ursa von Balthasara." In Štrukelj. *Teologia i świętość*. Lublin: Wydawnictwo Polihymnia, 2010, 9–21.

Russian: "Od 'sidjašego' bogoslovija—k bogosloviju 'koljenopriklonjenomu.'" In Štrukelj. *O slave Božjej*. Moscow: Izdatelstvo franciskancev, 1999, 9–24.

French: "De la chaire à l'oratoire: Théologie et prière selon Hans Urs von Balthasar." *Communio: Revue catholique internationale* 148, no. 3–4 (2000): 101–11.

Chapter 4. "Beauty Will Save the World": The Christian Message about Beauty according to Pope Benedict XVI and Hans Urs von Balthasar

Czech: "Co je krása? Pojetí krásy v díle Benedikta XVI a Hans Urs von Balthasara." Lecture for the international symposium "Jaká krása spasí svět" for the Catholic faculty of Charles University in Prague, May 13–14, 2014.

Slovenian: "Lepota ozdravlja svet: Krščansko sporočilo o lepoti pri Josephu Ratzingerju in Hansu Ursu von Balthasarju." *Communio: Mednarodna katoliška revija* 24 (2014): 174–84. Reprint: "Lepota bo rešila svet." In Štrukelj. *Zaupanje in pogum*. Ljubljana: Družina, 2015, 177–94.

German: "Was ist Schönheit? Christliche Botschaft von der Schönheit bei Joseph Ratzinger und Hans Urs von Balthasar." *Kirche heute* 21, no. 7 (2014): 16–19.

Polish: "Co to jest piękno? Chrześcijańskie orędzie o pięknie według Josepha Ratzingera i Hansa Ursa von Balthasara." In Štrukelj. *Zaufanie odwaga bycia chrześcijaninem.* Radom: Wydawnictwo Diecezji Radomskiej, 2019.

Chapter 5. Hans Urs von Balthasar and Adrienne von Speyr: The Unity of Two Works

Slovenian: "Hans Urs von Balthasar in Adrienne von Speyr: Enota dveh del." *Communio: Mednarodna katoliška revija* 15 (2005): 347–64.

Italian: "Hans Urs von Balthasar e Adrienne von Speyr: Unità di due opere." *Communio: Rivista Internazionale di Teologia e Cultura* 203–204 (2005): 27–43. Reprint in: *Solo l'amore è credibile: Una rilettura dell'opera di Hans Urs von Balthasar*, edited by Rino Fisicella, 75–93. Vatican City: Lateran University Press, 2007; Reprint in Štrukelj. *Teologia e santità.* Cinisello Balsamo, Milano: Edizioni San Paolo, 2010, 319–43.

German: "Hans Urs von Balthasar und Adrienne von Speyr: Die Einheit zweier Werke." *Identität und offener Horizont: Festschrift für Egon Kapellari*, edited by Franz Lackner and Wolfgang Mantl, 473–88. Vienna-Graz-Klagenfurt: Styria Verlag, 2006.

Polish: "Hans Urs von Balthasar i Adrienne von Speyr: Jedność podwójnego dzieła." In Štrukelj. *Teologia i świętość.* Lublin: Wydawnictwo Polihymnia, 2010, 283–302.

Chapter 6. A Continuing Legacy: Adrienne von Speyr

German: "Adrienne von Speyr ist lebendig." Lecture for the thirty anniversary from the death of Adrienne von Speyr. In Mariastein by Basel, September 20, 1997. In Štrukelj. *Kniende Theologie*, 2nd ed. St. Ottilien: EOS Verlag, 2004, 235–41.

Russian: "Adrienna fon Špejir živjot." In Štrukelj. *O slave Božjej.* Moscow: Izdatelstvo franciskancev, 1999, 175–83.

Slovenian: "Adrienne von Speyr živi." In Štrukelj. *Klečeča teologija*. Družina: Ljubljana, 2000, 301–10.

Polish: "Adrienne von Speyr żyje." In Štrukelj. *Teologia i świętość*. Lublin: Wydawnictwo Polihymnia, 2010, 275–81.

Chapter 7. Man and Woman under God: The Dignity of the Human Being according to Hans Urs von Balthasar

Slovenian: "Mož in žena v božji zamisli: Dostojanstvo človeka po Hansu Ursu von Balthasarju." *Communio: Mednarodna katoliška revija* 3 (1993): 101–10. Reprint in Štrukelj. *Klečeča teologija*. Družina: Ljubljana, 2000, 185–98.

English: "Man and Woman under God: The Dignity of the Human Being according to Hans Urs von Balthasar." *Communio: International Catholic Review* 20, no. 2 (1993): 377–88.

Dutch: "Man en vrouw in God: De waardigheid van de mens volgens Hans Urs von Balthasar." *Communio: Internationaal katholiek tijdschrift* 18, no. 2 (1993): 106–16.

Portuguese: "Dignidade do homem e da mulher no pensamento de Hans Urs von Balthasar." *Communio: Revista Internacional Católica* 10, no. 3 (1993): 229–35. Reprint: "Dignidade do homem e da mulher no pensamento de Hans Urs von Balthasar." *Communio: Revista International de Teologia, Ciência e Cultura* (Brasil) 27, no. 3 (2008): 813–20.

Polish: "Mężczyzna i niewiasta w Bogu: Godność człowieka według Hansa Ursa von Balthasara." *Communio: Międzynarodowy przegląd teologiczny* 13, no. 6 [78] (1993): 93–103. Reprint: "Mężczyzna i kobieta w Bogu." *Communio: Międzynarodowy przegląd teologiczny* 27, no. 2 [158] (2007): 53–63. Reprint: "Mężczyzna i kobieta w Bogu." In Štrukelj. *Teologia i świętość*. Lublin: Wydawnictwo Polihymnia, 2010, 185–97.

German: "Mann und Frau in Gott: Die Würde des Menschen nach Hans Urs von Balthasar." *Forum Katholische Zeitschrift* 10 (1994): 269–77. Reprint in Štrukelj. *Kniende Theologie*, 2nd ed. St. Ottilien: EOS Verlag, 2004, 157–68.

Russian: "Mužčina i ženščina v Boge: Dostoinstvo čeloveka po Hansu Ursu fon Baltazaru." In Štrukelj. *O slave Božjej.* Moscow: Izdatelstvo franciskancev, 1999, 107–20.

Chapter 8. The *Theo-Logic* of Hans Urs von Balthasar

Slovenian: "Resnica iz ljubezni: Teološka logika Hansa Ursa von Balthasarja." *Communio: Mednarodna katoliška revija* 3 (1993): 319–24. Reprint in Štrukelj. *Klečeča teologija*. Družina: Ljubljana, 2000, 61–69.

German: "Die 'Theologik' von Hans Urs von Balthasar." *Communio: Internationale katholische Zeitschrift* 22 (1993): 507–12. Reprint in Štrukelj. *Kniende Theologie*, 2nd ed. St. Ottilien: EOS Verlag, 2004, 31–37.

Dutch: "De 'Theologica' van Hans Urs von Balthasar." *Communio: Internationaal katholiek tijdschrift* 18, no. 6 (1993): 475–80.

English: "The *Theo-logic* of Hans Urs von Balthasar." *Communio: International Catholic Review* 20, no. 4 (1993): 616–22.

Russian: " 'Teologika' Hansa Ursa fon Baltazara." In Štrukelj. *O slave Božjej.* Moscow: Izdatelstvo franciskancev, 1999, 23–30.

Polish: "Teologika Hansa Ursa von Balthasara." In Štrukelj. *Teologia i świętość.* Lublin: Wydawnictwo Polihymnia, 2010, 31–37.

Chapter 9. Life in Christ: The Christian States of Life according to Hans Urs von Balthasar

German: "Leben in Christus: Christliche Stände als lebendige Mitte der Theologie Hans Urs von Balthasars." *Forum Katholische Theologie* 21, no. 3 (2005): 220–30.

Hungarian: "Krisztusban élt élet: Hans Urs von Balthasar teológiájának eleven középpontja: a keresztény életállapotok." *Vigilia* (Budapest) 70, no. 6 (June 2005): 457–66.

Polish: "Życie w Chrystusie: Stany chrześcijańskie jako żywotne centrum teologii Hansa Ursa von Balthasara." In Štrukelj. *Zaufanie odwaga bycia chrześcijaninem*. Radom: Wydawnictwo Diecezji Radomskiej, 2019.

Dutch: "Leven in Christus: Christelijke levensstaten centraal in de theologie van Hans Urs von Balthasar." *Communio: Internationaal katholiek tijdschrift* 40, no. 3–4 (2015): 260–72.

Chapter 10. Hope Does Not Disappoint

German: "Hoffnung trügt nicht." *Communio: Internationale katholische Zeitschrift* 25 (1996): 393–402. Reprint in Štrukelj. *Kniende Theologie*, 2nd ed. St. Ottilien: EOS Verlag, 2004, 207–18.

English: "Hope Does Not Disappoint." *Communio: International Catholic Review* 23, no. 3 (1996): 472–79.

Dutch: "Hoop wordt niet teleurgesteld." *Communio: International katholiek tijdschrift* 21, no. 5 (1996): 348–58.

Slovenian: "Upanje ne osramoti." *Communio: Mednarodna katoliška revija* 7 (1997): 74–83. Reprint in Štrukelj. *Klečeča teologija*. Družina: Ljubljana, 2000, 253–66.

Polish: "Nadzieja zawieść nie może." *Communio: Międzynarodowy przegląd teologiczny* 17, no. 5 [101] (1997): 44–57. Reprint:

"Nadzieja nie zawodzi." In Štrukelj. *Teologia i świętość.* Lublin: Wydawnictwo Polihymnia, 2010, 237–48.

Czech: "Naděje neklame." *Communio: Mezinárodní katolická revue* 3, no. 2 (1998): 45–54.

Russian: "Nadežda ne obmanet" (published in Moscow in 2019).

Hungarian: "A remény nem csal meg." *Communio: Nemzetközi katolikus folyóirat* 5, no. 2 (1997): 10–18.

Chapter 11. Lord Jesus Christ as Judge and Savior

Slovenian: "Nauk o sodbi pri Benediktu XVI." *Communio: Mednarodna katoliška revija* 19 (2009): 364–74.

German: "Die Lehre vom Gericht bei Benedikt XVI." *Kirche heute* 16, no. 11 (2009): 4–7. Reprint: "Der Herr als Richter und Retter." *Communio: Międzynarodwy przeglad teologiczny* 33 (2013): 23–32. Reprint in Štrukelj. *Vertrauen: Mut zum Christsein.* St. Ottilien: EOS Verlag, 2012, 203–16.

Polish: "Nauka o sądzie Bożym według Ojca Świętego Benedykta XVI." In Štrukelj. *Teologia i świętość.* Lublin: Wydawnictwo Polihymnia, 2010, 249–58.

Italian: "La Dottrina del Giudizio in Benedetto XVI." In Štrukelj. *Teologia e santità.* Cinisello Balsamo, Milano: Edizioni San Paolo, 2010, 278–90.

Dutch: "De Heer als Rechter en Redder." *Communio: Internationaal katholiek tijdschrift* 40, no. 6 (2015): 449–56.

Chapter 12. From Mutable to Immutable Life

Slovenian: "Iz minljivega v neminljivo življenje." *Communio: Mednarodna katoliška revija* 23 (2013): 48–58.

Chapter 13. "In God I Trust": Servant of God Archbishop Anton Vovk

Italian: "La fedeltà di monsignor Anton Vovk, servitore di Dio." *Communio: Rivista Internazionale di Teologia e Cultura* 214 (2007): 54–59. Reprint: *L'Arcivescovo Anton Vovk: Servo di Dio*. Ljubljana, 2008.

Polish: "Wierność arcybiskupa Antona Vovka, sługi bożego." *Communio: Międzynarodowy przegląd teologiczny* 27, no. 4 [160] (2007): 116–22. Reprint: *Arcybiskup Anton Vovk: Sługa Boży*. Ljubljana, 2008. Reprint: "Wierność Sługi Bożego abpa Antona Vovka." In Štrukelj. *Teologia i świętość*. Lublin: Wydawnictwo Polihymnia, 2010, 109–17.

German: "Erzbischof Vovk—der Fels im kommunistischen Slowenien." *Kirche heute* 15, no. 3 (2008): 4–9. Reprint: *Erzbischof Anton Vovk: Der Diener Gottes*. Ljubljana 2008 and 2017.

Slovenian: *Nadškof Anton Vovk: Božji služabnik*. Ljubljana, 2008 and 2017.

French: *Archevêque Anton Vovk: Le Serviteur de Dieu*. Ljubljana, 2008.

English: *Archbishop Anton Vovk: The Servant of God*. Ljubljana, 2008 and 2017.

Spanish: "Arzobispo Anton Vovk: Siervo de Dios." Ljubljana, 2008. Reprint: "La fidelidad del siervo de Dios Anton Vovk." *Communio Argentina: Revista Católica Internacional* 15 (2008): 43–56. Reprint: *Communio: Revista Católica Internacional de Pensamiento y Cultura* (Nueva época), no. 8 (2008): 145–55.

Chapter 14. "God in All Things": Servant of God Anton Strle

German: "Der theologische Beitrag von Prof. Dr. Anton Strle zur Marienverehrung in Slowenien." In *Mater fidei et fidelium:*

Collected Essays to Honor Theodore Koehler on His 80th Birthday. Marian Library Studies: A New Series, 17–23, Dayton, Ohio: 1991. Reprint: "Die Mariologie als Herzstück der Ekklesiologie." In Štrukelj. *Kniende Theologie*, 2nd ed. St. Ottilien: EOS Verlag, 2004, 127–36. "STRLE Anton." In *Biographisch–Bibliographisches Kirchelexikon*, vol. 32, 1357–1379. Nordhausen: Verlag Traugott Bautz GmbH, 2011.

Russian: "Mariologija kak serdce ekkleziologiji." In Štrukelj. *O slave Božjej*. Moscow: Izdatelstvo franciskancev, 1999, 83–94.

Slovenian: "Mariologija kot srčika ekleziologije." In Štrukelj. *Klečeča teologija*. Družina: Ljubljana, 2000, 143–54. "Povsod Boga: Življenje in delo prof. dr. Antona Strleta." *Communio: Mednarodna katoliška revija* 13 (2003): 291–306. "Povsod Boga: Prelat prof. dr. Anton Strle. In memoriam (21.1.1915 + 20.10.2003)." *Bogoslovni vestnik* 64 (2004): 211–25. "Profesor Anton Strle: Ob desetletnici smrti." *Tretji dan* 42, nos. 7/8 (2013): 91–102. "Gorečnost za sveto teologijo v spisih Božjega služabnika Antona Strleta." In *Brezjanski pogovori* (2015): 25–52. "Prizadevanje Antona Strleta za sveto teologijo." *Communio: Mednarodna katoliška revija* 25 (2015): 142–54.

Polish: "Mariologia jako centralna szęść eklezjologii." In *W służbie Bogurodzicy: 10-lecie Polskiego Towarzystwa Mariologicznego (1999–2009)*. Niepokalanów : Wydawnictwo Ojców Franciszkanów, 2009, 279–87. Reprint: "Mariologia jako centralna część eklezjologii." In Štrukelj. *Teologia i świętość*. Lublin: Wydawnictwo Polihymnia, 2010, 155–64.

Chapter 15. The Purification of Memory

Polish: "Oczyszczenie pamięci." *Communio: Międzynarodowy przegląd teologiczny* 36, no. 3 [195] (2016): 67–76. Reprint in Štrukelj. *Zaufanie odwaga bycia chrześcijaninem*. Radom: Wydawnictwo Diecezji Radomskiej, 2019.

Slovenian: "Očiščenje spomina." *Communio: Mednarodna katoliška revija* 28 (2018): 31–37.

English: "The Purification of Memory." *Communio: International Catholic Review* 45, no. 1 (Spring 2018): 85–92. Reprint *Bogoslovni vestnik* 78, no. 3 (2018): 721–27.

German: "Die Reinigung des Gedächtnisses: Rückblick auf die Vergebungsbitte der Kirche im Jubiläumsjahr 2000." *Kirche heute* 25, no. 6 (2018): 13–15.

Spanish: "La purificación de la memoria." *Communio Argentina: Revista Católica Internacional* 25, no. 3 (2018): 69–75.

Dutch: "De zuivering van het geheugen." *Communio: Internationaal katholiek tijdschrift* 43, no. 1 (2018): 13–19.

French: "La purification de la mémoire." *Communio: Revue catholique internationale* 256, no. 2 (2018): 69–75.

Croatian: "Čišćenje sjećanja." *Communio: Međunarodni katolički časopis* 44, no. 131 (2018): 107–11.

Czech: "Očištění paměti" *Communio: Mezinárodní katolická revue* 25, no. 1 (2020): 80–87.

BIBLIOGRAPHY

Works of Joseph Ratzinger / Pope Benedict XVI

Address of His Holiness Benedict XVI after the Concert for His 80th Birthday. April 16th, 2009.

Address to Heiligenkreuz Abbey. September 9, 2007.

Apostolic Journey to München, Altötting, and Regensburg: Meeting with the Representatives of Science in the Aula Magna of the University of Regensburg [Regensburg Address]. September 12, 2006.

Auf Christus schauen: Einübung in Glaube, Hoffnung, Liebe. Freiburg: Herder, 1989.

Auferstehung und ewiges Leben. JRGS 10. Freiburg: Herder, 2012.

Behold the Pierced One: An Approach to a Spiritual Christology: San Francisco: Ignatius Press, 1986.

"Biblical Foundations of Priesthood." *Communio: International Catholic Review* 17 (Winter 1990): 617–27. German: "Vom Wesen des Priestertums." In JRGS 12, 33–50.

Foreword to *Božja slava—živi človek: Teološka antropologija*, by Anton Strle. 5–6 (German), 7–8 (Slovenian). Ljubljana: Družina, 1992.

Called to Communion: Understanding the Church Today. San Francisco: Ignatius Press, 1996.

Church, Ecumenism, and Politics: New Endeavors in Ecclesiology. San Francisco: Ignatius Press, 2008.

Che Cos'è Il Cristianesimo [What is Christianity?]. Milan: Mondadori, 2023.

"Commento alla La lettera apostolica *Ordinatio Sacerdotalis*." *La Civiltà Cattolica* 145, no. 3 (July 2, 1994): 61–72.

"Die Dimensionen des Problems: These I-VIII. Kommentar von Joseph Ratzinger." In *Die Einheit des Glaubens und der theologische Pluralismus*, edited by Internationale Theologenkommission, 17–51. Einsiedeln: Johannes Verlag, 1973.

Diener eurer Freude: Meditationen über priesterliche Spiritualität. Freiburg: Herder, 1988, 2006. Reprinted in JRGS 12, 463–532.

Dogma and Preaching: Applying Christian Doctrine to Daily Life. Unabridged ed. San Francisco: Ignatius Press, 2011.

Einführung in das Christentum. JRGS 4. Freiburg: Herder, 2014. 1st ed.: München: Kösel Verlag, 1968.

Eschatologie. Regensburg: Pustet Verlag, 1977.

Eschatology: Death and Eternal Life. 2nd ed. Washington, D.C.: The Catholic University of America Press, 2007.

"The Feeling of Things, the Contemplation of Beauty": Message of His Eminence Card. Joseph Ratzinger to the Communion and Liberation (CL) Meeting at Rimini. August 24–30, 2002. http://www.vatican.va/roman_curia/congregations/cfaith/cti_documents/rc_cti_1976_pluralismo-teologico-index_ge.html

"Zur Frage nach dem Sinn des priesterlichen Dienstes." *Geist und Leben* 41 (1968): 347–76. Reprinted in *Künder des Wortes und Diener eurer Freude: Theologie und Spiritualität des Weihesakraments*. JRGS 12, 350–86. Freiburg: Herder, 2010.

God and the World: Believing and Living in Our Time. A Conversation with Peter Seewald. San Francisco: Ignatius Press, 2002.

"Grenzen kirchlicher Vollmacht: Das neue Dokument von Papst Johannes Paul II; zur Frage der Frauenordination." *Communio: Internationale Katholische Zeitschrift* 23 (1994): 335–45. Reprinted in JRGS 12, 139–53.

"Homily at the Funeral Liturgy of Hans Urs von Balthasar, Luzern, July 1, 1988." In Schindler, *Hans Urs von Balthasar: His Life and Work* (1991), 291–95.

Homily for the Holy Mass Concluding the Year for Priests. June 11, 2010.

"Identification with the Church." In *Living with the Church*, edited by Joseph Ratzinger and Karl Lehmann. Chicago: Franciscan Herald Press, 1978.

"Identifikation mit der Kirche." In *Kirche: Zeichen unter den Völkern*. JRGS 8/1, 178–92. Freiburg: Herder, 2010.

In the Beginning. . . A Catholic Understanding of the Story of Creation and the Fall. Grand Rapids: Eerdmans, 1995.

Introduction to Christianity. San Francisco: Ignatius Press, 1990. German: *Einführung in das Christentum*.

Jesus of Nazareth, Vol. 1. *From the Baptism in the Jordan to the Transfiguration*. Translated by Adrian J. Walker. New York: Doubleday, 2007.

Jesus von Nazareth: Beiträge zur Christologie. JRGS 6/1. Freiburg: Herder, 2013.

Kirche: Zeichen unter den Völkern. JRGS 8/1 and 8/2. Freiburg: Herder, 2010.

Künder des Wortes und Diener eurer Freude: Theologie und Spiritualität des Weihesakramentes. Joseph Ratzinger Gesammelte Schriften [JRGS] 12. Freiburg: Herder, 2010.

Zur Lehre des Zweiten Vatikanischen Konzils. JRGS 7/1 and 7/2. Freiburg: Herder, 2012.

"Life and Ministry of Priests." Congregation for the Clergy. International Symposium on the 30th Anniversary of the Promulgation of the Conciliar Decree *Presbyterorum Ordinis*. (October 24, 1995). http://www.vatican.va/roman_curia/congregations/cclergy/index_en_pres_ainterv.htm

With Hans Urs von Balthasar, eds. *Mary: The Church at the Source*. San Francisco: Ignatius Press, 2005.

Milestones: Memoirs, 1927–1977. San Francisco: Ignatius Press, 1998.

Ministers of Your Joy: Scriptural Meditations on Priestly Spirituality. Slough, U.K.: St. Paul Publications, 1989. German: *Diener eurer Freude*.

The Nature and Mission of Theology: Essays to Orient Theology in Today's Debates. San Francisco: Ignatius Press, 1995.

Ein neues Lied für den Herrn: Christusglaube und Liturgie in der Gegenwart. Freiburg: Herder, 1995.

"On Hope." *Communio: International Catholic Review* 12 (Spring 1985): 71–84. German: "Über die Hoffnung."

"Opfer, Sakrament und Priestertum in der Entwicklung der Kirche." *Catholica* 26 (1972): 108–25. Reprinted in JRGS 12, 83–106; English: "Sacrifice, Sacrament and Priesthood in the Development of the Church." In *Principles of Catholic Theology*, 250–67.

"Originalität und Überlieferung in Augustins Begriff der *confessio*." *Revue d'études augustiniennes et patristiques* 3, no. 4 (1957): 375–92.

"Perspektiven der Priesterausbildung heute." In *Unser Auftrag. Besinnung auf den priesterlichen Dienst*, ed. J. Ratzinger, P. W. Scheele, and Karl Hillenbrand. Würzburg: Echter, 1990, 11–38; new ed.: "Bereitung zum priesterlichen Dienst." In *Ein neues*

Lied für den Herrn. Christusglaube und Liturgie in der Gegenwart. Freiburg: Herder, 2007, 216–36; JRGS 12, 432–50.

Pilgrim Fellowship of Faith: The Church as Communion. San Francisco: Ignatius Press, 2005.

"Der Priester als Mittler und Diener Christi im Licht der neutestamentlichen Botschaft, in 100 Jahre Priesterseminar in St. Jakob zu Regensburg 1872–1972." In *Theologische Prinzipienlehre. Bausteine zur Fundamentaltheologie.* München: Wewel, 1982, 281–99. Reprinted in JRGS 12, 107–28. English: "The Priest as Mediator and Minister of Christ in the Light of Message of the New Testament." In *Principles of Catholic Theology*, 267–84.

"Der Priester im Umbruch der Zeit." *KIBI* 49 (1969): 251–54. Reprinted in JRGS 12, 387–401. English: *Priestly Ministry: A Search for Its Meaning.* New York: Sentinel Press, 1971.

"Das Problem der christlichen Prophetie." Niels Christian Hvidt im Gespräch mit Joseph Kardinal Ratzinger. *Communio: Internationale Katholische Zeitschrift* 28, no. 2 (1999): 177–88.

Principles of Catholic Theology: Building Stones for a Fundamental Theology. San Francisco: Ignatius Press, 1987. German: *Theologische Prinzipienlehre.*

Salt of the Earth: The Church at the End of the Millennium. An Interview with Peter Seewald. San Francisco: Ignatius Press, 1997.

"Some Perspectives on Priestly Formation Today: Keynote Address." *The Catholic Priest as Moral Teacher and Guide: Proceedings of a Symposium Held at St. Charles Borromeo Seminary, Overbrook, Pennsylvania, January 17–20, 1990.* San Francisco: Ignatius Press, 1990, 1–20. German: "Perspektiven der Priesterausbildung heute."

To Look on Christ: Exercises in Faith, Hope and Love. New York, Crossroad, 1991. German: *Auf Christus schauen.*

Spe salvi. Encyclical Letter. November 30, 2007.

Teaching and Learning the Love of God: Being a Priest Today. Selected Writings. With a Foreword by Pope Francis and an Introduction by Gerhard Cardinal Müller. San Francisco: Ignatius Press, 2017.

Theologische Prinzipienlehre: Bausteine zur Fundamentaltheologie. München: Wewel, 1982.

Theology of the Liturgy: The Sacramental Foundation of Christian Existence. Collected Works 11. San Francisco: Ignatius Press, 2014.

"Über die Hoffnung." *Communio: Internationale Katholische Zeitschrift* 13, no. 4 (1984): 293–305.

Das Werk: Veröffentlichungen bis zur Papstwahl. Edited by Vinzenz Pfnür. Augsburg: Sankt Ulrich Verlag, 2009.

The Yes of Jesus Christ: Exercises in Faith, Hope, and Love. New York: Crossroad, 2005.

"Zum Zölibat der katholischen Priester." *Stimmen der Zeit* 195 (1978): 781–83. Reprinted in JRGS 12, 154–58.

Works of Hans Urs Cardinal von Balthasar

"Address of Hans Urs von Balthasar." *L'Osservatore Romano*, Weekly Edition (July 23, 1984): 7–8.

"Adriennes Charisma." In *Adrienne von Speyr und ihre kirchliche Sendung: Akten des römischen Symposiums 27–29 September 1985*, edited by Hans Urs von Balthasar, Georges Chantraine, and Angelo Scola, 173–78. Einsiedeln: Johannes Verlag, 1986.

"Adrienne von Speyr (1902–1967): Die Miterfahrung der Passion und Gottverlassenheit." *Geist und Leben* 58 (1984): 61–66; reprint in: *Frauen des Glaubens*, edited by Paul Imhof, 267–77. Würzburg: Echter, 1985.

Der antirömische Affekt: Wie lässt sich das Papsttum in der Gesamtkirche integrieren? 2nd ed. Einsiedeln: Johannes Verlag, 1989.

Bernanos: An Ecclesial Existence. San Francisco: Ignatius Press, 1996. German: *Gelebte Kirche: Bernanos*.

Das betrachtende Gebet. Einsiedeln: Johannes Verlag, 1955.

Christen sind einfältig. Einsiedeln: Johannes Verlag, 1983.

Christian and Anxiety. San Francisco: Ignatius Press, 2000.

The Christian State of Life. San Francisco: Ignatius Press, 1983.

Der Christ und die Angst, 6th ed. Einsiedeln: Johannes Verlag, 1989.

Convergences: To the Source of Christian Mystery. San Francisco: Ignatius Press, 1983. German: *Einfaltungen*.

Credo: Meditations on the Apostles' Creed. New York: Crossroad, 1990. Ignatius Press ed. San Francisco, 2000.

Dare We Hope "That All Men Be Saved"? With a Short Discourse on Hell. San Francisco: Ignatius Press, 1988.
"Earthly Beauty and Divine Glory." *Communio: International Catholic Review* 10 (Fall 1983): 202–6.
Einfaltungen: Auf dem Wege christlicher Einigung, 3rd ed. Einsiedeln: Johannes Verlag, 1987.
Elucidations. San Francisco: Ignatius Press, 1998. German: *Klarstellungen*.
Engagement with God. San Francisco: Ignatius Press, 2008. German: *In Gottes Einsatz leben*, 2nd ed. Einsiedeln: Johannes Verlag, 1972.
Epilogue. San Francisco: Ignatius Press, 2004.
Explorations in Theology I. *The Word Made Flesh*. San Francisco: Ignatius Press, 1989. German: *Verbum Caro*.
Explorations in Theology II. *Spouse of the Word*. San Francisco: Ignatius Press, 1991.
Explorations in Theology III. *Creator Spirit*. San Francisco: Ignatius Press, 1993.
Explorations in Theology IV. *Spirit and Institution*. San Francisco: Ignatius Press, 1995.
Explorations in Theology V. *Man Is Created*. San Francisco: Ignatius Press, 2014.
Das Ganze im Fragment: Aspekte der Geschichtstheologie. Einsiedeln: Benziger Verlag, 1963.
First Glance at Adrienne von Speyr, 2nd ed. San Francisco: Ignatius Press, 1981.
Gelebte Kirche: Bernanos, 3rd ed. Einsiedeln: Johannes Verlag, 1988.
The Glory of the Lord: A Theological Aesthetics I. *Seeing the Form*. Edinburgh, T&T Clark, 1982. 2nd. ed., San Francisco: Ignatius Press, 2009.
The Glory of the Lord II. *Studies in Theological Style: Clerical Styles*. San Francisco: Ignatius Press, 1984.
The Glory of the Lord IV. *The Realm of Metaphysics in Antiquity*. San Francisco: Ignatius Press, 1989.
The Glory of the Lord VI. *Theology: The Old Covenant*. San Francisco: Ignatius Press, 1989.
The Glory of the Lord VII. *Theology: The New Covenant*. San Francisco: Ignatius Press, 1989.

Die grossen Ordensregeln. 7th ed. Freiburg: Johannes Verlag Einsiedeln, 1994.

Foreword to *Heilige Zeichen* by Egon Kapellari, 7–10. Graz-Wien-Köln: Verlag Styria, 1987.

In the Fullness of the Faith: On the Centrality of the Distinctively Catholic. San Francisco: Ignatius Press, 1988. German: *Katholisch*.

Katholisch: Aspekte des Mysteriums. Einsiedeln: Johannes Verlag, 1975.

Klarstellungen: Zur Prüfung der Geister, 4th ed. Einsiedeln: Johannes Verlag, 1978.

Kleine Fibel für unversicherte Laien, 3rd ed. Einsiedeln: Johannes Verlag, 1989.

Kostet und seht: Ein theologisches Lesebuch. Einsiedeln: Johannes Verlag, 1988.

The Laity and the Life of the Counsels: The Church's Mission in the World. San Francisco: Ignatius Press, 2003. Rev. ed. (with additional essays) of *Der Laie und der Ordensstand*. Einsiedeln: Johannes Verlag, 1948.

Life Out of Death: Meditations on the Paschal Mystery. San Francisco: Ignatius Press, 2012.

Love Alone Is Credible. San Francisco: Ignatius Press, 2004.

"Die marianische Prägung der Kirche." In *Maria heute ehren*, edited by Wolfgang Beinert, 263–79. Freiburg: Herder, 1977.

The Moment of Christian Witness. San Francisco: Ignatius Press, 1994.

Mysterium paschale: The Mystery of Easter. San Francisco: Ignatius Press, 1995.

My Work: In Retrospect. San Francisco: Ignatius Press, 1993.

New Elucidations. San Francisco: Ignatius Press, 1986.

Neue Klarstellungen, 2nd ed. Einsiedeln: Johannes Verlag, 1995.

Nochmals Reinhold Schneider. Einsiedeln: Johannes Verlag, 1991.

The Office of Peter and the Structure of the Church. San Francisco: Ignatius Press, 1986. German: *Der antirömische Affekt*.

Our Task: A Report and a Plan. San Francisco: Ignatius Press, 1994.

Pastoralbriefe des Heiligen Paulus: Für das betrachtende Gebet erschlossen, 2nd ed. Einsiedeln: Johannes Verlag, 1992.

Prayer. San Francisco: Ignatius Press, 1986. German: *Das betrachtende Gebet*.

Priestly Spirituality. San Francisco: Ignatius Press, 2013.
Razing the Bastions. San Francisco: Ignatius Press, 1993. German: *Schleifung der Bastionen*.
Rechenschaft. Einsiedeln: Johannes Verlag, 1965.
Romano Guardini: Reform from the Source. San Francisco: Ignatius Press, 2010.
Schleifung der Bastionen, 5th ed. Einsiedeln: Johannes Verlag, 1989.
A Short Primer for Unsettled Laymen. San Francisco: Ignatius Press, 1985. German: *Kleine Fibel für unversicherte Laien*.
With Michael Albus. "Spirit and Fire: An Interview with Hans Urs von Balthasar." *Communio: International Catholic Review* 32 (Fall 2005): 573–93.
With Angelo Scola. *Test Everything: Hold Fast to What is Good*. An Interview with Hans Urs von Balthasar. San Francisco: Ignatius Press, 1989.
Theo-Drama: Theological Dramatic Theory I: *Prologomena*. San Francisco: Ignatius Press, 1989.
Theo-Drama II. *Dramatis personae: Man in God*. San Francisco: Ignatius Press, 1990.
Theo-Drama III. *Dramatis personae: Persons in Christ*. San Francisco: Ignatius Press, 1992.
Theo-Drama V. *The Last Act*. San Francisco: Ignatius Press, 1998.
Theo-Logic: Theological Logical Theory I. *The Truth of the World*. San Francisco: Ignatius Press, 2000.
Theo-Logic II. *The Truth of God*. San Francisco: Ignatius Press, 2004.
Theo-Logic III. *The Spirit of Truth*. San Francisco: Ignatius Press, 2005.
A Theological Anthropology. New York: Sheed & Ward, 1968.
"Theology and Holiness." *Communio: International Catholic Review* 14 (Winter 1987): 342–50.
A Theology of History. San Francisco: Ignatius Press, 1994. German: *Theologie der Geschichte: Ein Grundriss*, new ed. Einsiedeln: Johannes Verlag, 1959.
The Theology of Karl Barth: Exposition and Interpretation. San Francisco: Ignatius Press, 1992. German: *Karl Barth: Darstellung und Deutung Seiner*, 4th ed. Einsiedeln: Johannes Verlag, 1976.

Thomas und die Charismatik: Kommentar zu Thomas von Aquin, Summa Theologica Quaestiones II-II 171–182, besondere Gnadengaben und die zwei Wege menschlichen Lebens, new ed. Freiburg: Johannes Verlag Einsiedeln, 1996.

The Threefold Garland: The World's Salvation in Mary's Prayer. San Francisco: Ignatius Press, 1982.

Tragedy under Grace: Reinhold Schneider on the Experience of the West. San Francisco: Ignatius Press, 1997. German: *Nochmals Reinhold Schneider*.

Truth Is Symphonic: Aspects of Christian Pluralism. San Francisco: Ignatius Press, 1987. German: *Die Wahrheit ist symphonisch*.

Two Sisters in the Spirit: Thérèse of Lisieux and Elizabeth of the Trinity. San Francisco: Ignatius Press, 1992.

Unless You Become Like This Child. San Francisco: Ignatius Press, 1991.

Verbum Caro. Einsiedeln: Johannes Verlag, 1960.

Die Wahrheit ist symphonisch: Aspekte des christlichen Pluralismus. Einsiedeln: Johannes Verlag, 1972.

Who Is a Christian? San Francisco: Ignatius Press, 2014.

The Whole in the Fragment: Aspects of the Theology of History. 2nd ed. San Francisco: Ignatius Press, 1990. German: *Das Ganze im Fragment*.

Foreword to *Življenje iz polnosti vere: Teologija krščanskih stanov pri Hansu Ursu von Balthasarju* by Anton Štrukelj. Ljubljana: Družina, 1981, 1986, 1995, 5–8. German: *Leben aus der Fülle des Glaubens: Theologie der christlichen Stände bei Hans Urs von Balthasar*, 7–8. Graz-Wien-Köln: Verlag Styria, 2002.

"Zugänge zu Christus." In *Wer ist Jesus Christus*, edited by J. Sauer, 9–25. Freiburg-Basel-Wien: Herder, 1977.

Writings of Anton Štrukelj concerning Anton Strle

"Der theologische Beitrag von Prof. Dr. Anton Strle zur Marienverehrung in Slowenien." *Mater fidei et fidelium: Collected Essays to Honor Theodore Koehler on His 80th Birthday*, Marian Library Studies. A New Series, Volume 17–23. Dayton, Ohio: University of Dayton, 1991, 380–87.

Reprint: "Die Mariologie als Herzstück der Ekklesiologie." In *Kniende Theologie*. St. Ottilien: EOS Verlag, 1999, 85–95. 2nd German ed.: 2004, 127–36.
Slovenian: "Mariologija kot srčika ekleziologije." In *Klečeča teologija*. Družina: Ljubljana, 2000, 143–54.
Russian: "Mariologija kak sjerdce ekkleziologiji." In *O slave Božjej*. Moscow: Izdatelstvo franciskancev, 1999.
Italian: "Mariologia come il cuore di mariologia." In *Teologia e santità*. Cinisello Balsamo, Milano: Edizioni San Paolo, 2010, 167–78.
Polish: "Mariologia jako centralna szęść eklezjologii." In *W służbie Bogurodzicy*. Niepokalanów: Wydawnictwo Ojców Franciszkanów, 2009, 279–87. Reprint: "Mariologia jako centralna część eklezjologii." In *Teologia i świętość*, Lublin: Wydawnictwo Polihymnia, 2010, 55–164.

"Biseromašnik prelat prof. dr. Anton Strle." *Tretji dan* 30 (June/July 2001): 101–3.

"Povsod Boga: Življenje in delo prof. dr. Antona Strleta, Conference at Faculty of Theology in Ljubljana, December 3, 2003." *Communio: Mednarodna katoliška revija* 13 (2003): 291–306.

"Povsod Boga: Prelat prof. dr. Anton Strle. In memoriam (21.1.1915 +20.10.2003)" *Bogoslovni vestnik* 64 (2004): 211–25.

"STRLE, Anton." In *Biographisch–Bibliographisches Kirchelexikon*, vol. 32. Nordhausen: Verlag Traugott Bautz GmbH, 2011, 1357–1379.

"Profesor Anton Strle: Ob desetletnici smrti." *Tretji dan* 42, no. 7/8 (2013): 91–102.

"Gorečnost za sveto teologijo v spisih Božjega služabnika Antona Strleta." *Brezjanski pogovori* (2015): 25–52.

"Prizadevanje Antona Strleta za sveto teologijo." *Communio: Mednarodna katoliška revija* 25 (2015): 142–54.

Additional Literature

Albrecht, Barbara. *Eine Theologie des Katholischen: Einführung in das Werk Adrienne von Speyrs*. Durchblick in Texten 1. Einsiedeln: Johannes Verlag, 1972.

Ambaum, Jan. "An Empty Hell? The Restoration of All Things? Balthasar's Concept of Hope for Salvation." *Communio: International Catholic Review* 18 (Spring 1991): 35–52.

Biser, Eugen. "Dombau oder Triptychon? Zum Abschluß der Trilogie Hans Urs von Balthasars." *Theologische Revue* 84, no. 3 (1988): 177–84.

Congregation for the Doctrine of the Faith. *Donum Veritatis: On the Ecclesial Vocation of the Theologian*. Instruction. May 24, 1990.

_____. *Letter to the Bishops of the Catholic Church on the Collaboration of Men and Women in the Church and in the World*. May 31, 2004.

Cottier, Georges. *Memoria e pentimento: Il rapporto fra Chiesa santa e cristiani peccatori, la purificazione della memoria, l'importanza della richiesta di perdono per l'ecumenismo*. Cinisello Balsamo: Edizioni San Paolo, 2000.

Crawford, David S. "The Gospel of Life and the Integrity of Death." *Communio: International Catholic Review* 39 (Fall 2012): 364–80.

Daniélou, Jean. *Essai sur le mystère de l'histoire*. Paris: Éditions du Seuil, 1953.

de Lubac, Henri. *The Church: Paradox and Mystery*. Shannon, Ireland: Ecclesia Press, 1969.

_____. "A Witness of Christ in the Church: Hans Urs von Balthasar." In Schindler, *Hans Urs von Balthasar: His Life and Work* (1991), 271–88.

Denzinger, Heinrich et al., ed. *Compendium of Creeds, Definitions, and Declarations on Matters of Faith and Morals*, 43rd ed. San Francisco: Ignatius Press, 2012.

Fisichella, Rino. "Hans Urs von Balthasar e Adrienne von Speyr: L'inseparabilità delle due opere." *Communio: Rivista Internazionale di Teologia e Cultura* 156, no. 4 (1997): 61–74.

Francis, Pope. Foreword to *Teaching and Learning the Love of God: Being a Priest Today*, by Joseph Ratzinger/Benedict XVI, 11–15. San Francisco: Ignatius Press, 2017.

Griesser-Pečar, Tamara. "Anton Strle v zaporu in pred sodiščem" [Anton Strle in prison and before the court]. *Communio: Mednarodna katoliška revija* 25, no. 2 (2015): 162–73.

_____. *Boj proti veri in Cerkvi (1945–1961): Razstava, September 5–December 2, 2007; Muzej novejše zgodovine Slovenije* [Fighting against religion and the Church (1945–1961): Exhibition, September 5–December 2, 2007; National Museum of Contemporary History]. Ljubljana: Družina, 2007.

Guardini, Romano. *Die letzten Dinge*. Kevelaer: Topos plus Taschenbuch, 2008. English: *The Last Things: Concerning Death, Purification after Death, Resurrection, Judgment, and Eternity*. Notre Dame: University of Notre Dame Press, 1965.

Guerriero, Elio. *Hans Urs von Balthasar*. Milan: Edizioni Paoline, 1991.

_____. *Hans Urs von Balthasar: Eine Monographie*. Freiburg: Johannes Verlag Einsiedeln, 1993.

Heim, Maximilian Heinrich. *Joseph Ratzinger: Life in the Church and Living Theology: Fundamentals of Ecclesiology with Reference to* Lumen Gentium. With a Foreword by Joseph Cardinal Ratzinger. San Francisco: Ignatius Press, 2007.

Henrici, Peter. “Hans Urs von Balthasar: A Sketch of His Life.” In Schindler, *Hans Urs von Balthasar: His Life and Work* (1991), 7–43.

_____. *Hans Urs von Balthasar: Aspekte seiner Sendung*. Freiburg: Johannes Verlag Einsiedeln, 2008.

Hribšek, Alojzij. *Blessed Aloysius Grozde: A Teenage Witness for Christ the King*. Ljubljana: Družina, 2012.

International Theological Commission. *Memory and Reconciliation: The Church and the Faults of the Past*. December 1999.

John Paul II. “Address for the Awarding of the International Paul VI Prize to Hans Urs von Balthasar.” June 23, 1984. English translation: *L’Osservatore Romano*, English Weekly Edition (July 23, 1984): 7.

_____. “Ansprache des Heiligen Vaters an die Teilnehmer.” In *Adrienne von Speyr und ihre kirchliche Sendung*, 181–82. Einsiedeln: Johannes Verlag, 1986. *Discorso ai partecipanti al convegno sulla personalità di Adrienne von Speyr* [Address to participants in the convention on Adrienne von Speyr]. September 28, 1985. https://www.vatican.va/content/john-paul-ii/it/speeches/1985/september/documents/hf_jp-ii_spe_19850928_adrienne-von-speyr.html.

_____. *Fidei depositum*. Apostolic Constitution. October 11, 1992.

_____. *General Audience*. September 1, 1999.

_____. *Homily on the Day of Pardon in the Holy Year 2000*. March 12, 2000.

_____. *Incarnationis mysterium*. Bull of Indiction of the Great Jubilee of the Year 2000. November 29, 1998.

_____. *Pastores dabo vobis*. Post-Synodal Apostolic Exhortation. March 25, 1992.

_____. *Tertio millennio adveniente*. Apostolic Letter. November 10, 1994.

Kempis, Stefan von. *Benedikt XVI.—das Lexikon: Von Ablass bis Zölibat*. Leipzig: Edition Radio Vatikan/Benno Verlag, 2007.

Koch, Cardinal Kurt. *Das Geheimnis des Senfkorns: Grundzüge des theologischen Denkens von Papst Benedikt XVI*. Ratzinger-Studien 3. Regensburg: Verlag Friedrich Pustet, 2010.

Karger, Michael. "'Nicht als ob wir von uns selbst etwas vermöchten'. . . Papst Benedikt XVI. im Licht seiner Primizsprüche." In *Benedikt XVI: Mit Christus für die Menschen: 60 Jahre Dienst im Weinberg des Herrn*, edited by Rudolf Voderholzer, 61–65. Regensburg: Verlag Schnell & Steiner, 2011.

Konda, Jutta. *Das Verhältnis von Theologie und Heiligkeit im Werk von Hans Urs von Balthasar*. Würzburg: Echter, 1991.

Krenski, Thomas. "Mit Handbuchwissen wäre Adriennes Theologie nicht aufzufangen gewesen: Hans Urs von Balthasar and Adrienne von Speyr." Mainz, Lecture: June 11, 2005.

Lehmann, Karl, and Walter Kasper, eds. *Hans Urs von Balthasar: Gestalt und Werk*. Cologne: Communio, 1989.

Lexikon für Theologie und Kirche. Vol. 3. Freiburg, Herder, 2009.

Levering, Matthew. *The Achievement of Hans Urs von Balthasar: An Introduction to His Trilogy*. Washington, D.C.: The Catholic University of America Press, 2019.

L'Osservatore Romano. *Biography of His Holiness, Pope Benedict XVI*. 2005. http://www.vatican.va/content/benedict-xvi/en/biography/documents/hf_ben-xvi_bio_20050419_short-biography_old.html

Maček, Matija. *Zapisniki politbiroja CK KPS/ZKS 1945–1954* [The records of Politburo Central Committee of the Communist Party of Slovenia 1945–1954], edited by Darinka Drnovšek, Arhivsko društvo Slovenije, Viri 15. Ljubljana: Darinka Drnovšek, 2000.

Marcel, Gabriel. *Trois pieces: Le regard neuf, Le mort de demain et La chapelle ardente*. Paris: Plon, 1931.

Ouellet, Marc. *Charismen: Eine Herausforderung*. Einsiedeln: Johannes Verlag, 2011.

_____. "L'existence comme mission: L'anthropologie théologique de Hans Urs von Balthasar." STD diss. Rome: Pontificia Universitas Gregoriana, 1983.

Péguy, Charles. *The Portal of the Mystery of Hope*. Translated by David L. Schindler. Grand Rapids: Eerdmans, 1996.

Roten, Johann G., SM. "The Two Halves of the Moon: Marian Anthropological Dimension in the Common Mission of Adrienne von Speyr and Hans Urs von Balthasar." In Schindler, *Hans Urs von Balthasar: His Life and Work* (1991), 65–86.

Sans Vala, Jorge, and Ramón María Sans Vala. *Por qué me hice sacerdote?* Salamanca: Ediciones Sigueme, 1959.

Schindler, David L., ed. *Hans Urs von Balthasar: His Life and Work*. San Francisco: Ignatius Press, 1991.

Schlier, Heinrich. *Nun aber bleiben diese Drei: Grundriß des christlichen Lebensvollzuges*. Einsiedeln: Johannes Verlag, 1972.

Servais, Jacques. "Per una valutazione dell'influsso di Adrienne von Speyr su Hans Urs von Balthasar." *Rivista Teologica di Lugano* 6, no. 1 (2001): 67–89.

Sicari, Antonio, OCD. "Hans Urs von Balthasar: Theology and Holiness." In Schindler, *Hans Urs von Balthasar: His Life and Work* (1991), 121–32.

Slovenian Bishops' Conference. *Katekizem katoliške Cerkve*. Slovenian translation of the *Catechism of the Catholic Church*. Ljubljana: Slovenska škofovska konferenca, 1993 and 2008.

Speyr, Adrienne von. *Der Christlicher Stand*. Einsiedeln: Johannes Verlag, 1956.

_____. *Erde und Himmel: Ein Tagebuch* II. Einsiedeln: Johannes Verlag, 1975.

_____. *Die katholischen Briefe I*. Einsiedeln: Johannes Verlag, 1961.

_____. *Das Hohelied*. Einsiedeln: Johannes Verlag, 1972.

_____. *Korinther I*. Einsiedeln: Johannes Verlag, 1956.

_____. *Das Wort und die Mystik.* Part I, *Subjektive Mystik;* Part II, *Objektive Mystik.* Einsiedeln: Johannes Verlag, 1970.

Strle, Anton. *Božja slava—živi človek: Teološka antropologija* [God's glory, the living Man: Theological anthropology]. Ljubljana: Družina, 1992.

_____. "Kaj mi pomeni Jezus iz Nazareta?" [What does Jesus of Nazareth mean to me?]. *Communio: Mednarodna katoliška revija* 30, no. 4 (2020): 299–324. Originally published in Družina on November 24, 1974.

_____. *Konstitucije, odloki, izjave, poslanice: Vatikanskega vesoljnega cerkvenega zbora (1962–1965)* [Second Vatican Council. Translation and introductions to all documents (1962–1965)]. 2nd ed. Ljubljana: Nadškofijski ordinariat, 1995.

_____. Over fifty articles. In *Leto svetnikov* [The year of saints]. 5 vols. 2nd ed. Edited by Marijan Smolik and Andrej Kropej. Celje: Mohorjeva družba, 1999–2001.

_____. *Lojze Grozde: Mladec Kristusa Kralja* [Lojze Grozde: The disciple of Christ the King]. Ljubljana: Salezijanci, 1944. French: *Un martyr des temps modernes: Alöis Grozďe* (1923–1943). Foreword by Bishop Gregorij Rožman. Paris: La Colombe, 1957.

_____. *Skrivnost Boga* [The mystery of God]. Ljubljana: Družina, 1977.

_____. *Teologi za prihodnost* [Theologians for the future]. Ljubljana: Družina, 1998.

_____. *Vem, komu sem veroval: Vera in razodetje* [I know whom I have believed: Faith and revelation]. Ljubljana: Družina, 1988.

_____. *Vera Cerkve* [The faith of the Church]. 2nd ed. Celje: Mohorjeva družba, 1997.

_____. *Živo upanje: Velikonočna skrivnost* [Living hope: Paschal Mystery]. Ljubljana: Družina, 1990.

Štrukelj, Anton. "Duhovnik Joseph Ratzinger." *Communio: Mednarodna katoliška revija* 19 (2009): 285–319.

_____. "Schönheit und Heiligkeit in der Theologie: Hommage an Papst Benedikt XVI aus slowenischer Sicht." In *Hommage an Papst Benedikt XVI: Aufsätze und Essays*, edited by Maximilian Heinrich Heim and Wolfgang Gottfried Buchmüller, 119–26. Heiligenkreuz im Wienerwald: Be&Be, 2018.

_____. Schönheit und Heiligkeit. *Papst Benedikt XVI. zum 95*. Geburtstag: EOS Verlag Sankt Ottilien, 2021.

_____. *Ti Si Peter Skala* [You are Peter the Rock]. Ljubljana: Družina, 1996.

_____. *Zakon in Devištvo* [Marriage and virginity]. Ljubljana: Družina, 1995.

_____. *Življenje iz polnosti vere: Teologija krščanskih stanov pri Hansu Ursu von Balthasarju*. Ljubljana: Družina, 1981, 1986, 1995.

Trippen, Norbert. "Joseph Ratzinger als Mitgestalter des II. Vatikanischen Konzils." *Communio: Internationale Katholische Zeitschrift* 35, no. 6 (2006): 541–44.

Vatican Council II. *Gaudium et spes: On the Church in the Modern World*. Pastoral Constitution. December 7, 1965.

_____. *Lumen gentium: On the Church*. Dogmatic Constitution. November 21, 1964.

Vovk, Anton. *V spomin in opomin: Osebni zapisi škofa Antona Vovka od 1945 do 1953* [For remembrance and warning: Personal records of Bishop Anton Vovk from 1945 to 1953]. Edited by Blaž Otrin. Ljubljana: Družina, 2003.

INDEX

Names

Subjects